T0330023

European Monetary Integration

European Monetary Integration

Past, Present and Future

Edited by

Eric J. Pentecost

Reader in Economics, Loughborough University, UK

and

André van Poeck

Professor of Economics, University of Antwerp, Belgium

Edward Elgar
Cheltenham, UK • Northampton, MA, USA

Published by
Edward Elgar Publishing Limited
Glensanda House
Montpellier Parade
Cheltenham
Glos GL50 1UA
UK

Edward Elgar Publishing, Inc.
136 West Street
Suite 202
Northampton
Massachusetts 01060
USA

A catalogue record for this book
is available from the British Library

Library of Congress Cataloguing in Publication Data
European monetary integration : past, present, and future / edited by Eric J. Pentecost, André Van Poeck
    p. cm.
    Includes bibliographical references and index.
    1. Monetary unions—European Union countries. 2. European Monetary System (Organization) 3. Money—European Union countries. 4. European Union countries—Economic integration. I. Pentecost, Eric J. II. Poeck, André van

HG925.E962 2001
332.4'566'094—dc21

2001033076

ISBN 1 84064 579 2

Typeset by Manton Typesetters, Louth, Lincolnshire, UK.
Printed and bound in Great Britain by MPG Books Ltd, Bodmin, Cornwall.

Contents

PART III   THE FUTURE: BEYOND 2000

Figures

Tables

Boxes

List of contributors

Frank Barry Assistant Professor, Department of Economics, University College Dublin, Dublin, Ireland.

Alain Borghijs Research Fellow, University of Antwerp, UFSIA, Antwerp, Belgium.

Heather D. Gibson Economist, Bank of Greece, Athens, Greece.

Jens Hölscher Senior Lecturer in Economics, University of Brighton, Brighton, Sussex, UK.

Anke Jacobsen Free University of Berlin, Berlin, Germany.

Hubert Kempf Professor of Economics, University of Paris 1, Paris, France.

Eric J. Pentecost Reader in Economics, Department of Economics, Loughborough University, Loughborough, Leicestershire, UK.

Friedrich L. Sell Professor of Economics, Munich University of the Armed Forces, Munich, Germany.

Horst Tomann Professor of Economics, Free University of Berlin, Berlin, Germany.

Euclid Tsakalotos Assistant Professor, Athens University of Business and Economics, Athens, Greece.

André van Poeck Professor of Economics, Department of Applied Economics, University of Antwerp, UFSIA, Antwerp, Belgium.

Lúcio Vinhas de Souza Tinbergen Institute, Rotterdam, The Netherlands.

Preface

This text is based on an EU-funded Intensive Programme on European Monetary Union. The three-year programme which ran in Antwerp, Loughborough and Berlin in 1998, 1999 and 2000 respectively, was coordinated by the University of Antwerp (UFSIA) with participation from Loughborough University (England), the Free University of Berlin, the University of Paris 1 and Athens University of Economics and Business. The editors are grateful to all of the participating academics who made this programme such a successful venture, and without the enthusiasm and cooperation of whom this book would not have reached fruition. The editors owe a special debt to Euclid Tsakalotos who made perceptive and constructive comments on most of the chapters that appear in this volume.

In addition to the academic lectures that the students received, which are included in this volume, the programme also involved a number of field trips to various European Union and national institutions to listen to talks and analysis from practitioners whose work involves them with different aspects of European Monetary Union (EMU). The local organizers are extremely grateful for the time and invaluable advice given to the students who participated in the various field trips. In Antwerp in 1998 visits were made to the National Bank of Belgium and the European Central Bank (ECB). In 1999 the programme in Loughborough took students to the Association of British Insurers, Lloyds Insurance Market and the Bank of England; and in Berlin in 2000, visits were made to the Deutsche Bank, the ECB and the Bundesbank.

The students who participated in these three intensive programmes and made such an invaluable contribution to their success are: Dimitris Apostolinas, Karl Bartels, Alex Becker, Karolin Borek, Peter Calon, Sven Craeynest, Steffen Daehne, Thomas Desmedt, Petra Gabriel, Michael Golde, Laura Goodall, Carla Gunnesch, Fotini Hamboulidou, Ludovic Hausman, Stefan Herzog, Paulina Karasiotou, Stilianos Katehis, Andreas Kogler, Nicolas Legrand, Sandy Linke, Alessandro Manfron, Tobias Marquart, Nancy Masschelein, Thomas Mayer, Chris McCullagh, Jurgen Monsieur, Matthias Paustian, Thomas Peccia-Galleto, Ramon Pernas Frias, Filip Perneel, Ellie Powell, Amelia Purdie, Nikolaus von Raggamby-Fluck, Fredrich Rheinheimer, Nicole Rosin, Tom Scheltjens, Michael Scholze, Christian Schwerdtner, Dirk Sebrecht, Ravinder Stephen Singh- Sud, Dimitra Sotiriou, Robert Spanheimer,

Maria Stiakaki, Nancy Thiry, Clare Tweed, Kirstan Van Bockstaele, lvan Van De Cloot, Peter Vanlerberghe, Heike Volmer, Bent Voorhoof, Wolf Wagner, Gillian Weekes, Nina Wright and Alessandra Almedida de Deus Zwinscher.

The biggest debts of all are to the EU Commission, who funded the entire project and to Marie-Anne Fivez (University of Antwerp, UFSIA) who dealt with the budgeting and other financial matters.

1. The historical background to European Monetary Union

Eric J. Pentecost and André van Poeck

1 EUROPEAN MONEY: A HISTORICAL PERSPECTIVE TO EMU

The introduction on 1 January 1999 of the euro for intra-banking sector transactions and the establishment of the European Central Bank (ECB), marked the beginning of a new era in European monetary arrangements. With a common currency for use as a medium of exchange to follow the introduction of the new unit of account in 2002, Western Europe will have a unified coinage system for the first time since Charlemagne in AD 800. This latest currency reform represents the end of a process that began in the late 1970s with the European Monetary System (EMS), which fixed the exchange rates of a number of the European Union (EU) member countries' currencies, and is the last of a long line of currency reforms in continental Europe. To place these recent monetary developments into their historical context, this chapter examines European monetary cooperation and development since the mid-nineteenth century when many of the modern European nation states first came into existence, up until the establishment of the EMS in 1979. Developments since 1979 are considered in the rest of book, as this date marks the modern beginnings of European Monetary Union (EMU).

Nineteenth-century Monetary Unions in Europe

At the end of the Napoleonic wars in 1815, Europe was a fragmented continent. Belgium, Italy and Germany were not single nations and Switzerland, although a federation of states, did not have a common national currency. Only Britain, which returned to the Gold Standard in 1821 following the 'suspension of payments' from 1797, and France were nations with a uniform means of payment and exchange. During the course of the nineteenth century as principalities became nation states, several monetary unions emerged in an attempt to provide a more consistent means of payment. Bordo and Jonung

(2000) have classified these monetary unions according to their scope as either national or multinational unions. The national monetary unions formed in Italy in 1862 and Germany in 1876, were essentially the result of the establishment of new nation states, whereas the formation of the Latin Monetary Union in 1865 and the Scandinavian Currency Union in 1873 were multinational arrangements and hence more like twenty-first-century EMU.

European national monetary unions

The establishment of Italy as a nation state in 1861 led swiftly to monetary unification one year later. In 1859 there were up to 90 different metallic currencies serving as legal tender, in addition to locally-issued bank notes. These arrangements were considered as a barrier to trade and by 1862 a new unified currency system was introduced based on the lira of Sardinia. All pre-unification coins and notes were abolished and exchanged for coins denominated in the new lira, which was equal in value to the French franc. A bimetallic currency standard was chosen to accommodate the prevalence of silver coins in southern Italy and to conform to the system used by Italy's trading partners, especially France, where the silver-to-gold ratio was set at 15.5:1.

There was no attempt to establish a central bank to run the Italian monetary union. The Banca Nazionale del Regno d'Italia (BNR) held a leading position among the banks, partly because it was the largest and partly because it was the bank of the state that had led the political unification process. This led at various times to competition between the note-issuing banks, especially in response to the fiscal deficits of the early 1860s, until the reform of the system in 1893. This reform led to the formation of the Banca d'Italia, by the merging of the BNR and the two remaining note-issuing Tuscan banks and the establishment of a rule that the banks agreed to limit the note issue to three times the volume of specie. This proved to be successful, because the Banca d'Italia was responsible for 75 per cent of the note issue and from 1893 there was a period of fiscal discipline.

The nineteenth century German Monetary Union, like the Italian monetary union, also proceeded in stages taking over three decades to establish. By the time of the Vienna Congress of 1815 the 39 principalities and free cities on German territory had full sovereignty to regulate and issue their own coinage and monetary system. As a result there were large numbers of different coins with different metal content, making exchange difficult and expensive. After the establishment of the *Zollverein* – customs union – in 1834 and the Dresden coinage convention in 1838, the principalities agreed to choose one of two currencies – the thaler or the gulden – as the basic monetary unit. The thaler and the gulden were fixed to a specific quantity of silver, such that one thaler was equal to 1.75 gulden. Under the 1857 Vienna Coinage Treaty,

Austria linked its coinage system to that of the *Zollverein*, but the basic weight in which the relationship of silver metal to number of coins was expressed was 500 grams. The new relationship was 500 grams of silver to 30 thaler, 52.5 gulden or 45 Austrian gulden. The Vienna Treaty included two other major steps towards monetary union. First, exchange of gold coins into silver coins was forbidden and no gold coins were minted except for the special *Vereinshandelsgoldmünzen* designed for foreign trade. Second, the treaty prohibited the granting of legal tender status to inconvertible paper money.

This system prevailed until the political unification of Germany in 1871. The Reichsbank was established in 1876 from the Prussian central bank and introduced a single coinage system, based on the mark (one-third of a thaler). With victory over the French in the Franco-Prussian war of 1870–71, Germany received 5 billion francs as an indemnity which was used to augment the gold reserves enabling Germany to join the Gold Standard. Very much like the monetary reunification of Germany in the 1990s political unification came first followed by monetary union.

Multinational monetary unions
The Latin Monetary Union (LMU) was formed in 1865, between France, Italy, Belgium, Sweden and Greece (who joined in 1868). It was designed to harmonize the gold and silver content of primary gold and silver coins of each country and to prevent arbitrageurs from taking the coins across national boundaries to be melted down into coins of a higher value. These common coins were made legal tender and circulated throughout the union, though token coins were legal tender in their home countries. The initial success of the LMU prompted the French to call another conference in 1867 to discuss plans to integrate the coinage systems of the US, Germany and the UK, so forming a global monetary union.

The German sovereign was worth just over 25 francs, so by devaluing the pound by 0.83 per cent one pound would exactly equal one sovereign. The French and their LMU partners would replace or augment their 20-franc gold coins with a 25-franc gold coin, but making no other change to their monetary arrangements. In the US the Americans were in the process of reintroducing gold coinage following the civil war. A half eagle (5 dollars) was equal to 25.85 francs, so with a small adjustment of some 3.5 per cent, it could have been brought into line with either the sovereign or a 25-franc coin. The French, however, vetoed the plan because they feared that a 25-franc coin would compete with their 20-franc gold coin and moreover that they would have to bear the cost of reminting, while being unable to impose the French standard on the rest of the world. Thus the global monetary union never materialized but the LMU continued.

After 1870, however, the LMU suffered two serious shocks, which meant that from 1878 until it finally collapsed in 1926 it was really a 'limping standard', which allowed the free coinage of gold, but provisionally suspended coinage of the silver five-franc piece. The first shock was the Franco-Prussian War, which saw France move to an inconvertible paper standard. The second shock was that Italy, who joined the LMU with one lira equal to one French franc, was forced to revert to an inconvertible paper standard due to the debts inherited from the former principalities (worth some 40 per cent of gross domestic product).

The Scandinavian Currency Union (SCU) was set up in 1873 between Denmark and Sweden (Norway joined later in 1875) and became part of the Gold Standard system, until the SCU was dissolved by Sweden in 1921. Initially the Scandinavian countries were considering joining the LMU, but with Germany victory in the Franco-Prussian War, they decided to form their own currency union. The SCU was based on gold and adopted as a common unit the krona, which was equal to the Swedish riksdaler. Unlike the LMU, from the beginning there were no gold coins, but notes were universally accepted at par. In 1885 the three central banks all allowed drafts to be drawn on each other at par, which effectively eliminated the gold points between the countries. The agreement was dissolved after the First World War, largely as a result of the effects of war on the respective economies.

There are two important lessons for EMU from this brief review of the nineteenth-century monetary unions. First, monetary union within a country is much more likely to be successful than is a monetary union between nation states. This is a result of two structural features: the existence of national central banks to support the currency, which did not exist in the multinational currency unions, and the national political will to enforce the union. Second, fiscal deficits in any single country can undermine the monetary union, as Italy's deficits damaged the LMU. Thus some form of fiscal constraint is likely to be needed if any multinational monetary union is to be successful.

European Money in the Twentieth Century up to 1979

The First World War brought the Gold Standard to an end and the suspension and eventually the end of both the LMU and the SCU. With the conclusion of hostilities, only the dollar was left pegged to gold and exchange rates were allowed to float freely. The wartime divergences in national price levels had greatly exceeded the divergences in exchange rates and therefore the restoration of some kind of international equilibrium required a further fall in the depreciated European currencies against the US dollar.

Indeed the old monetary units of Austria, Hungary, Poland, Germany and Russia were practically wiped out. By the end of their respective inflations, pre-war price levels had been multiplied by 14,000 in Austria, by 23,000 Hungary, 2.5 million in Poland and 4 billion in Russia. The situation was even worse in Germany. In 1923 a new mark was created with a conversion value of one new mark equal to 1,000,000,000,000 old marks. These facts notwithstanding policy makers seemed determined to return to the pre-war set of exchange rate parities so encouraging speculators, expecting a return to the gold standard, to buy the European currencies and so bid up their prices. The transition to fixed exchange rates took place in the mid-1920s – Sweden in 1924, Britain in 1925, France in 1926 and Italy in 1927. The gold standard was therefore effectively restored by 1927, but before the end of the decade doubts had already emerged as to its sustainability.

By 1931 both Germany and Austria had suspended gold convertibility and imposed exchange controls. The Bank of England devalued the pound in September 1931 which sparked off a further 12 devaluations and a gradual return to floating exchange rates. The US floated the dollar in 1933, soon followed by Belgium, France, the Netherlands and Switzerland in 1936. The important feature of the 1930s period of exchange rate flexibility is that there was heavy intervention in the foreign exchange markets by the authorities, who essentially followed beggar-thy-neighbour-type policies, leading to intensified economic nationalism. This in turn led to a plethora of quotas, increased tariffs and exchange controls. This period of non-cooperation and indeed outright economic warfare eventually gave way to hostilities of a more lethal kind.

After the Second World War economic circumstances dictated that the Western European nations entered into a period of monetary cooperation with one another and with the US. Industrial production in France, Germany and the Netherlands had fallen by 75 per cent on its pre-war level and trade was in an equally dismal state, with bilateral trading arrangements predominant. The solutions to these problems did not immediately come from the US, since convertibility of the European currencies was not an option. Thus they embarked on a programme to establish their own multilateral payments system, albeit with US backing. The Organization for European Economic Cooperation (OEEC) set up in 1948 allowed US aid to be more effectively linked to European trade and payments, which then led to the formation of the European Payments Union (EPU) in 1950. The EPU was a stop-gap measure to foster multilateral trade between the Western European economies until their economies were sufficiently strong to be fully convertible into the US dollar, under the Bretton Woods arrangements (see Coffey and Presley 1971). Full convertibility finally occurred in 1958, from which date the EPU was wound up. From the viewpoint of monetary integration, the undisputed success of the EPU was the impetus that it gave to further monetary cooperation.

Between 1958 and 1970 the Western European economies were part of a pseudo monetary union with the US, through the Bretton Woods fixed exchange rate system. Under this system the US dollar was pegged to gold and all other member countries pegged their currencies to the dollar, with small fluctuation margins of 1.25 per cent either side of the par value. Over this 12-year period, despite the removal of tariff barriers between members of the European Economic Community (EEC), as the EU was then called, the adoption of a common external tariff and the establishment of the Common Agricultural Policy (CAP), the EEC had few achievements in the monetary field. In particular, despite increasing economic integration there were no moves towards a common European monetary policy.

The catalyst for change was the monetary turbulence in the late 1960s. In particular, the devaluation of the pound by 14 per cent in 1967 and the subsequent devaluation of the French franc in 1968 led to much speculation regarding a revaluation of the German mark. Early in 1969 discussions were under way within the EU as how to handle the crisis. The outcome of these meetings was the Barre Plan (1969) and then the Werner Report (CEC 1970). The Barre Plan was simply an attempt to foster greater cooperation between the EU member states with regards to their monetary policies. At a summit in The Hague at the end of 1969, it was decided to embark on the creation of an economic and monetary union, the details of which were to be worked out during the following year by a committee chaired by Pierre Werner. The Werner Report famously set the objective of reaching economic and monetary union within ten years – that is by 1980. Like the Delors Report (Committee on the Study of Economic and Monetary Union 1989) some 20 years later, the Werner Report suggested a stage-by-stage process with national currency adjustments not ruled out until the final stage.

The Werner Plan for gradual transition to economic and monetary union did not however, come to fruition, due to developments elsewhere in the international monetary system. In particular, the plan to narrow the fluctuation bands between the EU currencies was jeopardized in May 1971 when capital inflows into (West) Germany put strong upward pressure on the Deutschmark–dollar peg, which resulted in a floating of the Deutschmark. Just three months later US President Richard Nixon announced the closing of the gold window and with it the convertibility of the US dollar into gold. Despite efforts to patch up the system in December 1971, the pound sterling was floated in June 1972, followed by generalized floating of all the main industrial countries' currencies by March 1973. With the subsequent turmoil caused by the OPEC (Organization of Petroleum-exporting Countries) oil embargo in 1973–74, any moves towards economic and monetary union were dead in the water.

The early floating rate period was characterized by great exchange rate volatility, which even by the late 1970s had shown little sign of abating. This led the EU member states to resurrect the idea of a currency union in the EU, which was independent of American influence and which would serve to deepen European economic integration. This process of European monetary union in the last quarter of the twentieth century is the theme of this book. The process began with the European Monetary System in 1979, which made exchange rates fixed but adjustable between member states. The number of central exchange rate realignments gradually reduced over time, so that from 1987 there were no major realignments. This confidence led to the Delors Report (1989), which set out the gradualist strategy and timetable for a complete economic and monetary union in Western Europe by the end of the twentieth century.

2   EMU: PAST, PRESENT AND FUTURE

This book is concerned with this latest phase of monetary cooperation and ultimately, currency reform, in Western Europe from 1979 and its economic implications for the individual EU economies. The chapters of this volume implicitly divide into three broad categories. First, those chapters that examine the route travelled on the road to monetary union since March 1979, with the setting up of the European Monetary System, up until the introduction of the euro on 1 January 1999. Second, there is a core group of chapters that examine different aspects of contemporary debates about EMU, especially the role of fiscal and monetary policy and the degree of labour mobility and labour market reform. Third, there is those chapters that are concerned with the likely future relationships between the euro area and the countries outside – both those within the EU, like the UK, Sweden and Denmark, and those outside the EU, like Poland, the Czech Republic and Hungary, *inter alia*, but with accession desires.

The Past: 1979–99

The transition from a loose, joint floating arrangement against the US dollar to complete monetary union, with a common central bank and a single currency over a period of a quarter of a century is an exercise in political economy. Three alternative theories of the transition process to monetary union are considered in Chapter 2 by Eric J. Pentecost – a market approach, an institutional approach and a shock-therapy approach. The transition to EMU, because it is a multinational currency union, has of political necessity been based on an institutional approach. This approach is in direct contrast to the German Economic and Monetary Union (GEMU) in 1989–90, when the West German Deutschmark replaced the East German Ostmark, which as explained by Friedrich Sell in Chapter 3, was based on the shock-therapy approach with political union occurring simultaneously. Although the transition processes have been very different, the problems faced by GEMU and EMU are not dissimilar, although the political homogeneity of Germany may make the resolution of some of these difficulties easier. For example, Sell notes that GEMU has resulted in a high demand for fiscal transfers because productivity levels were very different between East and West, and slow to converge. Similar problems may emerge within the larger, multinational EMU, but as yet there is no mechanism for extensive fiscal redistribution between states. Moreover with less labour mobility and labour market flexibility within EMU compared with GEMU, the demand for fiscal redistribution between regions is likely to be greater rather than less.

Furthermore, the larger the geographical area over which a single currency serves as a unit of account and medium of exchange, the less likely is that area to be an optimum currency area. Traditional theory, due to Mundell (1961), suggests that the size of an optimum currency area is defined by the degree of labour mobility. Labour mobility should be high within the currency area and relatively low outside the area. Anke Jacobsen and Horst Tomann argue in Chapter 4 that the low levels of labour mobility experienced in the EU since 1979 are not necessarily a problem for EMU, in that past performance is little guide to the future. The reason is that EMU creates beneficial economic externalities, such as the welfare gains from a credible monetary policy, which they conclude may lead to monetary union enhancing economic performance in the EU, simply because the institutional structures and adjustment mechanisms are very different under EMU than under the EMS. In particular, labour unions will be forced to change their behaviour, giving rise to more competitive labour markets and stimulating labour mobility across the continent.

Overall, the experience from the recent past indicates that national and multinational currency unions are really very different because the extent of political commitment is so much greater in a national monetary union. In a multinational union the lack of political union imposes limits on both the speed and the depth of integration. While this is not surprising, it does suggest that the costs of moving towards a monetary union, as has been the case in Germany and is likely also to be the case for EMU as a whole, are greater than economically necessary.

Present Issues for EMU

While there may be reason to doubt the success of the EMU project from a purely transitional perspective, EMU is up and running and so the present state of the union, its development and operation merit careful analysis. In general terms the established framework for macroeconomic policy is largely neoclassical. Monetary policy is therefore tied to an explicit low-inflation target; national fiscal policy is constrained to the pursuit of a balanced-budget policy over the economic cycle; and there are no specific economic policy measures to tackle the potential short-run problems of unemployment that may arise if prices are sticky in Keynesian fashion. The monetary and fiscal policy implications of currency reform for the operation of EU monetary and fiscal policy are considered in Chapters 5 and 6 and the implications for unemployment in EMU in Chapter 7.

In Chapter 5, Hubert Kempf explains the operation of the system of central banks and the objective of monetary policy – a low and stable inflation rate, defined by the European Central Bank itself to be no more than 2 per cent per annum. The inflation target is to be met by the ECB adjusting the short-term interest rate. Kempf notes that inflation targeting is a policy with additional difficulties for EMU because of the diversity between countries and regions. Thus there will be divergences between average EU inflation and national or regional inflation rates.

This inflation target policy is reinforced by the Stability Pact, which prevents national authorities from embarking on excessive fiscal deficits, which may then have to be monetized at the cost of breaching the inflation target. This arrangement with monetary policy set centrally by the ECB, but with fiscal policy being set nationally, within the constraints of the Stability Pact poses two major problems for the successful operation of EMU.

First, with fiscal policy constrained at the national level the effectiveness of the automatic stabilizers will be considerably reduced, thus the economic cycle will be more pronounced than if fiscal policy was set centrally. Second, public investment in infrastructure may enhance economic growth whereas public consumption does not, but the Stability Pact does not distinguish between the two types of fiscal policy. This is important because public investment is likely to be important for the cohesion of the peripheral countries, such as Greece, Portugal and Ireland. This leads Frank Barry (Chapter 6) to conclude that unless the Stability Pact constraining fiscal policy is loosened or the central EU budget increased, EMU is likely to result in greater regional diversity, especially in terms of unemployment, which, if left uncorrected, will lead to a fragmentation of EMU.

The mechanisms by which fiscal and monetary policy impinge on the EU labour markets, and especially on employment, is examined by André van Poeck and Alain Borghijs in Chapter 7. They argue that wage bargaining could eventually evolve in an unfavourable way, such that sector-level wage bargaining develops across the EU. To this extent unemployment will increase, since this reduces each sector's ability to withstand adverse shocks. On the other hand, unemployment could be reduced by the reduction in transactions costs for trade and the elimination of exchange rate uncertainty with positive effects on prices and wages. At the moment it is not possible to assess exactly how these effects will impact on national, or indeed regional, labour markets, although it is perhaps unlikely that real wage flexibility will increase, thus putting more of the burden on labour mobility.

Chapters 5, 6 and 7 all suggest that a low EU inflation policy together with highly constrained national fiscal policies could lead to serious nominal and real divergences between countries and regions of the eurozone. Unless the labour markets can respond to such regional diversity then it is likely that the restrictive policy stance will have to be relaxed if EMU is to be robust against defections.

The Future: Beyond 2000

Another issue that is important for the future of EMU is the expansion of the eurozone, particularly if the euro is to become, as many hope, an international currency to rival the US dollar. There are two potential directions of expansion: first, to the other EU member states who are not members of the eurozone (Denmark, Sweden and the UK); and second to the non-EU Eastern European economies (*inter alia*, Bulgaria, the Czech Republic, Hungary, Poland, Slovakia and Slovenia).

Heather Gibson and Euclid Tsakalotus (Chapter 8) discuss the ERM-II exchange rate arrangements that exist for non-euroland EU economies. They argue that although the ERM-II system is designed to facilitate monetary cooperation between the so-called 'ins' and the 'outs', the outs may still face the alternating problems of either excess credibility on the one hand, or speculative attack on the other. Thus the countries that remain outside the euro could face highly volatile nominal and real exchange rates and thus be in for a bumpy ride en route to full EMU membership.

In Chapter 9, Jens Hölscher and Lúcio Vinhas de Souza consider the exchange rate implications for the Eastern European economies and their potential future membership of EMU. They conclude that initially a mix of exchange rate policies are required, ranging from currency board arrangements to crawling peg arrangements linked to monetary targets, given the diversity of economic structures found in the former Eastern bloc countries. In addition they argue that to assist convergence, some kind of exchange rate undervaluation could be used to transfer resources from the original EMU members to the accession economies, perhaps as part of the transitional arrangements.

In conclusion, to use an aviation analogy, an experimental EMU has been assembled and towed out of its hangar for its maiden flight. From January 1999 the EMU plane has been taxying down the runway, ready to take off.

Whether the plane will take off and remain airborne, still remains an open question. Some of the difficulties noted in this text will have to be addressed to the satisfaction of all participants in the project for the flight to be a long one. The level of economic and political policy coordination required will be high and not all member states of euroland will necessarily be long-run beneficiaries of the monetary reform. Although it is far too early to pass judgement on a process which even after 25 years is still really only in its infancy, it is not premature to make a critical assessment of the performance and prospects of EMU as we enter the twenty-first century. This is the purpose of this book.

PART I

EMU: The Past, 1979–99

2. The political economy of transition to monetary union in Western Europe

Eric J. Pentecost

1 INTRODUCTION

The Oxford English Dictionary defines 'transition' as 'the passage from one state, subject, or set of circumstances to another'. In the context of European Monetary Union (EMU) the passage is from a state of separate national currencies with national central banks – referred to as a *pseudo* monetary union – to a common, single European Union currency with a single central bank – that is, a *complete* monetary union. The distinction between a pseudo currency union and a complete monetary union is very important. In a pseudo union the various member countries still have their own central banks and foreign exchange reserves and hence still determine their own money supply or credit policies. The members of a pseudo union, however, agree to manage their monetary and credit policies so as to maintain fixed exchange rate relationships between the participant currencies. There may also be some arrangements where surplus countries provide limited short-term financing for deficit countries and where capital controls prevail to limit speculative attacks on member currencies. By contrast in a complete exchange rate union, foreign exchange reserves are pooled and there is a central monetary authority. There is therefore complete assurance that the fixed exchange rate relationships will be maintained, without the need of capital controls, and the central monetary authority operates a union-wide monetary policy.

The transition from a pseudo to a complete exchange rate union in Western Europe is the principal concern of this chapter. Such a transition, however, is not merely about the transition from one type of monetary arrangement to another, but crucially also requires a transfer of some economic and political power from national monetary authorities and governments to the European Union (EU) and especially to the European Central Bank (ECB). By definition, the setting of monetary policy will pass from the control of national central banks to the ECB. Although the national central banks will have a role in the implementation of the chosen policy and be able to lobby the ECB for a particular monetary stance, national central bank governors will no longer be able to determine monetary policy independently. This transfer of economic power also implies a transfer of some political power away from national governments to a supranational authority, since traditionally national central banks have been the operational arm of national economic policy. In complete monetary union, national central banks are largely independent of national governments and responsible only to the supranational central bank and the implementation of its policies. This suggests that there are two major uncertainties about EMU. The first uncertainty concerns the likely policy to be pursued by the new supranational central bank: all countries have to be satisfied that it will follow a sensible, low-inflation monetary policy. The second uncertainty concerns the likely effects of this common policy on different nations within the union and to what extent national governments will be able to adjust other policy instruments to offset any local deleterious economic consequences.

These uncertainties go a long way to explaining why the transition from a pseudo to a complete monetary union in the EU has taken nearly a quarter of century and why all member states of the EU are not members of EMU. They also explain why the transition process has been determined at each stage by political practicalities, rather than by economic considerations. This latter point also means that the net economic gains from complete monetary union are uncertain in terms of both their magnitude and distribution. It is likely that some regions or sectors will be adversely affected while other areas may benefit, making the aggregate net benefits difficult to quantify and their distribution politically sensitive.

This chapter on the transition process from national monetary hegemony to European monetary control is organized as follows. Section 2 evaluates three alternative theoretical transition paths to EMU. Section 3 then traces the institutional route to EMU followed in Western Europe since the late 1970s, culminating in the establishment of the ECB in January 1999. Section 4 evaluates the role of the economic convergence criteria established in 1991 to determine which countries were to be allowed to proceed to EMU and the potential future problems that this criteria may cause. Section 5 offers an appraisal of the transition process as of March 2000, and Section 6 provides a brief summary of the main arguments.

2   ALTERNATIVE TRANSITIONAL PATHS TO COMPLETE MONETARY UNION

There are two principal approaches by which individual countries can move towards monetary unification: 'all at once' or gradualist. The latter comprises

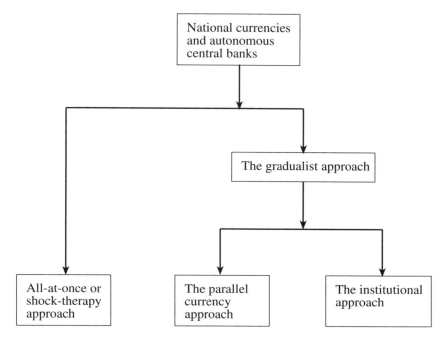

Figure 2.1   Alternative routes to EMU

two approaches: the market (parallel currency) and the institutional. These three theoretical approaches are considered in turn and summarized in Figure 2.1.

The All-at-once or Shock-therapy Approach

The all-at-once approach eliminates the need for a transition period and prevents any single nation from delaying the introduction of the common currency. For example, if it was agreed on a particular day that the UK should join the euro then the government would simply fix the pound's exchange rate against the euro. This rate could be the market rate prevailing on that day or some other arbitrarily chosen exchange rate. The point is that all pounds would become euros overnight and the monetary reform would be complete. All outstanding monetary contracts would be translated into euro contracts at the announced exchange rate and gradually the supply of pounds would be replaced with euro notes and coin. This is the most common kind of monetary reform in practice and is effectively the kind of monetary reform undertaken by Germany in 1989–90 when East and West were reunited.

The advantage of this approach is that a common inflation rate now exists for both countries without any prior convergence of inflation rates before the monetary reform. For this approach to be relatively costless, however, it is important that prices and wages are fully flexible. Inertia in prices and wages could lead to divergence between prices and wages within the union with a consequent misallocation of resources. In Western Europe, of course, wages and prices are not very flexible, hence the shock-therapy approach to monetary union would have been risky and most likely unsuccessful, for at least two reasons. First, that high unemployment in one country, because of the absence of high labour mobility, would be politically unacceptable to national electorates. Second, the sudden transfer of economic power to an untested supranational institution would have been very risky and therefore also politically infeasible. The crucial problem is that monetary union in the EU is about more than just a common currency or a monetary reform within a country, but about the partial transfer of both economic and political power from national policy makers to EU policy makers.

The Market Approach

The parallel-currency proposal was put forward in 1975 by a group of EU academics in *The Economist* magazine, but was resurrected in the late 1980s by the British government (HM Treasury 1989). The idea is that a common EU-wide money be issued by a central EU institution and allowed to circulate alongside other national currencies. Each government would permit its residents to use and hold this common currency in competition with national money. Exchange rates of national moneys relative to the common currency would fluctuate, essentially on the basis of rates of inflation. If this common currency is made sufficiently more attractive, in that it has a lower rate of depreciation compared to the other national currencies, then it will drive the national currencies out of circulation. Thus a process of currency substitution will see a gradual displacement of national currencies by the low-inflation common currency.

The advantages of this approach are twofold. First, the speed towards EMU is determined by market forces and not by politicians and bureaucrats. Second, if agents choose to hold the common currency rather than national currencies, the rate of inflation in the common-currency area will fall.

There are also, of course, some disadvantages of this approach. The first is that the mere existence of a common currency does not ensure its acceptance as a medium of exchange and store of value, because national currencies have established network effects (see Dowd and Greenaway 1994). That is, the common currency has no natural market advantages – even if it is never devalued – which means it is not a close substitute for existing currencies.

The second disadvantage is that the common currency would only work if it were declared legal tender by the national governments, so that it could be used as final payment and for settlement of debts. This would create a double standard of measure. For example, if UK residents could pay taxes in either pounds or the common currency, they would be inclined to pay in the currency which was falling in value and hold on to the currency that was the best store of value. If, by definition, the common currency has the lowest inflation rate, then residents will pay all taxes in domestic currency. Thus the common currency could be driven out of circulation by the bad national money, as Gresham's Law suggests. A third disadvantage is that there remain the institutional problems as to who controls the issue of the common currency and the objectives of the supplying institution.

The ideas of currency competition and substitution are therefore unlikely to be sufficient to bring about a single, common currency in the EU. Not only is the theoretical mechanism suspect, but there is little evidence that EU national currencies are close substitutes (see Pentecost 1997). Without specific help from national governments a common currency is very unlikely to emerge in the EU.

The Institutional Approach

The institutional approach to monetary union is also gradualist in nature, like the market-based approach, but in contrast to the market mechanism it is based on institutional development. Institutions are established whereby currencies are made to be closer substitutes and then simultaneously withdrawn and replaced by a common currency at some time in the future. Given the political nature of EMU this was probably the only way forward for the EU to have a common, single currency.

The first reason for this is that the process is wholly within the control of politicians, who decide and agree on the institutions required and the speed of reform. This is in contrast with the market approach discussed above, where the market decides the speed of reform. Second, the early stages do not necessarily involve any major political commitments or loss of economic autonomy. For example, by agreeing to fix the exchange rates between national currencies, national currencies effectively become perfect substitutes on the supply side without any loss of political autonomy, especially if exchange rate realignments and capital controls are permitted within the pseudo exchange rate agreement. Third, in order to maintain a fixed exchange rate arrangement, the national central banks will have to liaise with one another and by so doing foster greater mutual respect and cooperation that can be used in time to extend or harden the arrangements. Thus the institutional approach is akin to creeping inflation – the process goes on almost unnoticed in the early stages, by which time the institutional structure is sufficiently strong to resist challenges.

The principal difficulty with the institutional approach to monetary union is that not only may the switchover to a common currency be deferred indefinitely, but also the longer the transitional process the less likely that the process will be completed, due to either economic instability or diminution of political interest. Hence the Werner Report (CEC 1970) proposals for a common currency by 1980 were shelved when the Bretton Woods system collapsed and generalized floating emerged in the early 1970s. A second difficulty is that the kinds of institutional reforms agreed and implemented during the transition process are likely to be the easiest ones for the politicians to agree on, rather than the reforms that are most important for the operation of a common currency. Thus either the common currency never takes off because the speed of reform is too slow, constrained as it is by political compromise, or the currency is launched before the necessary reforms have been completed. In the latter case, the whole process may not only be brought to a sudden halt, but the whole 50-year process of European integration could be forced into reverse, leading to a fragmentation of the EU itself.

Furthermore, the reforms that are required are much wider than simple monetary reform: because a complete monetary union removes the exchange rate as an instrument of adjustment between regions (countries) it is important for any potential regional imbalances to be accommodated or alleviated by other policies or mechanisms. For example, if the exchange rate cannot be used to switch demand between countries then it is important for the factors of production to be relatively mobile between sectors of the economy and between regions of the EU. Thus if there is a shortfall of demand for one region's products, leading to unemployment, then either the workers have to switch to other lines of production where there is demand, or the workers have to move to other regions where their skills are required. This suggests that a common labour market structure is required, with similar or at least transferable social insurance systems, tax systems and housing policies. In the absence of such policies, national fiscal policies must have an important role in assisting and facilitating the management of regional demand. Without structural reform, the monetary union is unlikely to possess an efficient adjustment mechanism, which may lead to economic and political problems.

3   THE EUROPEAN MONETARY SYSTEM

The Origins

The notion of monetary union first appeared in the Werner Report (1970), which set the objective of complete economic and monetary union in the EU by 1980. These proposals quickly became unrealistic when the Bretton Woods system collapsed in August 1971 and the dollar's convertibility into gold was suspended, and was quickly followed by a move to floating exchange rates. Even with the collapse of the Bretton Woods pseudo monetary union, many members of the EU were reluctant to give up fixed exchange rates completely. The reasons are complex, but probably linked to the relationship between floating exchange rates and the interwar depression and rise of nationalism, together with the more practical problem of how to maintain the Common Agricultural Policy (CAP) in a floating exchange rate environment. Although the oil crises of 1973–74 led to hopes of any early return to fixed exchange rates being abandoned, Germany, Belgium, the Netherlands and Luxembourg participated in a joint float against the US dollar, known as 'the snake'. Although British, French and Italian membership of the snake was brief and spasmodic during the 1970s, the snake nevertheless served as a prologue for the European Monetary System (EMS).

With most of the real adjustment to the oil shock complete by the end of the 1970s, the British President of the EU Commission, Roy Jenkins (now Lord Jenkins of Hillhead), decided that the time was again right for a political initiative to further European integration. With the close cooperation of the German Chancellor Helmet Schmidt and the French President Valéry Giscard d'Estaing, the European Monetary System was launched three months late in March 1979. The EMS was a pseudo exchange rate union, with three institutional features: a fixed but adjustable exchange rate system, known as the exchange rate mechanism (ERM), the European currency unit (ECU) which served as a unit of account and the European Monetary Cooperation Fund (EMCF).

The Arrangements

The ECU was defined as a weighted basket of currencies of the countries that were members of the EU. It was originally designed as the numeraire of the system and as the potential ultimate reserve asset. The value of the ECU in terms of a national currency, i, equals the sum of the values of each member currency, j, in terms of currency i, multiplied by the amount of currency j in the ECU, that is:

$$P^i_{ECU} = \sum_j E_j z_j \qquad\qquad (2.1)$$

where P^i_{ECU} is the value of the ECU in terms of currency i, E_j is the currency i's cross-rate with currency j and z_j is the amount of currency j in the ECU. The weights of each currency in the ECU were designed to reflect the economic importance of each country in the EU. The weights w_j, are calculated by dividing (2.1) by P^i_{ECU}, which gives:

$$1 = \sum_j \frac{E_j z_j}{P^i_{ECU}} = \sum_j w_j. \qquad\qquad (2.2)$$

Thus the weights change as the cross-exchange rates change. To correct for this, the ECU is reweighted every five years to ensure that the weights again reflect relative national economic importance.

The ERM was an adjustable peg-type exchange rate system whereby currencies had a central value against the ECU, which in turn set the central rates against all other ERM currencies, but fluctuations of 2.25 per cent either side of the par value were permitted.[1] Countries had an obligation to intervene at the margins of this band to keep their currencies within the band. Hence if two currencies reach one of their bilateral exchange rate margins, then the monetary authorities of the weaker currency must intervene to purchase the currency, preventing further depreciation, while simultaneously the stronger currency country sells its currency to prevent further appreciation. Thus the currencies are maintained within their permitted fluctuation bands. Another feature of the ERM was the divergence indicator for each currency, which served to indicate which country was diverging from its central rate and hence on which country the burden of adjustment should fall. The value of the divergence indicator for each currency i, is given by the weighted sum of the divergence of currency i from each of the other currencies:

$$a^i = \sum_j w_j d^i_j, \qquad\qquad (2.3)$$

where w^j is the weight of currency j in the ECU basket and d^i_j is the deviation of currency j from its central parity with respect to currency i. The threshold for the indicator is 75 per cent of the divergence which would have occurred had the currency i deviated by the full 2.25 per cent from all other currencies. If the actual indicator a^i, was above the threshold then country i was supposed to take action by adjusting macroeconomic policy to be consistent with its exchange rate commitment. The divergence indicator, however, was not used and countries in the ERM have not been forced to adjust their macroeconomic policies if their currency breached the threshold.

It was also possible, however, for ERM members in conjunction with other member countries to realign their par values. Indeed in the early years of the ERM, realignments were relatively common. There were in fact seven realignments up to the end of 1983 and a further four up to January 1990.[2]

The EMCF was set up to facilitate the circulation of credits between central banks, which it was anticipated would evolve into a European central bank, like the International Monetary Fund (IMF). Arrangements were made for ECU official credits through the EMCF to countries with weak currencies. Each EU country deposited 20 per cent of its foreign exchange reserves with the EMCF, which could then be lent out to countries in need of foreign exchange. These loans were made for repayment over a range of different time horizons. For example, the very short-term financing facility was available to ERM members and provides funds for 45 days only. At the other end of the spectrum the medium-term financing facility offered loans of between two and five years to help countries tackle structural balance of payments problems.

An Evaluation of the Operation of the ERM

The EMS has passed through five broad phases on the road to complete monetary union as follows:

1. The trial phase (1979–83): This led to strongly diverging economic conditions, seven exchange rate realignments and the official ECU becoming marginalized.
2. The consolidation phase (1983–87): During this period the Deutschmark emerged as the anchor currency and common economic policies began to emerge around it.
3. The reorientation phase (1987–91): In this phase, the asymmetrical operation of the EMS was questioned and the need for commonly defined policies as set out in the Delors Report (1989) identified.
4. The crises phase (1992–93): This begins with the abolition of capital controls and the pursuit of divergent monetary policies between a reunified Germany and other ERM members.
5. The final stage (1993–99): During this period, there was a softening of the exchange rate target zone and the implementation of a nominal convergence criteria in preparation for EMU.

Throughout these five phases the crucial objectives of the ERM were to create a zone of exchange rate stability and to reduce inflation in the EU economies. There is now considerable empirical evidence that confirms a reduction in exchange rate volatility during phases 1 to 3, despite the number of exchange rate realignments. Moreover, this reduction in exchange rate volatility was not obtained by increased interest rate volatility (Artis and Taylor 1988, 1994). This is probably due to the existence of capital controls over this time period, which enabled countries to maintain a degree of monetary independence. The lack of exchange volatility leads Holmes and Pentecost (1995, 1996) to find evidence of closer financial integration between the EU economies up to the early 1990s, with the exception of the UK, which remained outside of the ERM.

Phases 2 and 3 of the EMS also witnessed a sharp fall in EU inflation, from about 11 per cent annum in 1982 to about 3 per cent in 1990. This convergence of inflation rates was achieved by the higher inflation countries of the ERM pegging their exchange rates to the Deutschmark, such that the ERM worked asymmetrically as a Deutschmark zone. The evidence for this German dominance view of the ERM is that inflation was reduced to German levels, rather than German inflation rising to ERM levels, and that the burden of exchange rate intervention largely fell on the non-DM currencies. In addition, Giavazzi and Giovannini (1989) note that at times of expected exchange rate realignment German interest rates were unaffected, whereas in contrast, French and Italian offshore interest rates increased indicating that they felt the effect of the expected depreciation of their currencies.[3] German dominance emerged partly as a response to the nth currency problem common with fixed exchange rate regimes, combined with the ineffectiveness of the ECU to serve as an appropriate numeraire for the system. The ECU, unlike gold, is not an independent entity and so it could not easily take on the role of numeraire (Giavazzi and Giovannini 1989). As pegging to an outside currency such as the dollar was out of the question, one of the EMS currencies had to be chosen. The DM was the obvious choice due to the Bundesbank's low-inflation record, but also because of the increasing prominence of the DM in international financial markets and the prior existence of a subgroup of countries which looked to Germany for monetary leadership.

The achievements of the EMS through the 1980s led the UK to join the system in October 1990 and enhanced political confidence that EMU could be reached. This gave rise to the demand for plans for the completion of the transition to full monetary union emerged. The result was the Delors Report (Committee on the Study of Economic and Monetary Union 1989), which subsequently formed the basis of the Maastricht Treaty (1992).

The Delors Report emphasized a continuation of the gradualist approach, but crucially set out a timetable by which complete monetary union was to be achieved. Fundamentally, it contained a three-stage plan for a single currency and a single central bank for the EU and hence implicitly, for the transfer of political and economic power from national governments to the EU itself. In

Stage 1, which was to begin on 1 July 1990, all countries were to join the ERM with the 2.25 per cent bands, all remaining capital controls were to be abolished and the degree of monetary cooperation among the EMS central banks was strengthened. Stage 2 was to start on 1 January 1994 and set up the European Monetary Institute (EMI), to operate as a precursor of the European Central Bank (ECB), which would be set up in Stage 3. The EMI was charged with strengthening monetary cooperation. The third stage was to begin at the latest in January 1999 when all exchange rates would be irrevocably fixed and the ECB would start its operations. The final stage, however, was made conditional on member countries meeting the so-called convergence criteria, which will be considered in the next section.

As noted above, the ERM was built around the Deutschmark and so it was Germany's responsibility to manage its monetary conditions with some respect for the preferences of the other members. Failure to do so would cause a dilemma for other members: either to follow the Deutschmark lead or to break free from the DM by devaluing against it. Following the abolition of all capital controls in the late 1980s and German reunification in 1989, the German budget deficit and nominal interest rates rose sharply, posing a dilemma for other members. Whereas the German need for continued low inflation required higher interest rates, other member states were in recession and required lower interest rates. In this sense the reunification of Germany was the underlying cause of the ERM crises of September 1992, when a speculative attack on sterling and the lira resulted in them leaving the ERM, devaluing by some 14 per cent against the DM. Simultaneously, Spain devalued the peseta and Ireland raised overnight interest rates to 1000 per cent to protect the punt. In the following week, France spent some $10 billion – over half of its foreign exchange reserves – to maintain the franc parity with the DM. One year later in August 1993, there was another crisis when a speculative attack on the French franc led to the collapse of the ERM in all but name. The exchange rate bands were widened to 15 per cent on either side of the central rates – giving a spread of 30 per cent between the two currencies at the top and bottom of the bands – and a period of enforced floating commenced as phase 5 started.

To an extent these ERM crises should have been predictable. By making the ERM more stringent – all countries to be in the narrow band and all capital controls to be abolished – it meant that there was no longer any flexibility in the system, which had been at least part of the secret of its success. Without capital controls and little exchange rate flexibility, the authorities faced the impossibility triangle, illustrated in Figure 2.2. In this triangle only two of the three objectives can be achieved simultaneously. Under the EMS of the 1980s, with capital controls, both exchange rate stability and autonomy monetary policy were feasible, but the abolition of capital controls meant that these two objectives were no longer possible. The

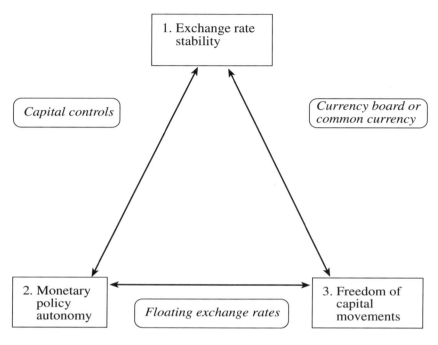

Figure 2.2   The impossibility triangle

UK chose a floating exchange rate, so preserving both freedom of capital movements and an autonomous monetary policy. While the wider exchange rate bands effectively led the other ERM members down the same road in the short run, there was even greater political pressure for full monetary union so that exchange rate stability and freedom of capital movements could coexist. Autonomy over monetary policy was therefore surrendered. Thus during phase 5 the widening of the exchange rate bands made EMU more likely by relaxing the exchange rate constraint, while at the same time showing that a pseudo union was not feasible without some form of capital controls or exchange rate flexibility. This prospect added impetus to the drive for complete monetary union as set out in Stage 3 of the Delors Report.

4   AN EVALUATION OF THE CONVERGENCE CRITERIA FOR MEMBERSHIP OF EMU

The Maastricht Treaty included five convergence criteria, not in the initial Delors Report, which were insisted upon by some member states, especially

Germany, in an attempt to restrict the size of the monetary union and to ensure that the eventual monetary union would be a low-inflation union. The five convergence criteria that a country must meet in order to join the union are:

1. its inflation rate is not more than 1.5 per cent higher than the average of the three lowest inflation rates in the EMS;
2. its long-term interest rate is not more than 2 per cent higher than the average observed in the three lowest inflation countries;
3. it has not experienced a devaluation during the two years preceding the entry in the union;
4. its government budget deficit is not higher than 3 per cent of its GDP; and
5. its government debt has moved significantly towards the norm of 60 per cent of its GDP.

The Treaty makes it clear that the budgetary convergence criteria are subject to interpretation. For example, the condition that the government debt-to-GDP ratio should 'decline sufficiently' and 'approach the reference value of 60 per cent at a satisfactory pace', is sufficiently vague to be allow for wide-ranging interpretations. The Treaty also stipulated that the European Commission and the EMI will both report on the progress each country has made towards convergence, which was to include the independence of the national central bank, and will propose whether the country be admitted into EMU. The final decision, however, rests with the Council of Ministers, who will decide about membership for each country on a qualified majority basis.

At the subsequent Madrid Summit in December 1995, the EU members agreed to call the common currency the euro, and to subdivide Stage 3 of the Maastricht Treaty into three further stages. These are as follows:

1. The membership of EMU would be determined in mid-1998, based on which countries satisfied the convergence criteria set out in the Maastricht Treaty.
2. On 1 January 1999 national currencies will be defined in terms of the euro at irrevocably fixed exchange rates. Commercial banks will use the euro in the interbank market and new government bond issues will be in euros. This stage will last until 31 December 2001.
3. Between 1 January and 1 July 2002 the euro will replace the national currencies, which lose their status as legal tender. Therefore EMU begins on 1 July 2002 with the supply of euros being managed by the ECB. During this final six-month phase both national currencies and the euro will be legal tender.

The national central banks will not completely disappear after 2002; rather they will be part of the European System of Central Banks (ESCB). These national banks, however, will not make monetary or exchange rate policy decisions. They will be used solely to implement the policy of the ECB.

The convergence criteria enshrined in the Maastricht Treaty are novel and largely without foundation in economic principles. As noted above, the primary motivation for these criteria was the concern of some member states, especially Germany, that EMU would have an inflationary bias. Therefore, by insisting on all countries meeting specific criteria prior to membership it was hoped that any inflationary bias could be prevented from the outset. The argument is as follows. Suppose there are two countries about to form a monetary union. The inflation rate in one country is 8 per cent per annum and in the other, 2 per cent per annum. If they form a monetary union the common inflation rate is likely to be the average of the two rates, that is 5 per cent, which is higher than desired by the low-inflation member. Therefore, unless other benefits of monetary union exceed this cost, the low-inflation partner will not want to join. Thus the low-inflation country will not want to participate in EMU unless it can guarantee a low-inflation union. To try to secure this aim, barriers are put in the way of potentially high-inflation members, so as to prevent them from joining the union.

This strategy, however, is flawed on two counts. First, even if a potential EMU member keeps inflation low prior to membership, to ensure that it meets the entry requirements, this does not mean that in future its representatives will subscribe to the same low-inflation policy. Once inside EMU the country's representatives could vote for a more expansionary monetary policy and a higher rate of inflation. In other words the entry requirements do not pre-commit the countries to low inflation for ever. Second, the inflation criterion became more difficult for the relatively high-inflation countries to meet as competitive disinflation[4] resulted in the inflation rate of the lowest three members falling quickly. Thus the deflation was sharper than anticipated and the resulting output losses were consequently greater than intended for the higher-inflation countries.

The interest rate criterion is quite unnecessary since it is bound to be satisfied for members who are eligible to join the union and unlikely to be met for countries who will be ineligible to join EMU. The real rate of interest is defined as the nominal rate less the expected inflation rate; that is $r = i - \pi$ or $i = \bar{r} + \pi$, where $\bar{r}$ is the constant long-run real interest rate. If the real rate is approximately constant, reflecting productivity and thrift, then the only difference between the nominal interest rates is the difference in expected inflation rates. Thus a country which satisfies the inflation criterion must also satisfy the nominal interest rate criterion. Similarly, countries with large differences in expected rates of inflation are likely to have large differences in nominal interest rates. Moreover, since nominal interest rates are determined in the financial markets, the question of which countries are able to join EMU is left in the hands of the financial markets. That is, the countries they believe will join will be allowed to join because they will meet the interest rate criterion.

The exchange rate convergence criterion of no devaluation for two years prior to entry is straightforward. This rule is to prevent countries from manipulating their exchange rate just before entry to gain competitive advantage over other members. When the Maastricht Treaty was signed this requirement was that the rates must remain with the 2.25 per cent band around the central rate. The ERM crises in August 1993 increased the width of the band to ± 15 per cent around the central rate and so this criterion became very soft and largely ineffective.

The budgetary criteria have come under specific attack from economists (see, for example, Buiter and Kletzer 1991). The motivation is again the need to achieve and maintain low inflation within the monetary union. The rationale is that countries with a high debt-to-GDP ratio are more likely to want to engineer inflation surprises so as to reduce the real value of their debt outstanding, thus securing a gain for the government and a loss for bond holders. Even within the monetary union a high-debt economy is more likely to favour a high-inflation policy than a country with a low debt-to-GDP ratio. A second criticism of the budgetary criteria is that the numbers chosen (3 per cent and 60 per cent) are completely arbitrary and a strong case can be made for higher numbers. Furthermore compared to the US, the EU countries have found it particularly difficult to reduce their debt-to-GDP ratios. Indeed over the 1991–96 period the average debt-to-GDP ratio actually rose in the EU, due to the restrictive budgetary and monetary policies. A tight monetary policy to constrain inflation will suppress nominal GDP which, by lowering the denominator, will serve to raise the debt-to-GDP ratio. Thus the tight budgetary and monetary policies make the achievement of the convergence criteria even more difficult than they need have been.

A third problem with the budget criteria is that even if the countries do meet the criteria for entry into EMU there is again no guarantee that they will adhere to these restraints once admission has been gained. For this reason it was agreed at the Dublin Summit in December 1996 to introduce a Stability Pact, which is to be implemented after the start of EMU. There are three points to this pact:

1.   Countries will aim to achieve budget balance.
2.   Countries with a budget deficit exceeding 3 per cent of GDP will be subject to fines, which can be as much as 0.5 per cent of GDP.
3.   These fines will not be applied if the country in question experiences a

natural disaster or other exceptional circumstances, defined as a decline
in GDP greater than 2 per cent in a single year. In cases where the fall in
GDP is between 0.75 and 2 per cent the application of the fine will be
subject to the approval of the EU finance ministers. Countries where
GDP falls by less than 0.75 per cent of GDP have agreed not to invoke
exceptional circumstances and to pay the fine, although even in this case
the imposition of the fine will require a decision of the Council of
Ministers.

The problem with the fiscal criteria is that they give the national authorities
little scope for flexibility. With monetary policy centrally controlled and
aimed at securing low inflation and fiscal policy being confined to balanced
budgets, the national authorities will in effect have given up almost all discretion over macroeconomic policy. This is likely to lead to conflicts between
EU objectives (low inflation) and national government objectives (high levels
of employment). Furthermore, it may also seriously reduce the automatic
stabilizing effect of allowing the budget deficit to vary over the economic
cycle, so intensifying recessions. If the experience in the 1990s is a guide
then there are some serious implications. Table 2.1 shows that in the recession of the early 1990s many EU countries experienced a decline in real GDP,
and for six of these countries (Belgium, France, Sweden, Spain, Portugal and
Italy) the structural budget deficit rose to levels greater than 3 per cent of

Table 2.1   Budget deficits and GDP (selected countries and years)

	Year	Change in real GDP (%)	Fine applicable	Budget deficit as % of GDP	
				Financial balance	Structural balance
Belgium	1993	−1.5	yes	−7.1	−3.3
Finland	1993	−1.2	no	−7.9	−1.6
France	1993	−1.3	yes	−5.7	−3.8
Germany	1993	−1.2	no	−3.2	−2.9
Italy	1993	−1.2	yes	−9.5	−8.4
Portugal	1993	−1.1	yes	−6.1	−5.7
Spain	1993	−1.2	yes	−8.4	−6.2
Sweden	1993	−2.2	no	−12.3	−9.2
UK	1991	−1.5	no	−2.8	−2.7

Source: Organization for Economic Cooperation and Development (1999), *Economic Outlook*, Paris: OECD.

GDP. Although some of these economics could claim special circumstances France, Portugal and Spain could not have done so and would have been eligible for fines.

This in turn may lead to the problems of enforcing the fines and measuring the deficits. Experience with budgetary rules, such as the Gramm–Rudman legislation in the US, is that it is unsuccessful since the authorities find ways of circumventing the rules. Von Hagen (1991), for example, has found evidence that US states employed 'off-budget' expenditures when they were constrained by constitutional limits. Thus constitutional rules may have little effect on the size of the budget deficits, which may make the fiscal criteria irrelevant.

Finally the Maastricht Treaty makes no reference at all to the need for a common set of labour market institutions and social security systems between the member states. Because the Treaty has nothing to say about real economic convergence, it is possible that the consequences of EMU, if it goes ahead as planned, will result in more divergent economic performance between the nation states, at least in the short run. This is likely to lead to political tensions within EMU, which, if sufficiently strong, could lead to the fragmentation of the EU. A slower, but arguably safer approach would have been to agree a series of graduated structural reforms *before* EMU, rather than hoping that EMU would bring pressure on recalcitrant states to undertake such reform subsequently. Nominal convergence is of course an easier objective on which to obtain political agreement, but less important for the real economy, whereas real convergence, which is vital for the success of EMU, is much harder to bring about because of political and social inertia.

5   THE PROGRESS OF THE TRANSITION PROCESS

The big step in the transition process is with the start of Stage 3. The convergence criteria discussed in Section 4, were used in May 1998 according to the Maastricht Treaty, to determine the 'ins' and the 'outs' of EMU and it was decided that EMU would go ahead with 11 member states. Greece would be excluded for not satisfying the criteria[5]. Sweden was not a member of the ERM and so was excluded and the UK and Denmark chose to use their opt-out from the first phase of EMU. Table 2.2 shows how these decisions were reached. There are several features that stand out from this table.

1.   With the exception of Greece all countries satisfy the inflation and long-term interest rate criteria. As noted above these criteria are not mutually exclusive.
2.   Sweden and the UK are excluded by the non-membership of the ERM from membership, although the UK satisfies all of the other criteria.

3. All of the countries that had an excessive budget deficit for at least one
    year since 1994 were abrogated by the Council.
4. The UK, Finland and Luxembourg are the only countries to pass the
    debt-to-GDP ratio, set at 60 per cent. Moreover, of the 'in' countries both
    Belgium and Italy have debt-to-GDP ratios exceeding 100 per cent.

It is clear that the Maastricht convergence criteria have been interpreted
generously, especially in the case of Italy. This makes something of a nonsense of the initial criteria. It is well known that for France the budget
deficit-to-GDP ratio was only below 3 per cent because of some creative
accounting. The debt-to-GDP ratios of both Belgium and Italy exceed 100
per cent, but the fact that both countries' debt-to-GDP ratios had been falling,
albeit very slowly in the case of Italy, was deemed sufficient for entry. This,
of course, again emphasizes the political nature of EMU, rather than the
economic nature, although as noted before, the nominal convergence criteria
are not really based on any sound principles of economics.

With effect from 1 January 1999 the exchange rates between the 11 national currencies taking part in EMU have been irrevocably fixed (see Table
2.3 for the conversion rates agreed) and the interest rate on euro deposits
initially set by the ECB at 3 per cent annum. During the course of 1999,
uncertainty arose about the appropriate level of euro interest rates. In March
1999 interest rates were cut to 2.5 per cent annum, ostensibly to boost
economic growth, but by early 2000 they had been raised on three occasions
to stand at 3.5 per cent in March, as inflation rose above 2 per cent in the euro
area. At the end of 2000, euro interest rates stand at 4.75 per cent with some
analysts forecasting further euro interest rises during 2001 – perhaps to 5 per
cent by the middle of 2001.

These interest rate changes partly reflect the underlying tensions within
EMU caused by differential economic performance between the member
states when faced with a common monetary policy. Table 2.4 shows the
OECD's prediction of output gaps and unemployment in the EU countries.
Ideally interest rates need to be lower in Spain and Italy where unemployment is about 17 and 12 per cent, respectively, but higher in Ireland, where
inflation is running at about 6 per cent per annum as of December 2000.
While the recent rises in interest rates may eventually ease EU-wide inflation,
this policy is likely to make the unemployment problem worse. The monetary
mechanism whereby adjustment can take place – devaluation of the Spanish
peseta against the Irish punt, for example – is ruled out and so adjustment
must operate through the real side of the economy. That is, Ireland loses
competitiveness to Spain, which gains jobs at the expense of the Irish. Thus
Irish jobs are exported to Spain. The problem is not that the job opportunities
move location, but that the workers do not move to follow them. In other

Table 2.2   Current performance of member state in relation to convergence

	Inflation HICP (harmonized consumer price index)	Government budgetary position						Exchange rates ERM participation	Long-term interest rates
		Existence of an excessive deficit	Deficit (% of GDP)	Debt (% of GDP)	Change from previous year				
	Jan. 1998		1997	1997	1997	1996	1995	March 1998	January 1998
Reference value (%)	2.7		3	60					7.8
Belgium	1.4	yes	2.1	122.2	-4.7	-4.3	-2.2	yes	5.7
Denmark	1.9	no	-0.7	65.1	-5.5	-2.7	-4.9	yes	6.2
Germany	1.4	yes	2.7	61.3	0.8	2.4	7.8	yes	5.6
Greece	5.2	yes	4.0	108.7	-2.9	1.5	0.7	yes	9.8
Spain	1.8	yes	2.6	68.8	-1.3	4.6	2.9	yes	6.3
France	1.2	yes	3.0	58.0	2.4	2.9	4.2	yes	5.5
Ireland	1.2	no	-0.9	66.3	-6.4	-9.6	-6.8	yes	6.2
Italy	1.8	yes	2.7	121.6	-2.4	-0.2	-0.7	yes	6.7
Luxembourg	1.4	no	-1.7	6.7	0.1	0.7	0.2	yes	5.6
Netherlands	1.8	no	1.4	72.1	-5.0	-1.9	1.2	yes	5.5
Austria	1.1	yes	2.5	66.1	-3.4	0.3	3.8	yes	5.6
Portugal	1.8	yes	2.5	62.0	-3.0	-0.9	2.1	yes	6.2
Finland	1.3	no	0.9	55.8	-1.8	-0.4	-1.5	yes	5.9
Sweden	1.9	yes	0.8	76.6	-0.1	-0.9	-1.4	no	6.5
UK	1.8	yes	1.9	53.4	-1.3	0.8	3.5	no	7.0
EU	1.6		2.4	72.1	-0.9	2.0	3.0		6.1

Source: CEC (1998b).

Table 2.3 Euro conversion rates on 1 January 1999

1 euro is equal to	
Austrian schillings	13.7603
Belgian/Luxembourg francs	40.3399
Dutch guilders	2.20371
Finnish markka	5.94573
French francs	6.55957
German marks	1.95583
Irish punts	0.78756
Italian lira	1936.27
Portuguese escudo	200.482
Spanish peseta	166.386

Table 2.4 Unemployment rates and output gaps in Western Europe

	Unemployment rates			Output gaps		
	1998	1999	2000	1998	1999	2000
Austria	6.1	6.0	5.6	−0.8	−0.7	−0.6
Belgium	11.8	11.5	11.3	−1.2	−1.0	−0.7
Denmark	6.5	6.0	5.9	0.8	0.2	−0.4
Finland	10.9	9.7	8.8	1.3	0.8	0.3
France	11.8	11.2	10.6	−1.2	−0.9	−0.4
Germany	11.2	10.8	10.3	−1.4	−1.4	−1.2
Ireland	9.1	8.4	7.9	2.0	1.0	0.4
Italy	12.2	12.1	11.9	−3.2	−3.2	−2.7
Netherlands	4.1	4.2	4.4	1.4	1.0	0.4
Portugal	5.1	5.3	5.3	0.1	0.2	0.3
Spain	19.1	17.8	16.8	−1.0	−0.8	−0.8
Sweden	6.5	6.3	6.0	−1.2	−1.0	−0.9
UK	6.5	7.4	8.0	0.9	−0.4	−0.9
EU	10.6	10.3	10.1	−1.0	−1.2	−1.0
Eurozone	11.7	11.3	10.8	−1.3	−1.2	−1.0

Source: Organization for Economic Cooperation and Development (1999), *Economic Outlook*, Paris: OECD.

words because labour mobility is low, Irish workers become redundant whereas formally unemployed Spanish workers will gain employment.

The distribution of economic gains and losses from EMU if significant and uncorrected may ultimately undermine the political will to continue with EMU. To ensure that this does not happen more flexibility is needed in the operation of fiscal and regional policy. The case for a greater centralized fiscal budget together with regional transfers is economically overwhelming, but politically a non-starter. Regional policy is tied partly by the constraints on national budget deficits and partly by the lack of significant central funds to assist depressed areas (see Button and Pentecost, 1999). Greater labour market flexibility is also needed to help reduce unemployment – as the Dutch experience illustrates – but again there seems to a general lack of political urgency in tackling this problem. Thus, at least in the short to medium term a widening of real regional economic performance can be expected, which is not encouraging for the long-term future of the monetary union.

6   CONCLUSIONS

This chapter has outlined the transition from a joint floating exchange rate system through a pseudo union (the EMS) to full monetary union (EMU). This transition has been gradualist and politically motivated at almost every stage. The relevant economic criterion, as set out by the optimal currency literature, has been put to one side. Because of this, structural reform of the EU economies, especially with regard to labour markets and intra-EU labour mobility, has not been addressed, although nominal convergence has in the main been achieved prior to membership. The potential problem facing EMU is how to bring about the necessary structural reform and in the meantime to redistribute the gains to compensate the losers adequately. Without such reforms and a transfer mechanism, the monetary reform may eventually turn out to have undesirable economic consequences, which will lead to its abandonment.

NOTES

1. There was a wider fluctuation band of ± 6 per cent for inflation-prone economies such as Italy.
2. See Gibson (1996) for specific details of these realignments.
3. Note, however, that the German leadership view of the ERM is contested by Fratianni and von Hagen (1990b), who argue that German monetary policy did respond to policy changes in France and Italy.
4. The policy of competitive disinflation was followed actively in France. Jean-Claude Trichet, the governor of the Bank of France, admitted that this was France's primary policy objective (see Connolly 1995).
5. Greece was admitted into the euro in January 2001.

3. German monetary unification and its implications for EMU

Friedrich L. Sell*

1   INTRODUCTION

On 1 July 1990, a monetary union was implemented between West and East Germany. By the next day, all stocks of Ostmarks were converted into D-Marks. Different conversion rates were applied according to the age of the Ostmark owners, the 'liquidity' of deposits and the speculative character of the Ostmark acquired in the year of conversion. Most of the bank deposits, firm and household debts and financial claims were converted at an exchange rate of 2:1 (Ostmark/D-Mark), whereas price and wage contracts as well as old-age pensions enjoyed an exchange rate of 1:1 (see Sinn and Sinn 1991, p. 34).

Before and after this remarkable event a lively discussion took place that centred on the following issues: did a monetary union actually make sense from the theory of optimum currency areas' point of view? This question was raised mainly by the economics profession. Should the conversion use a much higher exchange rate given the fact that the monetary union had to be accepted politically? This position was maintained primarily by the Deutsche Bundesbank. Finally, should there be a unique conversion rate of 1:1 just to avoid any kind of bad feelings from East Germany's population and to stop East–West migration? These issues are addressed in Section 2.

By the end of 1990, the federal government organized general elections with great emphasis on winning the majority not only of the West German, but also of the East German vote. West German trade unions and business associations formulated their vested interests in the East German wage formation process, while European neighbours expressed their fears of an even stronger economic hegemony by the Germans, and made reference to the historical situation in Europe before the Second World War. These important aspects of the conversion controversy will be discussed in Section 3.

When observing more closely the impact the then chosen conversion rate of exchange had on the economic development inside and outside Germany for about nine years, a more distanced evaluation of the economic repercussion (Section 4) seems to be possible. In particular, in this chapter, three major problems will be elucidated. First, the deindustrialization tendencies in East Germany; second, the huge transfers from West to East Germany as well as the dramatic increase in public deficits and public debt in Germany since the early 1990s; and finally, the asymmetric shock caused by the economic and monetary union between East and West Germany to the European partners participating in the European Monetary System (EMS).

The chapter then continues with policy conclusions and with an attempt to draw some lessons from the German case – though very special indeed – for the ongoing process of monetary integration in Europe (European Monetary Union: EMU). Finally, a mathematical annex completes the exposition.

2   THEORETICAL ASPECTS

Was (West + East) Germany a Case for an Optimum Currency Area?

The theoretical debate on the monetary union between East and West Germany mixed up two aspects which, though intimately linked with each other, should not be confused. One aspect deals with the question whether the exchange rate of the two currencies (D-Mark, Ostmark) should be fixed at all – that is if a *monetary union* should be entered – while the other aspect questions *the rate* at which the fixing of the exchange rate was to be done. First the issue as to whether East and West Germany were good candidates to build an optimum currency area is considered.

The theory of optimum currency is far away from being a comprehensive piece of international monetary economics. It merely offers some preconditions that have been identified 'as relevant for choosing the likely participants in an optimum currency area' (Tavlas 1993, p. 666). These more or less 'traditional' criteria have received competition from, or at least some sort of complementarity by, 'modern' strands of the new macroeconomic theory. In the following, the German monetary union is tested on both of these criteria.

Traditional criteria

1. *Similarity of inflation rates*   Although East Germany was not affected by a significant open inflation, its repressed economy embedded a considerable monetary overhang, that is, a large *potential* inflation. However, this was not a wilful monetary overhang, so it is difficult to assess differences in the economic preferences with regard to the goal of price stability between East and West Germany. Kindleberger (1967) and Haberler (1971) stressed the fact that the more countries resemble each

other in their economic preferences the easier they will find it to build a common currency area. This may be reflected in similar rates of inflation (Magnifico 1973) and/or fiscal integration (Johnson 1970, see below).

2. *Degree of factor mobility*   Factor mobility between East and West Germany did not provide a substantial substitute for exchange rate flexibility as Mundell's (1961) criterion requires for prospective optimum currency areas. Although there was a unidirectional readiness to migrate (East–West) and an asymmetrical propensity to invest (West–East),[1] these facts were primarily caused by the unification effect and do not prove a lasting interregional mobility of factors of production between West and East Germany.

3. *Openness and size of the economy*   By the time of the monetary union East Germany – though a small economy – was not well integrated either in international (monetized) trade or in international finance. Hence, it was not a good candidate for a monetary union according to McKinnon's (1963) criterion.

4. *Degree of commodity diversification*   East Germany did not show a diversified economy, forestalling the need for frequent changes in the terms of trade via the exchange rate (Kenen 1969). Hence, according to Kenen, it was not prepared to renounce the instrument of flexible exchange rates.

5. *Price and wage flexibility*   Neither East nor West Germany fulfilled this precondition, which enables adjustment between regions when the exchange rate is no longer a variable. This statement holds especially for West Germany's wages in the last 25 years and for the wage policy in East Germany since 1990.

6. *Degree of goods market integration*   Both parts of Germany were equipped with quite different production structures so that they were not prone to symmetric terms-of-trade shocks. The benefits of eliminating currency exchanges in a monetary union will be greater, the larger the proportion of common rather than country-specific shocks (Grubel 1970; Currie 1992).

7. *Fiscal integration*   In the beginning, there was almost no fiscal integration; however, fiscal transfers from West to East Germany began to flow quite soon after the new *Länder* began functioning as government entities. One should be cautious, however, about taking this as a 'harmony' in economic preferences (see above).

8. *Existence of a hegemonic power*   This criterion was surely met as the West German government and the Deutsche Bundesbank were confined to active leadership (Ogrodnick 1990, p. 247) in the process of (re)unification. As Putnam and Bayne put forward in 1987, without such a dominant member, other factors would have to emerge to consolidate the union.

Modern criteria

9. *The nominal anchor issue*   Countries in a monetary union need to agree on how monetary policy should be conducted as fixed exchange rates impose identical interest rates (Tavlas 1993, pp. 670–71). In this respect, there was no discussion about the Deutsche Bundesbank taking immediate responsibility for both parts of Germany.
10. *The credibility issue*   By joining the union with the low-inflation West Germany, East Germany could reap the benefits of a high reputation, without any loss of output and employment, at least in the medium to long run. Moreover, the monetary union served to signal to the East Germans that the German reunification would be irrevocable and offered no incentive for a huge East–West migration.
11. *The terms-of-trade issue*   East Germany suffered from a negative terms-of-trade shock when it liberalized its trade and was confronted with 'internationalized' prices for important inputs; participation in the monetary union with West Germany, however, did not allow for an expansion in the money supply to fight against the contraction in real income.
12. *The incentives for the hegemon issue*   The fear of a loss of reputation of the Deutsche Bundesbank and/or of the capital market bonus of Germany with regard to Europe and the rest of the world with West Germany engaging in the very costly task of restructuring a former socialist country was largely unfounded.

As it is impossible to weigh up these very different criteria, the theoretical evaluation of the costs and benefits of a monetary union between West and East Germany remains ambiguous. While a majority of the *traditional* criteria would not have favoured proceeding to monetary union as it was done, some of the *modern* criteria – at least *ex post* – tend to support the policy chosen by the East and West German authorities.

The Conversion Rate Issue

Once it was clear that German monetary union would occur, discussions about the appropriate exchange rate at which the conversion should be carried out became widespread. There were three main strands in the debate: first, several research institutes, governmental offices and others started to compute purchasing power parities between the Ostmark and the D-Mark. Second, the focus of the Bundesbank, of the federal government and of various scientific councils was on the 'right conversion rate' for goods, wages and pensions and, third (with the same discussants), bank deposits, financial claims and debts were at stake.

From a theoretical perspective, the conversion rates for stocks and current payments for goods and factor prices must not coincide (Clausen and Willms 1994, p. 199). In an ideal world of perfectly flexible factor and goods prices the conversion rate chosen for *current payments* should not affect the real variables of the economy. Given the well-known relevance of wage/price rigidity in Germany, however, negative repercussions on income and employment from the 'wrong choice' could be expected. As far as the conversion rate for stocks was concerned, the most important aspect was that it would determine 'the East German citizens' initial endowment with financial assets' (ibid., p. 199) and the East German company's burden with debt. The conversion rate chosen would have to avoid an inflationary push and help eliminate the existing monetary overhang. In principle, the choice of the stocks' conversion rate does not affect 'the steady-state rate of inflation. It determines the long-run equilibrium price level and therefore has transitory implications for the rate of inflation' (ibid., p. 200). The actual discussion in Germany during 1990 did not strictly follow this structure; instead, three different aspects of the current payments' conversion rate were debated on the one hand and the stocks' conversion issue on the other hand. In the following we aim to refocus those strands of discussion.

Current payments' conversion rate

1. *The (consumer) purchasing power parity (PPP) point of view* The estimated purchasing power parities ranged from 100 Ostmarks = 94 D-Marks to 100 Ostmarks = 132 D-Marks for a bundle of East German consumer (*traded and non-traded*) goods and centred on 100 Ostmarks equal to 88 D-Marks for a bundle of West German goods (Sinn and Sinn 1991, p. 37). Both computations were most likely biased as Sinn and Sinn (ibid., pp. 38–9) explain: after the monetary union a typical East German household would have needed less than 132 D-Marks, as with a changed price structure it could have bought more from the now cheaper, but less from the now more expensive goods. *Mutatis mutandis*, 88 D-Marks would not have been enough to compensate for the fact that its preferences (still) differed from the West German taste. The geometric mean between those two extremes – in the neighbourhood of 108 – might have been the 'utility equivalent solution' (ibid., p. 39).

2. *The foreign exchange revenue point of view* Another important aspect of the conversion rate issue dealt with the foreign exchange productivity of East German exports. In 1989, the implicit exchange rate was close to 4.5:1. Hence, it seemed rather plausible to make use of an equivalent conversion rate. After the currency conversion, one Ostmark was equal to one D-Mark. East German exporters, however, now received only one

unit of the new money instead of 4.5 units of the old money. Their export prices, thus, had fallen. But how to explain the vast difference between the implicit exchange rate of 4.5:1 and the above PPP rates? The main explanation originates from Bela Balassa's (1982) analysis of biased exchange rates: countries with a low productivity of labour and low prices of non-tradables (as was the case with East Germany) will experience an upwards bias in their exchange rate (undervalued), if the exchange rate only reflects the (producer) purchasing power parity for *traded* goods.

3. *The adequate wages and pensions point of view* During the intense discussion on the right conversion rate for wages and old-age pensions, the Deutsche Bundesbank maintained the strongest position against a 1:1 change; it argued that a wage–price spiral could well begin. The German government was much less sceptical about it and tried to make out of the issue a matter of its own credibility and of social justice towards the East German population. Most economists were quite critical about the decision then taken: many East German households would have perceived a conversion at 2:1 as already an improvement in their real wages. On the other hand, with the then realized conversion rate of 1:1, wage costs (per unit of production) rose considerably measured by units of export goods: while the export prices had fallen (see above), wages denominated before in Ostmarks now had to be paid in D-Marks. *Real* (export) product wages, hence, rose by 450 per cent (Hoffmann 1993, p. 28). This became one of the major factors to explain the subsequent decline in the competitiveness of East Germany's tradables sector.

The stocks' conversion issue

The Deutsche Bundesbank was the leading defender of the position to 'devalue' East Germany's deposits and (intranational) debts by a conversion rate of 2:1. If not, the fear was of an inflationary pressure on the goods markets due to a revaluation of assets, of an 'excess burden' for firms and households with outstanding debt and, in the case where the federal government would take over the debt, of a large increase in the government's deficits and indebtedness. Surprisingly, the inflationary effects of the East German backlog demand were not very pronounced. The savings ratio soon returned to ordinary levels so that apparently there was more of a secular *shift* in East Germany's consumption towards West German goods than of a secular *increase*. From today's point of view and given the negative balance of the Treuhandanstalt – which was assigned to transfer as many as possible of the former GDR state-run companies into private ownership (Schmidt 1994, p. 3) – in terms of net revenues, it was a very wise decision to halve firm and household debt in East Germany.

Alternatives to a Premature Monetary Union

Meanwhile, German monetary union and the applied conversion rates belong to economic history. None the less, it is more than an academic question to think of possible alternatives that economic theory offers. We shall examine the scenarios: a free trade zone with a flexible exchange rate between the Ostmark and the D-Mark; a free trade zone combined with a currency board system in East Germany with the D-Mark serving as the 'backing currency'; and a free trade zone with the D-Mark circulating in East Germany as a parallel currency.

1. *A flexible exchange rate* between the Ostmark and the D-Mark could in principle have helped to neutralize – by continuous depreciations of the Ostmark – wage and price inflation in East Germany. In this case, East Germany's tradables sector might have 'survived' with low- and medium-quality manufactured goods for some time. Also, East Germany might have been much more appealing to some of the foreign private investors. Most likely, what Sinn and Sinn (1991) have called the 'high wage–high tech' strategy which has dominated since 1990, could not have had such an overwhelming influence on the transformation of East Germany.

2. *A currency board* is an institution that issues bank notes and coins in domestic currency, which can be exchanged on demand at a fixed exchange rate into a foreign reserve currency; that is, domestic notes and coins are backed 100 per cent by a reserve (Hoffmann and Sell 1993, p. 14). In the case of East Germany, the reserve currency would have been the D-Mark. The Deutsche Bundesbank would have provided the former GDR 'Staatsbank' with the necessary amount of D-Mark reserves. Coupling the Ostmark to a reserve currency like the D-Mark would have guaranteed equally stable prices in the area of the Ostmark and – of course – made the Ostmark fully convertible.

3. *A parallel currency* to the Ostmark – with the D-Mark being the 'natural' candidate of choice – would have meant a fully flexible exchange rate between the two currencies and freedom to denominate contracts in one of the two moneys (Fuhrmann 1994, p. 14). In this case, there is no need for official reserves of gold and/or foreign exchange. Under normal circumstances, private agents will prefer the more stable currency with the consequence that the East German 'Staatsbank' would have had to adapt to the course of the Deutsche Bundesbank, or the Ostmark would have disappeared from the markets in the wave of continuous depreciation and inflation.

The flexible exchange rate and the parallel currency approaches can be viewed as interim solutions on the road to monetary union. As Siebert puts it, compared with instant monetary union they would have had the advantage of:

- using the exchange rate as a shock absorber for the East German firms, thus giving them competitiveness temporarily,
- easing the transnational difficulties involved in adapting the social security system and in adjusting wages,
- delegating the conversion of debt, liabilities and wages to the market exchange rate prevailing at the end of the transitional period, and uncoupling the GDR-Mark from the European Monetary System (EMS) for the transitional period. (Siebert 1990, p. 8)

All these alternatives, however, suffer from the following shortcomings compared with the solution selected by the federal government of Germany:

- only a monetary union was a credible signal to the agents that political union between East and West Germany was imminent; without a monetary union, emigration of people from East Germany might not have stopped;
- given the long mutual economic and cultural history of East and West Germany, political union was widely desired;
- there was only a short 'historical' period of time in which the former USSR could be 'convinced' to agree to Germany's (re)unification;
- even a large devaluation of 400 to 500 per cent perhaps, would have been only the lower bound of a much larger depreciation with flexible exchange rates.[2] This sort of overshooting would have fuelled inflation in East Germany.

3   PUBLIC CHOICE ASPECTS

The Political Business Cycle of the German Currency Conversion[3]

From the methodological viewpoint of international competitiveness, the East–West German conversion of July 1990 had to ensure that East Germany's average costs per unit in the production of tradables were not lifted up beyond West Germany's level. The dilemma was that once the decision was taken on the conversion rate, the rate of adjustment of East German to West German wages was no longer 'free' to be chosen. Apparently, the economic logic behind this statement had not been recognized and/or considered by that time. In the following, we shall present a graphical model of the German

general elections of 1990, which draws on Sell (1994, pp. 128–31) and aims
at explaining 'why' politicians systematically violated the existing boundary
economic conditions. Formal details can be found in the mathematical annex.

Figure 3.1a shows the relationship between the (non-)adjustment rate of East
German wages to the level of West German wages $(1 - \gamma)$, on the one hand, and
the conversion rate between the Ostmark and the D-Mark (w), on the other,
which guarantees neutrality of the average costs per unit of production *vis-à-vis*
the level in West Germany. This is a trade-off relationship in the tradition of the
Phillips curve framework. It is downward sloped, which means that a total
adjustment of nominal wages in East Germany to the level in West Germany $(\gamma
= 1)$ was only feasible in exchange for a maximal conversion rate between the
Ostmark and the D-Mark of w^*. *Mutatis mutandis*, the feasible exchange rate
goes to zero when the rate of wage (non-)adjustment approaches $(1 - \gamma)^*$. An
increase in East Germany's capital productivity, π_K, shifts the graph towards the
origin. This reflects the fact that a higher capital productivity allows *ceteris
paribus* for a lower rate of conversion and a higher rate of wage adjustment.

The optimization problem for East Germany, therefore, consisted in maxi-
mizing a utility function under the constraint of the above boundary condition.
Such a utility function included the rate of wage adjustment (γ), the inverse of

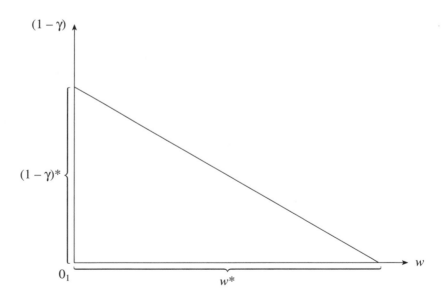

Source: Sell 1994

Figure 3.1a   Cost–neutrality function

the conversion rate (w^{-1}) and the rate of economic growth (dy/y). Higher values of the mentioned determinants would in principle have increased East German utility, *ceteris paribus*.

As in Nordhaus (1975), any utility function can easily be transformed into an aggregate voting function, where the government reduces the set of economic variables that are put to vote to three or less (preferably two) items. The two major variables that were put to the vote in East Germany during 1990 in various elections were the speed of adjustment of East German to the level of the West German wages and the (reciprocal of the) conversion rate. If the voting function is well behaved, the so-called iso-voting curves have the general shape as in Figure 3.1b.

In Figure 3.2, a graphical solution of the constrained optimization problem is presented. If we identify k_0 to be the level of average costs per unit of production in East Germany which would have guaranteed neutrality with respect to the level in West Germany, the federal government might have lost the main elections with the East German electorate and also the general elections *in toto*. To give an example: with a conversion rate of 2:1, a wage adjustment rate of 50 per cent might have given the same price competitiveness to East Germany's tradables as to West Germany's. Therefore, politicians

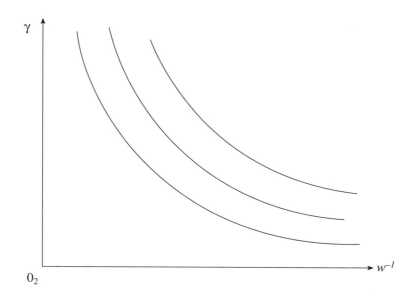

Source: Sell 1994

Figure 3.1b   Iso-voting curves

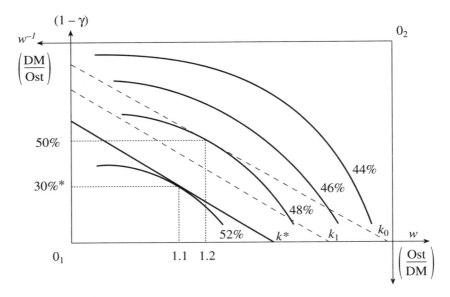

Note: $^*\gamma = 0.7 \Rightarrow$ wage adjustment rate of 70 per cent.

Source: Sell (1994).

Figure 3.2   Equilibrium

of the ruling parties, who did not care too much about these considerations but wanted to be re-elected, cheated by announcing the rather irrelevant or soft budget constraint k^* to be achievable although they knew that it would lead to a severe output loss and a reduction in the competitiveness of East Germany's tradables. But a promise of a wage adjustment rate of 70 per cent coupled with a conversion rate of 1:1 was smart enough to win elections.

3.2   The Role of Interest Groups

Germany's monetary and economic union was accompanied by very active lobbying initiatives: West German entrepreneurs and unions as well as East German and West German households put pressure on the decision makers in Bonn (see Alexander 1994, pp. 11–15):

1.   *West German entrepreneurs*   This group was particularly interested in securing East Germany as an additional market for their products; for this reason, they had no great interest in potential competitors from the

East, but rather wanted to take over East German plants. Hence, they favoured a low conversion and a high wage adjustment rate.

2. *East German entrepreneurs*   By the time of the monetary and economic union there was not a single 'East German entrepreneur'.

3. *West German trade unions*   The unions were interested in presenting the inherent costs of German monetary and economic union to their West German members as rather low; on the other side – given that there were no East German trade unions by this time – they defended a low conversion and a high wage adjustment rate, hoping to win new members in East Germany.

4. *East German trade unions*   In practice, this group did not exist by the time of monetary and economic union.

5. *West German households*   These were mainly concerned with the possible fiscal burden(s) emerging from the unification process and with the likelihood of losing the high standard(s) of the West German social security system during the process of social and economic 'harmonization' between East and West Germany.

6. *East German households*   Their major interest was to achieve a low conversion rate for their monetary assets. They did not expect that many of their jobs would become obsolete with a low conversion and a high wage adjustment rate.

In sum, there was not a single pressure group who favoured a high conversion and a low wage adjustment rate by the time of monetary and economic union.

The Role of Foreign Countries

West Germany's European partners were generally unenthusiastic about the imminent monetary and economic union; basically, there were two major sources of scepticism. The first one was formulated by Margaret Thatcher on 26 January 1990 in a *Wall Street Journal* interview (see Teltschik 1993, p. 115). She blamed German politics for pursuing nationalistic goals rather than subordinating to European interests. Furthermore, German monetary and economic union would – according to Mrs Thatcher – destabilize the *economic equilibrium* within the European Community. In order to fully appreciate this statement, one should remember that the British government's agenda at that time was still to exert an influence over the prospective European Monetary Union to further its own interests, and was far from its later 'opt-out-clauses' point of view. A larger zone of command for the Deutsche Bundesbank – which the German monetary and economic union would necessarily imply – would allow even more 'monetary leadership' by the Deutsche Bundesbank in Europe which may predispose the design of the prospective European Central Bank.

There was a second area of reservation, deriving mainly from the historical experiences of Germany's European neighbours, with François Mitterrand as the most prominent representative. In December 1989, the French president visited the GDR and pointed out that free elections in East Germany should precede any negotiations on a German (re)unification. Also, he claimed the right of Germany's neighbours and the four Second World War allies to participate in the decision-making process. The notion of the 'invulnerability of national borders' became a means of questioning the abolition of the Wall between East and West Germany.

Neither strand of reasoning was concerned with the conversion issue in the first place; however, a German monetary and economic union was recognized as a necessary prerequisite for the political union.[4] The reaction of the West German government to both of these objections was to ensure that German unification would be seen as part of the European political and economic convergence process (Teltschik 1993, p. 99) and – more implicitly – that Germany was prepared to relinquish some of its high demands for price stability as the major goal of the prospective European Central Bank in exchange for the acceptance of Germany's (re)unification and a more emancipated role for (re)unified Germany in the 'concert of nations' in future.

4   ECONOMIC REPERCUSSIONS

Deindustrialization in East Germany[5]

Within the framework of the well-known Salter–Swan–Meade analysis, East Germany's economic situation on the eve of German monetary and economic union is characterized by Figure 3.3. Given the initial transformation curve, *EE*, and the full-employment locus, *S*, the factor allocation was represented by *P*. The former GDR consumed a bundle of (tradable and non-tradable) goods as represented by point *C*, where the income-consumption line (*Z*) and the real absorption line (*A*) intersect. Hence, there was a moderate deficit in the balance of trade[6] (corresponding to the distance $D_T - S_T$) and – much more pronounced – a considerable amount of hidden unemployment (corresponding to the distance $S_N - D_N$).

The full-employment locus (*S*) in Figure 3.3 merely stands for potential outputs.[7] What is important, is that the slope of *S* signals to the producers the relative price between tradables and non-tradables, according to which they will allocate their factors of production. The eventually used real output (*Y*) of the former GDR is represented by point *D* and consisted in the rectangle $0S_TDD_N$. Hence, it was smaller than real absorption (*A*) at a size of $0D_TCD_N$.

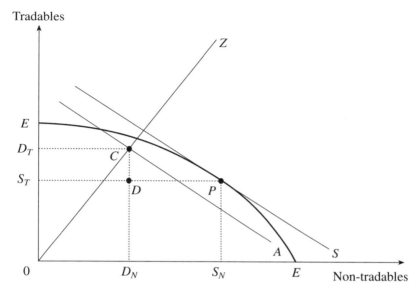

Source: Greiner et al. (1994).

Figure 3.3   *East Germany's economy on the eve of monetary and economic union with West Germany*

Thus, the condition for open (in the case of the former GDR more or less) economies, $Y - A = X - M$, was fulfilled.

In the subsequent analysis of the revaluation effects of the Ostmark due to the chosen conversion rate, we shall ignore negative terms-of-trade effects (such as the higher oil price at world market conditions) which had to be accommodated by the East German economy in the early phase of transformation. As we have seen above, the conversion rate chosen for economic flow variables during the German monetary and economic union resulted in a considerable nominal and real appreciation of the Ostmark with the (producer) purchasing power parities as a point of reference.

It was clear that the sector most affected by the real appreciation was the production of tradables. With the simultaneous accession to the European Common Market, East German products were also in full competition with highly advanced western companies. Hence, it was no surprise that East German exporters experienced considerable difficulties. As Balassa (1982) and Edwards (1984) expressed it in the 1980s with reference to reforms in developing countries: trade liberalization should never be accompanied by an appreciation of the real exchange rate.[8] But this is

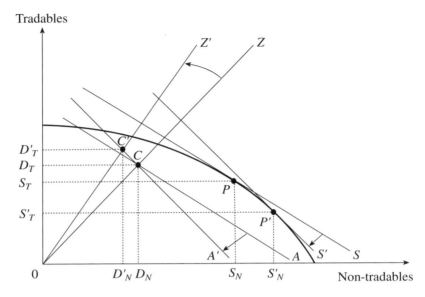

Source: Greiner et al. (1994).

*Figure 3.4   Impact of the low conversion rate between the D-Mark and the
Ostmark on East Germany's (non-)tradables sector*

precisely the kind of shock that the East German economy had to face
right from the beginning!

When analysing the effects of the real exchange rate appreciation in the
framework of the Salter–Swan–Meade diagram (see Figure 3.4), one has to
rotate the absorption line (A) as well as the income line (S) to the left (to A'
and S', respectively) so that they become steeper; also, the expansion path 0Z
will have to move – due to the change in relative prices – to its new position
0Z', that is, closer to the axis of the now relatively cheaper tradables. The new
equilibrium consumption point is now C' and the new equilibrium production
point is P'.

As a result, production in the tradable sector falls from S_T to S'_T. (*indirect
deindustrialization*) whereas the demand for tradables increases from D_T to D'_T.
The latter causes an additional deficit in East Germany's balance of trade. More
precisely, the regional[9] demand for tradables exceeds the regional supply. Hence,
the positive balance of trade for West *and* East Germany *vis-à-vis* the rest of the
world will have to diminish! In the non-tradables sector, demand decreases
from D_N to D'_N; the supply of non-tradables, on the other hand, increases from
S_N to S'_N, so that a significant rise in open unemployment occurs.

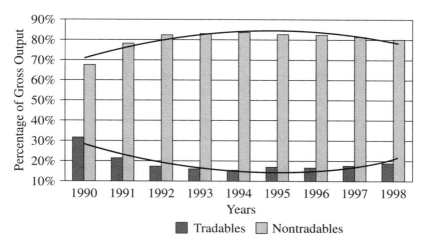

Sources: Statistisches Bundesamt; Greiner et al. (1994), IfW (1999), own calculations.

Figure 3.5   *Shares of tradables and non-tradables in gross output of East Germany, 1990–1998*

Between 1990 and 1998, one can observe a remarkable change in the sectoral structure of the East German economy, that is, in the contribution of tradables and non-tradables to total output. As Figure 3.5 demonstrates, the share of the tradables' sector in total gross output declined considerably until 1993–94, while the share of the non-tradables sector increased accordingly. This was primarily due to the growing importance of the construction industry, the housing sector, construction-related industries and the services sector. Since 1994, the share of the tradables' sector has increased slightly. This effect is based among other things on the moderate expansion of the industrial sector (that is, it is caused by improvements in the competitiveness of firms), and on the declining activity in the construction and housing industry (Institute für Weltwirtschaft, IfW 1999, p. 11).

It should be added that the deindustrialization effect caused by the conversion rate of 1:1 between the Ostmark and the D-Mark, which represented an appreciation of the Ostmark in the neighbourhood of 450 per cent, was enhanced by additional factors: the supply shock triggered by the wage policy of West German trade unions 'on behalf' of the almost non-existing East German trade unions,[10] the absorption of high fiscal transfers from West Germany ('direct industrialization'); the liberalization of East Germany's trade when joining the trade area of West Germany and, hence, of the European Economic Community; the abrupt cessation of export demand stemming

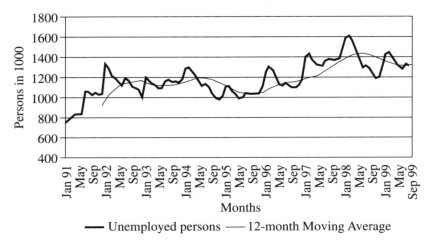

Months

—— Unemployed persons —— 12-month Moving Average

Sources: Statistisches Bundesamt; own calculations.

Figure 3.6   Unemployment in East Germany, January 1991 to September
1999

from East Europe; and, last but not least, the inefficiency and obsolescence of the capital stock inherited from the socialist planning system (Siebert 1994, p. 5). While the last three items are typical for former socialist economies transforming into market economies, the first two shed light on important aspects of EMU.

How did the East German economy absorb these supply and demand shocks? There has been a tremendous loss of jobs in East Germany in absolute terms: 'the number of persons employed in Eastern Germany fell from 9.9 million in the second half of 1989 to 5 million at the end of 1992' (Siebert 1993, p. 4). Since then, a large number of employees have withdrawn from the labour market; unemployment has now 'stabilized' at significantly above one million (see Figure 3.6).

This result has a lot to do with the failure of wage policy during the transformation process of the East German economy; once the 1:1 conversion rate was introduced for mainly political reasons (see above), wage contracts were confronted with the full 'burden' of overcoming the employment problem. Instead of adjusting wages smoothly to the level of West Germany, trade unions – constrained neither by strong counterparts in the bargaining process nor by attempts of the government to control the wage increases (Siebert 1993, p. 8) – pushed for higher wages and competed against one another with regard to the speed of wage adjustment. Because of strong objections from

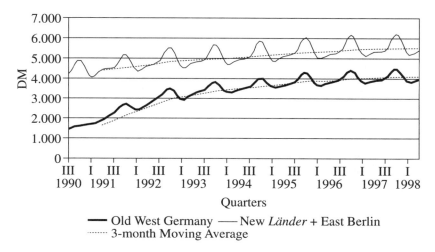

Sources: Statistisches Bundesamt; own calculations.

Figure 3.7   Gross income of employed persons per employee and month, III/1990–II/1998 (DM)

East German business associations, the speed of wage adjustment to the West German level has slowed down since 1994–95. Full wage adjustment was no longer envisaged for the end of the twentieth century as it had been until the mid-1990s.

As is depicted in Figure 3.7, the 'wage gap' between 'Old West Germany' and the 'New Länder + East Berlin' – measured by the respective gross income of employed persons per employee and month – has narrowed considerably since 1990.

As wage restraint in East Germany has been – if at all – much less enthusiastic in the non-tradables sector and given that this sector is traditionally less successful in producing recordable and accountable productivity gains, one could expect the total wage bill in East Germany to become increasingly dominated by the local goods sector. This is precisely what Figure 3.8 shows.

As a matter of fact the quick decision on a monetary union between East and West Germany and the chosen conversion rate for current payments was intended to slow down if not stop the migration from East to West Germany. However, the strong appreciating effect of the currency conversion had two contradictory effects *ex ante* on the direction and the intensity of migration. According to the very simple calculus of Todaro (1977), the decision of the labour force to migrate depends primarily on the difference between the *expected* wage rates

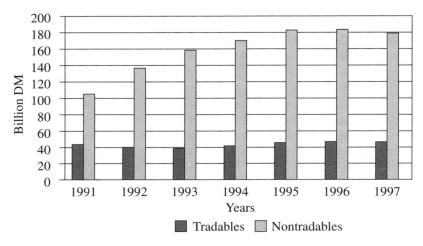

Sources: Statistisches Bundesamt; own calculations.

Figure 3.8   Total wage bill in East Germany, 1991–1997

of the two (or more) regions: whereas the nominal wage-increasing effect of the conversion rate for current payments tended to pull the labour force back into East Germany, it could be seen that – coupled with unsound wage adjustment plans – the impact on the level of wages in East Germany would necessarily reduce the likelihood of finding a job in East Germany (again). *Ex post*, the figures show that East–West migration had dropped considerably by the second quarter of 1990, when monetary union took place: 'Migration was close to 400,000 people in 1989 and 1990. Most of this took place in the fourth quarter of 1989 and the first quarter of 1990. Since then, a declining trend has been observed' (Clausen and Willms 1994, p. 208). (See Figure 3.9.)

Clausen and Willms (1994, p. 204) attribute the slowdown of emigration to West Germany and the stimulated immigration from West Germany to the rise of unemployment in West Germany (since 1992) and the more and more visible improvement in the enterprise and infrastructure capital stock of East Germany. H-W. Sinn has offered a different, but perhaps the most relevant explanation: the high-wage policy pursued in East Germany induced massive lay-offs and the latter

> were a strong, incentive to migrate to the west where jobs for skilled easterner's were easily available. Because it was afraid of migration, the west German government decided to pump huge sums of public money into East Germany. The social support given to the East Germans can be seen as a 'stay-put premium', as a subsidy for not migrating to the west'. (Sinn 1999, p. 15)

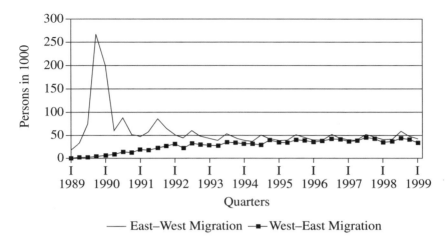

Sources: Clausen and Willms (1994); Statistisches Bundesamt; own calculations.

Figure 3.9   Migration in Germany, I/1989–I/1999

The German case of 'avoiding immigration,' is by no means a 'programme' for EMU and the EU: it would induce huge costs and would require subsequent policy interventions to patch up undesired consequences (ibid., pp. 18–19).

Prior to the currency union, East German productivity was estimated at one-third of the West German level (Siebert 1993, p. 8). Until 1994, productivity increased rapidly as a result of the drastic reduction in employment (see Figure 3.6); afterwards the rise was also caused by the modernization of equipment. In 1998, East German productivity achieved nearly 60 per cent of the West German level (IfW 1999, pp. 80–81).[11] It is clear that it may be another 10–15 years until the productivity levels in West and East Germany are equalized. Fortunately, from 1994–95 onwards (see above), unions in many cases abandoned the wage adjustment corridor with a view to parity with West Germany. Instead, they have sought decentralized firm-by-firm or region-by-region agreements with particular business sites. Hence,[12] unit labour costs were pushed up considerably in the first five years of German monetary and economic union. Since then, there has been a moderate decline. Figure 3.10 demonstrates this point.

What can we learn from these experiences for EMU? First of all, the East German case shows that wage policy must be particularly productivity orientated in a monetary union: there is no more room for exchange rate manipulation to compensate in the short run for losses in competitiveness as

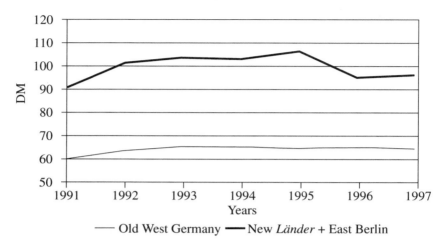

Sources: Clausen and Willms (1994); Statistisches Bundesamt; own calculations.

Figure 3.10   *Nominal unit labour costs in West and East Germany, 1991–*
1997 (per 100 DM)

measured by unit labour costs (increases). In the absence of huge transfer
schemes (which were available during Germany's monetary unification, see
below), there is no viable way to quickly reduce existing differences in per
capita income among European countries. Migration has been a weak shock
absorber even in a country with the same language, history and cultural
background under conditions of high structural unemployment. This points to
the necessity for flexible wages and a considerable degree of wage dispersion
within EMU. Given the strong pressure on prices and quality of tradables in a
globalized world economy, much responsibility rests upon wage formation in
the non-tradables sector. In contrast to the example of East Germany (at least
in the first years after economic and monetary union), wage restraint is a
'must' for these sectors on the European level.

West–East Transfers and Accumulation of Debt in West Germany

The conversion of the Ostmark to the D-Mark –whether for flows or for
stocks – implied a transfer of purchasing power to East Germany which the
East Germans used in the first place to buy West German goods (Siebert
1990, p. 27). As a consequence, the aggregate demand for West German
products increased, creating what was later called the '*Sonderkonjunktur für
Westdeutschland*' (special economic upswing for West Germany). At the

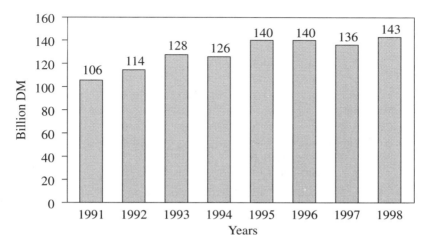

Sources: Statistisches Bundesamt; own calculations.

Figure 3.11   *Amount of net transfers from West to East Germany, 1991–*
1998

same time, there was a lack of demand for East German goods, depressing
the economy in East Germany. Hence, a sort of split business-cycle situation
emerged (ibid., p. 27). The economic recovery in West Germany was a kind
of 'Keynesian demand boost' (Siebert 1993, p. 13), whereby the large net
transfers launched from the West to the East of the country (see Figure 3.11)
created additional deficits in the federal budget.

Net public transfers to the eastern *Länder* were in the range between 106
and 143 billion Deutschmarks per year over the 1991–98 period, an amount
which corresponds to 4–5 per cent of the annual West German GDP (Canova
and Ravn 1998, p. 5): 'Of these transfers social insurance related payments
account for about 45% while investment subsidies account for 12% and
direct investment for infrastructures for the rest' (ibid.). Although a 'solidar-
ity tax' was introduced in 1991, the overwhelming part of these transfers
were financed by public borrowing (Sinn 1999).

In fact, since 1990 the public deficits and public debt of unified Germany
have risen dramatically (for a thorough analysis of the consequences, see
Bröcker and Raffelhüschen 1997). The debt of the total public sector, which
amounted to 925 billion D-Marks in 1989 increased to 2191 billion D-Marks
by the end of 1997 (Statistisches Bundesamt 1998). The following important
factors explain the development of public deficits and public debt (see Figure
3.12):

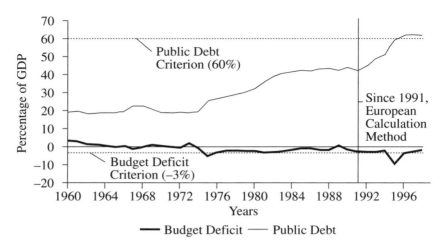

Sources: Statistisches Bundesamt; own calculations.

*Figure 3.12   Public debt and budget balance in Germany, 1960–1998
             (percentage of GDP)*

- governmental transfers from West to East Germany;
- interest payments on the additional debt burden;
- the accumulated debt of the Treuhandanstalt (THA) (the federal privatization agency); and
- the accumulated debt of the Credit Processing Fund (*Kreditabwicklungsfonds*), the German Unity Fund (*Fonds Deutsche Einheit*) and the public housing sector.

Most of these debt 'sources' are linked directly or indirectly to the currency conversion issue:

1. The occurrence of monetary and economic union between East and West Germany and the fact of the chosen conversion rate(s) have been important reasons for the size of the annual fiscal transfers from West to East Germany since 1990. This type of 'involuntary fiscal integration' (see above) would not have gained such a dimension with a flexible exchange rate of the Ostmark *vis-à-vis* the D-Mark at hand. Also, with a flexible exchange rate there would have been a high demand in East Germany for infrastructure capital and large parts of the existing capital stock would have been obsolete; however, the financing of these projects might have had a higher share of private risk

capital and the total amount of social insurance transfers might have been kept lower.

2. As the costs of the German monetary and economic union are and were primarily financed by state bonds, it is fair to say that the additional supply on the bond market induced an upward pressure on interest rates and thereby aggravated the burden of interest payments and of total debt for the German government.

3. In the meantime, we all know that there existed a significant 'capital stock illusion' between the federal government of West Germany and the THA with regard to non-labour factors of production in East Germany: the market prices of the privatized socialist firms were much lower than expected and in some cases even negative. But this is also an outcome of the conversion rate chosen and cannot be taken *ex post* as an exogenous factor. The appreciation of the Ostmark increased the liabilities of East Germany's firms while at the same time it rendered their products less competitive. Old debts were taken over by the THA; in addition, compensating claims of firms 'for losses due to currency conversion' of 20 billion D-Marks were satisfied by the THA (Siebert 1992, p. 21).

Asymmetric Shock for the EMS

The German monetary and economic union of 1990 has not only been a real shock to (West and East) Germany, but also to the world economy, and especially to the European economy and the European Monetary System (Siebert 1993, p. 15; Sinn 1996, p. 10). It had – as Hughes Hallett and Ma (1993, p. 418) put it – two major effects on the partners in the EMS:

1. an increased demand for their products caused by West Germany's increased fiscal expenditures (see above);
2. higher interest rates due to the higher fiscal deficits in Germany and the restrictive monetary policy of the Deutsche Bundesbank which were transmitted through the exchange rate mechanism (ERM).

While the trade effects, whereby European countries' current accounts *vis-à-vis* Germany's became positive, had an expansionary effect on their demand and income, the interest rate effects worked in the opposite direction, and they more than offset any positive stimulus through trade. Before summer 1992, countries participating in the ERM tried to avoid realignments by 'adjusting' their monetary policy to the restrictive course of the Deutsche Bundesbank (Alexander 1994, pp. 8–9). As a consequence, they had to face higher interest rates and a shortage of liquidity; both factors slowed down their economic recovery. Sinn (1997, p. 10) adds a third effect:

3. German interest rates increased the Deutschmark's attractiveness and created strong appreciation pressure on the D-Mark.

At first, the EMS prevented the Deutschmark from appreciating after unification. In the late summer of 1992, however, the English pound was forced out of the exchange rate mechanism and a number of other currencies had to realign their exchange rates, something that had not happened in the ERM for almost five years. Among them was the peseta, which was first devalued in August, then the Spanish government (re)introduced capital controls in October and, finally, devalued the peseta again in December 1992 (Sell 1993, p. 71).[13] The ERM system practically collapsed only six months later (summer 1993) when the exchange rate bands were broadened to a range of +/– 15 per cent. The system operating until the end of 1998, was much closer to floating exchange rates than to any derivative of fixed exchange rates.

As a result, it is fair to say that Germany's European partners suffered from an asymmetric shock that was primarily induced by the economic implications of the German monetary and economic union. Clearly, the currency conversion and the rate at which it was carried out, were not the only important factors. But the unrealistic mix of the conversion rate and the degree of wage adjustment (see above) explain to a considerable extent the amount of fiscal transfers necessary to keep East Germany 'alive'. However, one has also to blame Germany's European neighbours for their own high fiscal deficits as well; without these, the pressure on the interest rates would have been much less pronounced given that the interest elasticity of savings in the Organization for Economic Cooperation and Development is quite modest (Hughes Hallett and Ma 1993, p. 418).

On the other hand, perhaps many of the negative repercussions for Germany's European partners could have been circumvented by an early appreciation of the D-Mark in 1990 or 1991, 'allowing other countries a lower interest rate. Moreover, the recession in Europe in 1993 could have been softened considerably' (Siebert 1994, p. 14). When the D-Mark was finally free to revalue in 1993, this was the result of a high capital demand, particularly by the public sector of Germany, which raised German interest rates (and, later on, foreign interest rates) and, in turn, attracted foreign capital (Sinn 1997, p. 10). It was not the result of an increased attractiveness of Germany as a location for foreign private investment.

5   CONCLUSIONS AND LESSONS FOR EMU

A review of the East German–West German currency conversion debate has brought about the following main results:

1. With traditional and modern criteria as a point of reference, it was *ex ante* not clear whether East and West Germany were to form an optimum currency area in 1990; *ex post* one can definitely deny the question.

2. The conversion rate chosen in extending the currency area of the D-Mark to East Germany did not have serious inflationary effects, however, it amounted to an appreciation of the Ostmark of more than 450 per cent *vis-à-vis* the D-Mark.

3. There were no viable alternatives to the monetary and economic union, above all because of the expectations formed in East Germany by political promises.

4. The 1990 general elections in Germany are a good case for a public choice explanation of business cycle(s): by promising a high speed of wage adjustment to the East German electorate, the federal government violated the 'neutrality of unit costs of production rule' in East Germany and contributed to the high demand for fiscal transfers from West Germany.

5. As a result of the expenditure effects of West Germany's fiscal transfers to East Germany and the relative price effect of the Ostmark appreciation, the non-tradables sector in East Germany increased its contribution to East Germany's GDP and is about to reach its former index of value added.

6. East Germany's tradables sector grows slightly in the meantime, but still suffers from the Ostmark appreciation, and also from the upward pressure on wage costs, the full exposure to international competition, the loss of markets in Eastern Europe and 'Dutch disease' effects triggered by West Germany's fiscal transfers.

7. The fiscal transfers from West to East Germany, coupled with the appreciation of the Ostmark led to a short-lived economic recovery in West Germany in the early 1990s. This economic upswing, however, was followed by a deep recession and by a revision of long-term growth expectations for Germany, the doubling of the government debt within five years and an increased tax burden for households and enterprises.

8. Germany's monetary and economic union had negative spillovers for the EC partners via the interest rate channel and the ERM which outweighed positive spillovers from trade and growth (in the early 1990s) in Germany.

In the case of the monetary union between East and West Germany it will be important to subsequently reduce the net volume of fiscal transfers from the west to the east of Germany in order to monitor total government debt and at the same time to raise income generation and the tax base in East Germany. In the long run, the resurgence of new regional and sectoral imbalances should be avoided: West Germany must not fall behind East Germany in terms of the modernization of its physical capital stock, while the mobility of labour and human capital will have to increase throughout all regions in Germany.

As far as lessons for EMU are concerned, the case of East Germany's currency conversion shows that:

1. A monetary union leads to a high demand for fiscal transfers when productivity levels are quite different and convergence of levels is low[14] while wage levels are quite similar and convergence of levels is high (see Hughes Hallett and Ma 1993, p. 417).
2. Convergence of productivity levels is likely to take a long time, so that the financing of investment (private and public) may induce long-term pressure on real interest rates. Hence, much 'responsibility' rests upon the task to increase the interest elasticity of savings.
3. European governments are, in addition, confronted by the restrictions of the stability pact which limits the scope for building up public infrastructure and, at the same time, reduces the flexibility of fiscal policy.
4. As far as the so-called 'pre-ins' of EMU are concerned, the case of East Germany has shown that a currency board (similar to a monetary union) can be helpful in the transformation process in that it instantly provides credibility to the monetary authorities of the country in concern, as long as the anchoring currency, that is, the euro, is devoted to price stability. In comparison, flexible exchange rates and/or a participation in an EMS II, may be a much more time-consuming way to enhance the reputation of the authorities of the economies in transition.
5. However, when wages and prices are sticky downwards, flexible exchange rates and/or a participation in an ERM-II should have a comparative advantage over a currency board (and a premature monetary union) with regard to the costs of adjustment (output, employment losses) and the applicability of economic instruments (monetary, fiscal policy).

Finally, it should be mentioned that the real economical and social conditions which prevailed in East Germany on the eve of German monetary union are really rather different from those in EU countries. Hence, the various effects of European Monetary Union may be different in intensity and character from those that prevailed in Germany at the onset of unification. There is no doubt that the similarity between the two unions is limited, as, for example, the European conversion rates applied at the end of 1998 have not destroyed the competitiveness of any of the EMU member countries as was the case with East Germany (Sinn 1997, p. 24) in 1990. Nevertheless, with regard to the heterogeneity of the EMU members and the necessary integration of poor countries like Portugal, Greece and Ireland (not to speak of the future integration of countries in Central and Eastern Europe), there is much to learn from the policy mistakes made on the occasion of German monetary union.

NOTES

*   I am indebted to Silvio Kermer for his excellent research assistance.
1.   'Germany after unification is characterized by a high capital demand ... At the same time, there is an excess supply of labor' (Siebert 1993, p. 10).
2.   Remember that the black market exchange rate was between 7:1 and 9:1!
3.   The following exposition closely follows Sell (1994, pp. 128–31).
4.   Note that this is precisely how EMU is now advocated as a necessary precondition for political union in Europe.
5.   The following exposition closely follows Greiner et al. (1994, pp. 277–82).
6.   In 1989, East Germany's imports from third countries equalled its exports; imports from West Germany, however, surpassed exports by about 12 per cent. Hence, there was a moderate deficit in East Germany's balance of trade (Hoffmann 1993, p. 72).
7.   Not to be confused with Robert Lucas's (1973) concept of potential output.
8.   '[A] successful liberalization of the trade account will require a *real depreciation,* in order to help the exportables sector to expand as the new structure of relative prices replaces the old protective structure' (Edwards 1984, p. 4 italics added).
9.   With the former GDR taken as a region within unified Germany.
10.   A comprehensive analysis of the cumulative effects of all of these deindustrializing factors is presented by Greiner et al. (1994).
11.   The productivity, here, is measured by actual prices. This is adequate because the development of prices was an essential element of the East German catching-up process (IfW 1999, p. 80).
12.   As a result of the periodical centralized collective bargaining in the early years of Germany's monetary and economic union, labour costs nearly doubled between 1991 and 1998 (IfW 1999, p. 81).
13.   From late August 1992 onwards, the Bundesbank started to ease monetary policy in response to 'emerging tensions in the European Monetary System' (Mishkin and Posen 1997, p. 30).
14.   This implies that labour migration is weak and/or unable to reduce labour productivity differences sufficiently.

MATHEMATICAL ANNEX

A formal presentation of the graphs depicted in Section 3 has the following components: equation (3A.1) defines equality of total average costs per unit of production (of tradables) between East and West Germany:

$$k = (lA/Y + qK/Y)_{OST} \frac{1}{w} = (l^*A^*/Y^* + q^*K^*/Y^*)_{DM} \qquad (3A.1)$$

where:

$$w = OST/DM. \qquad (3A.2)$$

The variables have the following definitions:

k	=	total average costs per unit of production
$l(l^*)$	=	average wage rate in East (West) Germany
$q(q^*)$	=	average interest rate in East (West) Germany
$A(A^*)$	=	labour input in East (West) Germany
$K(K^*)$	=	capital input in East (West) Germany
$Y(Y^*)$	=	output in East (West) Germany
$\pi_K(\pi_K^*)$	=	average productivity of capital in East (West) Germany
$\pi_A(\pi_A^*)$	=	average productivity of labour in East (West) Germany
w	=	exchange rate between Ostmark and D-Mark, at which the conversion is carried out.

Equation (3A.2) inserted in equation (3A.1) yields equation (3A.1a):

$$k = (lA/Y + qK/Y)\frac{1}{w} = (l^*A^*/Y^* + q^*K^*/Y^*). \qquad (3A.1a)$$

For simplicity, the following assumptions shall hold

$$q = q^* \qquad (3A.3)$$

$$\pi_A = \lambda \pi_A^* \qquad (3A.4)$$

$$l = \gamma l^* \text{ with } 0 < \gamma < 1; 0 < \lambda < 1; \gamma > \lambda. \qquad (3A.5)$$

Hence, we assume that the financial market is fully integrated so that (average) interest rates are the same in West and East Germany (3A.3), average productivity of labour is less in East Germany than in West Germany (3A.4), and, the level of wages in East Germany is not fully adjusted to the level prevailing on average in West Germany (3A.5). Also, it is maintained that wage adjustment occurs faster than adjustment of labour productivity levels.

Inserting (3A.3), (3A.4) and (3A.5) into (3A.1a) leads to:

$$\left[\frac{\gamma l^*}{\lambda \pi_A^{\ *}}+\frac{q^*}{\pi_K}\right]\frac{1}{w}=\left[\frac{l^*}{\pi_A^{\ *}}+\frac{q^*}{\pi_K^{\ *}}\right] \tag{3A.1b}$$

$$\frac{\gamma l^*}{\lambda \pi_A^{\ *}}=\left[\frac{l^*}{\pi_A^{\ *}}+\frac{q^*}{\pi_K^{\ *}}\right]w-\frac{q^*}{\pi_K}\cdot\frac{\lambda \pi_A^{\ *}}{l^*} \tag{3A.1c}$$

$$\gamma=\left[\frac{l^*}{\pi_A^{\ *}}+\frac{q^*}{\pi_K^{\ *}}\right]w\frac{\lambda \pi_A^{\ *}}{l^*}-\frac{q^*\lambda \pi_A^{\ *}}{\pi_K l^*}$$

$$\gamma=\left[\lambda+\frac{q^*\lambda \pi_A^{\ *}}{l^*\pi_K^{\ *}}\right]w-\frac{q^*\lambda \pi_A^{\ *}}{\pi_K l^*}$$

$$\gamma=\lambda\left(1+\frac{q^*\pi_A^{\ *}}{l^*\pi_K^{\ *}}\right)w-q^*\lambda\frac{\pi_A^{\ *}}{\pi_K l^*}|\cdot(-1) \tag{3A.1d}$$

$$-\lambda=-\lambda(1+\ldots)w+\frac{q^*\lambda \pi_A^{\ *}}{\pi_K l^*}|+1 \tag{3A.1e}$$

$$(1-\gamma)=-\lambda\left(1+\frac{q^*\pi_A^{\ *}}{\pi_K^{\ *}l^*}\right)w+\frac{\pi_K l^*+q^*\lambda \pi_A^{\ *}}{l^*\pi_K}. \tag{3A.6}$$

Equation (3A.6) has the following properties:

$$\frac{\delta(1-\gamma)}{\delta w}=-\left[\lambda\left(1+\frac{q^*\pi_A^{\ *}}{\pi_K^{\ *}l^*}\right)\right]<0 \tag{3A.6a}$$

$$\frac{\delta(1-\gamma)}{\delta \pi_K}=-\left(\frac{q^*\lambda \pi_A^{\ *}}{l^*}\right)\cdot\frac{1}{\pi_K^{\ 2}}<0. \tag{3A.6b}$$

The graph of (3A.6) is depicted in Figure 3.1a (see above).

The relevant macroeconomic utility function for East Germany is represented by:

$$U = U\left(\gamma, w^{-1}, \frac{dY}{Y}, \ldots\right) \tag{3A.7}$$

The respective aggregate voting function takes the form:

$$V = V(\gamma, w^{-1}) \text{ with } \frac{\delta V}{\delta \gamma} > 0; \frac{\delta V}{\delta w^{-1}} > 0. \tag{3A.8}$$

4. The theory of monetary union and EMU

Anke Jacobsen and Horst Tomann

1 INTRODUCTION

The history of European monetary integration, as discussed in Chapter 2, shows that there have been political as well as economic forces driving the process of integration. In this chapter the theory of monetary union is considered, with its implications for the European Union (EU). If politicians decide on issues of monetary integration, what economic reasons should they take into account? In particular, if they are free to decide on a monetary regime, what would be the size of the optimum currency area?

In dealing with these questions in a theoretical framework we should be aware, however, that politicians may not be as free as it might seem. There is an immanent logic of economic integration. Whenever trade opportunities are realized in international trade, rules and agreements are required concerning the convertibility of the currencies involved. Moreover, with expanding international markets for tradable goods firms recognize their specific financial requirements. Furthermore if a substantial market share is obtained in export markets, foreign direct investment may become a more attractive option than exporting. Thus trade, finance and direct foreign investment induce an increasing demand for deregulation of financial markets. National authorities may, however, be reluctant to deregulate financial markets. The liberalization of international financial flows requires perfectly convertible currencies. Governments must therefore be in a position to defend their exchange rates. If, by contrast, they fear that private agents are not prepared to hold their money balances in the national currency, deregulation could lead to a financial crisis, triggered off by capital flight. Consequently, financial markets are liberalized only gradually – even Germany had not fully liberalized its financial markets until stage two of the European Monetary Union (EMU).

The cumulative logic of economic integration implies a necessity to coordinate economic policies. This, in turn, requires that national authorities abandon parts of their sovereignty. There are two compelling reasons for policy coordination in economies integrating their trade, direct investment and financial markets. First, economic integration does not necessarily lead to an overall macroeconomic equilibrium. It is true that there is an elaborate theoretical literature explaining that balance of payments disequilibria are offset by exchange rate variations. So, as to trade relations, the monetary equilibrium will require exchange rate movements according to purchasing power parity. Similarly, taking financial markets into account, external monetary equilibrium can be defined as uncovered interest rate parity. In reality, however, the demand for national money is not stable, and as a consequence the demand for currencies varies with the substantial variations in real exchange rates. Real exchange rates are in turn dependent on the structural characteristics of the economy as well as exchange rate expectations. Therefore one of the important objectives of monetary policy coordination is the stabilization of expectations. This requirement is independent of the exchange rate regime. Whether in a regime of 'no commitments' (flexible exchange rates) or in a regime of fixed, but adjustable exchange rates (Bretton Woods or the European Monetary System (EMS)), the need to stabilize expectations is ubiquitous.

Second, it is the outcome of the economic policies themselves that produce imbalances in interrelated markets, if these policies are not coordinated. In particular, in international monetary relations, monetary disequilibria are far more often induced by differing national monetary policies than by shifts in the money demand (Niehans 1984). Against this background, a common monetary policy that is institutionalized in a monetary union may prove to be a device best fitted to stabilize expectations in integrated markets. In particular, a monetary union sets up new rules which exclude piecemeal deviations from the joint course of policy. This creates the credibility of the common monetary policy.

In this chapter, the theory of optimum currency areas is reviewed in Section 2, followed by an analysis of the recent debate on the credibility of monetary regimes in Section 3. The implications of the discussion for European economic and monetary union are considered in Section 4.

2   THE THEORY OF OPTIMUM CURRENCY AREAS

The theory of optimum currency areas is an offshoot of the debate in the 1960s on the merits of fixed versus flexible exchange rates. It poses the fundamental question that if it is true that flexible exchange rates provide for autonomy in stabilization policies, how should an economic region be defined for which a common currency and, consequently, an autonomous common monetary policy, is an optimal policy device? This question is addressed by the theory of optimum currency areas which – contrary to what one might suppose – is rooted in the Keynesian tradition. It is, therefore, based on the assumption that the price level and the wage level of an economy are rigid. With this assumption, an economy seems to need flexible exchange rates to adjust to destabilizing international shocks. This leads to the two central questions of the theory of optimum currency areas. First, if prices and wages are rigid, are there other mechanisms in the economy to adjust to external shocks? Second, how effective are these mechanisms compared to flexible exchange rates? To respond to these questions two criteria are examined: the degree of factor mobility (Mundell 1961) and the degree of openness of the economy (McKinnon 1963). Another criterion which is relevant for the constitution of a currency union, the coordination of fiscal policies, will be addressed in Chapter 6.

Benefits and Costs of a Common Currency

Economic textbooks usually present the decision to establish a common currency or – from the point of view of a single country – the decision to enter a currency union on the basis of a benefit–cost analysis (see, for example, De Grauwe 1994). Also, the Commission of the European Communities, preparing the Council's decisions on monetary integration, has conducted benefit–cost analyses (see the contributions in *European Economy*, CEC 1990). Each member state has to compare the benefits expected from a currency union and the costs. Evidently, an economic case in favour of a currency union requires that for all participating countries the benefits exceed the costs. Apart from problems of measuring and evaluating benefits and costs of a monetary union, this approach has shortcomings. To evaluate the validity of the methodology let us consider benefits and costs of a monetary union in more detail.

An evident benefit of a common currency is that transaction costs are reduced. In a currency union there is no need to calculate prices in different currencies and to hold cash balances in different currencies. Transaction costs are particularly important, if the currencies involved are not perfectly convertible. Moreover, the uncertainty of the value of money is reduced. A monetary union creates more reliability in credit contracts and reduces the liquidity premium 'which we require to make us part with money' (Keynes 1936, p. 226). The instability of money demand is diminished or, at least, does not interfere with the course of monetary policy. There are two reasons for this. First, because the 'within-area' foreign variables are included in the EMU-wide money demand function, so reducing the specification errors which make the estimated parameters more stable. Second, there is a possibility that negatively correlated national shocks to the demand for money will at least partly offset one another. Therefore for most countries the demand for money becomes more stable, which implies that monetary policy gains credibility.

On the other hand, it is supposed that the loss of national autonomy in monetary policy implies costs. Two aspects are important. First, governments participating in a monetary union cannot claim their own seigniorage but have to share the common central bank surplus. In particular, monetization of public deficits is no longer at the discretion of national fiscal authorities. The exclusion of national inflation taxes is the very argument by which a common currency gains credibility. We should not, therefore, speak of costs in an economic sense. Second, member states of a currency union dispense with their national exchange rate policies as instruments of economic stabilization. To evaluate these costs we have to take a closer look at the value of exchange rate policy as a remedy against asymmetric real shocks. There are two reasons why the value of this policy is less than we might expect. First, according to McKinnon (1963), although exchange rate policies do help mitigate against monetary shocks, they do not offer any protection against real shocks. Second, the flexibility of prices and wages will increase within a monetary union. Let us elaborate these arguments in more detail.

Wage Rigidity and Money Illusion

First, what is the value of exchange rate flexibility as a remedy against wage rigidity? Mundell (1961), in his famous paper 'A theory of optimum currency areas' addresses this question by analysing asymmetric, real shocks in a simple one-product model of two economies, each with a separate currency. Suppose there is a decline in the demand for country A's output and a simultaneous rise in the demand for country B's output. With a flexible exchange rate, a depreciation of A's currency relative to B's, will reduce the real wage rate in A relative to that in B, by raising the price level in A relative to that in B, and so restore employment.

On the other hand, suppose both countries are divided into two regions which do not correspond to national boundaries – the East, which produces goods such as cars, and the West, which produces goods such as furniture. In this model, an exchange rate policy cannot help mitigate the effects on output of asymmetric real shocks. Suppose there is a general fall in the demand for cars and a rise in the demand for furniture. Since this change in tastes affects both economies there is nothing that national exchange rate policy can do to mitigate the effect of the shock, both countries will suffer from unemployment in the car industry. In the absence of money wage flexibility, the solution is either that workers have to move from car to furniture production – that is, there must be mobility of labour – or there has to be regional, rather than national currencies, so the exchange rate adjustment is again viable. Thus Mundell concludes that 'if the case for flexible exchange rates is a strong one, it is, in logic, a case for flexible exchange rates based on regional currencies, not on national currencies. The optimum currency area is the region' (Mundell 1961, p. 660).

It is, however, another question to evaluate exchange rate policies in the case of countries which are not one-product countries, but which participate in extensive intra-industry trade with each other. Consider the example of France and Germany. It is unlikely that these countries would be exposed to asymmetric real shocks, say as a consequence of productivity differences or a shift in preferences. None the less, there are differences which, in a monetary union, might be regarded as real shocks but actually do concern the monetary equilibrium of both countries. In particular, there are national differences with regard to how labour markets are organized and with regard to fiscal policies. These differences have an influence on both the price level and the rate of interest. To analyse these monetary consequences, the exchange rate must be considered as a monetary instrument, that is, following McKinnon (1963) and the monetary approach to the balance of payments as an instrument to balance national differences in monetary expansion (and not, as Mundell did, as an instrument to balance differences in relative prices). With that changed perspective, we recognize that the value of exchange rate policies is not determined by asymmetric real shocks but by the fact that countries respond differently to those shocks.

To give an example, consider the role of the labour market. Let us suppose that two countries which are different with respect to the trade unions' bargaining power form a monetary union. The country with comparatively aggressive trade unions, which demand high real wages – say France – will lose its competitiveness in the internal market. On the other hand, the country with cooperative trade unions (for example, Germany) will gain accordingly. As a consequence, an external imbalance develops, with increasing absorption in France (relative to real income) and relatively decreasing absorption in Germany. If the monetary regime allows exchange rate adjustments, France could devalue its currency and thus reduce its absorption relative to real income. The precondition for this kind of restoration of the external balance is, however, the reduction of real wages in France. That is, the trade unions have to accept that real wages are reduced by an increase in import prices. Although nominal wages are rigid as a consequence of the trade unions' bargaining power, it is the trade unions' money illusion with respect to the increase in import prices that provides the necessary reduction in real wages. This soft way to reduce absorption is excluded in a monetary union. It is now the role of wage policy to reduce real wages. Therefore the value of exchange rate policies depends on the assumed degree of money illusion of trade unions.

BOX 4.1   ASYMMETRIC SHOCKS AND THE MONETARY REGIME

1. An asymmetric demand shock in a two-country case (France, Germany) is responded to by an exchange rate adjustment.

y	production, real income
a	real absorption

    The demand shock induces a balance of payments disequilibrium.

France	Germany
$y < a$	$y > a$

    A devaluation of the French franc restores the balance of payments equilibrium.

    $$y\uparrow \qquad\qquad a\downarrow$$

    The reduction of a in France requires that real wages decrease. With rigid nominal wages the required real wage flexibility results from the trade unions' money illusion with respect to the price effects of the exchange rate adjustment.

2. In a monetary union, an asymmetric demand shock and the resulting balance of payments disequilibrium does not lead to a monetary imbalance. The regional imbalance can be resolved by:

    a. *Creditor–debtor relations*   If German lenders are prepared to invest in France, a real transfer ($a\downarrow$) is not required.
    b. *Fiscal transfers*   A system of equalizing fiscal revenues by transfers is in economic terms an insurance against asymmetric real shocks; without an insurance system, every region would have to provide for asymmetric shocks on its own account. Tax increases to finance fiscal transfers are not a necessary implication, therefore.
    c. *Factor mobility*   In the long run, Germany will experience a wage pressure and a relative rise in real absorption.
    d. *Wage flexibility*   An increase in the credibility of the monetary regime results in an increased wage flexibility.

In this case McKinnon's argument dominates. In small and open economics, the weight of import prices in the price-level index is so large that the assumption of money illusion fades. If the trade unions have bargaining power to secure real wages, they will not accept the loss of purchasing power which results from exchange rate adjustments. Consequently, absorption will not decrease. A devaluation of the franc results in purely monetary effects (accelerated inflation), and the external imbalance remains unchanged.

Thus if we assume national differences in labour market conditions, exchange rate policies seem to perform only real adjustments. To compensate for asymmetric shocks, the trade unions have to accept a reduction in real wages, independent of the monetary regime. The less their money illusion, the less flexibility is gained by exchange rate policies. Accordingly, the economic adjustment costs of a monetary union are low. So, asymmetric shocks in a monetary union are of less importance for stabilization policy than has been usually assumed. (These arguments are summarized in Box 4.1.)

Adjustment Requirements and Asymmetric Shocks

Following the debate concerning the optimality of currency areas, the adjustment of an economy to an asymmetric shock is independent of the monetary regime. The actual mechanism of adjustment, on the other hand, will differ between monetary regimes, hence under one regime adjustment may take the form of exchange rate changes, while under another adjustment may take place through the labour market. Empirical studies that examine the optimality of EMU refer to those older models. They investigate whether tendencies of a decrease in asymmetry between potential members of a currency union can be observed.

A first group of empirical studies use the criterion of similarity of economies, deducted from Kenen's criterion of diversification (Kenen 1969). The single economic market has already influenced symmetry. If we assume that the internal market leads to increasing specialization and therefore to increasing intra-industry trade, the production structures of the EU economies will adjust and the probability of asymmetric shocks will decrease (CEC 1990). The probability will rise, however, in the case of a realization of increasing returns to scale which results in an increasing regional concentration (Krugman 1991). Krugman (1993) compares the US and European countries concerning their structures of regional specialization and concludes that the regional industrial concentration in the US is stronger than in Europe. Krugman forecasts that a deepening of integration in Europe will increase the probability of the appearance of asymmetric shocks in a potential EMU. Critical in this comparison is the assumption that the ability to adjust is independent of the monetary regime. The experience after the ratification of the Maastricht Treaty has shown that the parameters of economic policy are strongly adjustable and, therefore, the adjustment processes are not deductible from past data.

Following Vaubel (1976), other empirical studies use the variability of real exchange rates as an indicator of asymmetric shocks. Real exchange rates are changing if nominal exchange rates are fixed but inflation rates diverge in the countries concerned. A change in the terms of trade between two countries can be caused by asymmetric disturbances or by asymmetric reactions to shocks.[1] It is assumed in these studies that the extent of fluctuations of the real exchange rate shows the adjustment requirement by indicating differences in regional competitiveness. Eichengreen (1991) compares the US and European countries and examines the optimality of the EU as a currency area. The periods from 1971 to 1979 and from 1980 to 1987 show a standard deviation of the fluctuations of the real exchange rate that is three to four times higher in the EU countries compared to the regions of the US. Eichengreen concludes from this result that the EU is subject to asymmetric shocks to a larger extent than the US, or that adjustment mechanisms in Europe are rather weak. Therefore, the EU countries do not form an optimum currency area.

Von Hagen and Neumann (1994) use the same type of analysis. They compare the fluctuations of the real exchange rate of different groups of EU countries to the relative price deviations of six German *Länder*. From their analysis, the authors recommend a 'Europe of two speeds', because the core countries of the EU show a smaller degree of real exchange rate fluctuations.

To put the emphasis on real exchange rate fluctuations is rather critical, because it is not clear whether these fluctuations are generated by an asymmetric shock or by reactions to a shock. For instance, real exchange rate fluctuations can be the result of trade union reactions to demand shocks, in which case it might be advantageous being a member of a currency union in which demand shocks may be reduced. Moreover, not all fluctuations in real exchanges rates are the consequence of demand shocks. They can also be the result of diverging monetary or fiscal policies in the case of fixed nominal exchange rates. As long as real exchange rate fluctuations are not clearly traced to asymmetric shocks, this analysis cannot deliver arguments for or against a currency union.

To avoid these problems Eichengreen (1991) proposes a correlation of bond prices at different stock exchanges in Europe and the US. If it is assumed that bond prices show actual and expected profits, asymmetric shocks which influence profits will have different consequences for bond prices in the regions. The study shows that the asymmetry of disturbances in Europe has been decreasing since the foundation of the EMS in 1979. Although the analysis tells us about the adjustment requirements, it is not able to identify the ability to adjust. Eichengreen presumes that the single economic market and the liberalization of capital markets in Europe contribute to an adjustment of bond prices in European countries. An increasing ability to adjust results in a decreasing adjustment requirement. Whether or not such a development ends up in providing the case for an optimality of a currency union cannot be clearly deduced from the analysis.

Therefore, Bayoumi and Eichengreen (1993) separately examine adjustment requirements and adjustment abilities. Moreover, the authors distinguish between effects of supply-side and demand-side disturbances in both the short and the long terms. The results indicate a 'Europe of two speeds'. Because of smaller correlations of disturbances among European countries compared to US regions, it is not admissible to conclude that the EU is not an appropriate currency area. This criterion does not permit the testing of a hypothesis concerning Europe's ability to adjust in the case of asymmetric shocks in a future currency union. An analysis that is based on past data cannot evaluate future developments especially if fundamental structural or institutional changes, like a common European monetary policy, have to be taken into account. By abolishing national monetary policies in a currency union demand shocks, caused by national monetary policies, must also disappear. Therefore, there may arise a tendency for demand shocks to be symmetric shocks in a currency union.

Erkel-Mousse and Melitz (1995) use econometric techniques in order to identify shocks which are classified into fiscal and monetary policy shocks. By this differentiation the authors try to investigate the costs of a loss of monetary autonomy. The authors investigate shocks that cause observed fluctuations in employment and inflation. If a monetary shock results mainly in price rather than employment effects in the short run, the loss of monetary autonomy is linked to low costs. On the other hand if a monetary shock results mainly in employment effects in the short run, then the loss of monetary autonomy is linked to high costs. When analysing the symmetry of the disturbances among the EU countries, high employment differences are ascertained, which presumes high costs of a currency union. However, when monetary shocks are observed, the empirical analysis shows that only in Germany are there strong fluctuations in employment. In other EU countries, the influence of monetary shocks on employment is very low. Therefore, the abolition of monetary autonomy in these countries is linked to relatively low costs, because it means giving up an already ineffective instrument. This impression is strengthened by an analysis of monetary policy shocks in France and the Netherlands. In these countries monetary shocks mainly explain unexpected inflation so that a common monetary policy in a currency union would be an advantage.

Conclusions

Our analysis has showed that a monetary union is judged wrongly if it is evaluated from a status quo point of view. The introduction of a common currency has to be regarded as an institutional innovation which has implications for the functioning of other policy areas and which changes the assignment of objectives to policy areas. Finally, we have to conclude that it is not correct to decide on a currency area on the basis of a country's cost–benefit analysis. It is true that, from a country's point of view, entering a monetary union is an 'all-or-nothing' decision. However, there are externalities to be taken into account, in particular on the benefit side. Each country's decision to enter implies an externality to other countries which in terms of economic theory is called a 'depletable external effect'. For that reason, the benefit of a monetary union for one country depends on the decision of other countries to participate. Consequently, as far as a monetary union has properties of a public good, a collective decision-making process would be appropriate from an economic point of view. We conclude that in economic terms decisions taken by the European Council should provide better results than country-by-country decisions. Otherwise, compensation payments could be provided to compensate for the externalities which are not taken into consideration by a single country. This conclusion to provide an admission grant has an interesting parallel in the debate on the European Central Bank (ECB). The United Kingdom was offered a seat on the board of governors of the ECB. This proposal was supported by France and Germany, but it was opposed by smaller countries. It is not difficult to see the economic rationale in that offer, which was a stimulus to enter.

3   CREDIBILITY OF A COMMON CURRENCY

Let us now turn to the second argument in favour of a common currency. The degree to which prices and wages are flexible is not independent of the monetary regime. We suggest that the introduction of a common currency increases the flexibility of markets. Accordingly, the capability to compensate for asymmetric shocks rises. If this is so, the costs of a loss of exchange rate flexibility are again lower than has usually been assumed.

The increased flexibility of prices and wages in a monetary union is based on the assumption of imperfect competition. This is a paradox, since price flexibility is regarded as being a typical feature of perfect markets. In practice, however, we observe that generally suppliers have the power to set prices in both goods and labour markets. If price-setting behaviour prevails, the outcome is price rigidity. In particular the effect of price setting in oligopolistic markets is to stabilize the market structure. The introduction of a monetary union, so the argument runs, changes the conditions of strategic behaviour in these markets and hence may have an impact on price and wage rigidity.

Let us consider again labour markets. Trade unions use their bargaining power predominantly by setting nominal wages. Their objective is to enforce real wage claims. Although the resulting real wage depends on the price-setting behaviour of firms, trade unions have an incentive to use their bargaining power. We know from the NAIRU (non-accelerating inflation rate of unemployment) model that competing real wage claims which are inconsistent, that is, which sum to more than is available in output per head, may result in rising inflation. The single trade union – and the workers it represents – may, however, still benefit.

Calmfors and Driffill (1988) have shown in their empirical investigation that this bargaining strategy dominates, in particular if wages are collectively bargained at branch level. The counterpart to this strategy is played by monetary policy. However, monetary policy can only indirectly influence the bargaining positions on the labour market by changing conditions on the goods market. It does so by restricting monetary expansion and hence the room for manoeuvre for price increases in the aggregate, rather than on the individual market. In addition, a restrictive monetary policy raises the rate of interest and restricts investment opportunities. In this indirect way, via reduction of aggregate demand and employment, monetary policy has an impact on the bargaining positions of the labour market parties.

The threat of a restrictive monetary policy, however, is not always credible. In particular, a single trade union may not feel restricted in its bargaining power by the threat of an increase in the general rate of unemployment. The introduction of a monetary union changes this constellation, since the monetary authority is shifted from the national to the supranational level. Thereby, the conditions for a conflict between wages policy and monetary policy are changed. In a monetary union, collective wage bargaining in one country is exposed to the competition of collective wage bargaining in the other countries. There is no escape from this competition, since an inflationary monetary policy assisted by exchange rate variations is no longer an option for the national authorities. Thus monetary policy credibility increases. In particular, trade unions have to recognize that the result of wage negotiations will have an immediate impact on employment.

Credibility and Institutional Change

The empirical study of Erkel-Mousse and Melitz (1995) has shown that the abolition of national monetary policies is associated with very low costs.

National monetary policy is not a necessary instrument for adjustment. This result is the principal focus of models that analyse the credibility aspects of monetary policy (Giovannini 1990, 1991 and Eichengreen 1993). The basic argument in these models refers to the way the EMS functioned. A system of fixed exchange rates and the perfect integration of markets for capital and goods imply adjustment costs that are relatively high in those countries with a weak currency, compared to the country with the anchor currency. The costs of adjustment in the weak currency country are indicated by the requirement to maintain a real interest rate differential to the country with the anchor currency – Germany – in the case of the EMS. On the other hand, a so-called quasi currency union existed, that is, a group of countries that showed a strong propensity to exchange rate pegging that resulted in extremely low differentials in interest rates and inflation rates compared to the anchor currency. In the case of the EMS these countries were Austria, Belgium, Denmark, Luxembourg and the Netherlands, and to a lesser extent France and Ireland, all of whom fixed their currencies to the DM. This kind of policy can be characterized as being a monetary policy comparable to that within a currency union. An indicator for a perfectly credible policy is the sustainable disappearance of a very small differential of nominal and real interest rates between these countries (De Grauwe 1994; Eichengreen 1993). Indeed interest rate differentials between the core EMS countries had nearly disappeared by the late 1990s, although Spain and Italy were forced to incur higher stabilization costs in terms of differentials in their inflation rates and interest rates compared to Germany.

The foundation of an independent European central bank that is obligated to maintain price stability and is, therefore, not forced to stabilize the exchange rate, can be interpreted as a first step in creating a credible institution (Cukierman 1992). Moreover, the independence of the central bank signals the policy change from a regime of full employment guarantee to a regime of price stability.

Adjustment Mechanisms and Institutional Change

If such a change in the policy regime can be credibly transmitted to the wage-bargaining partners, we should expect that wage policy will become more cooperative because of a reduction in unexpected inflation. As long as fiscal transfers cannot be excluded, a credible policy can be endangered. Assuming that economic agents form expectations concerning economic policy options, we can deduce that an institutional change generates reactions on their side. As a consequence, the foundation of a European central bank that pursues a credible monetary policy will lead to changes in wage policies in most member countries. This implies that a rational wage policy can be an aggressive one in a non-credible monetary regime. A wage policy that is confronted with a non-credible monetary policy anticipates the possibility of a change in an announced monetary policy strategy, in terms of rising inflation or a devaluation after a wage-bargaining process. The change of regime is evident in the case of countries with weak currencies. Membership of a currency union offers them the possibility of stabilizing expectations concerning inflation and exchange rates and consequently, of installing a credible regime that results in lower real interest rates and more flexible nominal wages. On the other hand, the wage-bargaining strategy will not change fundamentally in those countries that have already formed a quasi currency union.

Figure 4.1 shows inflation and growth rates of real wages for the years 1991 and 1995, respectively. A comparison shows that both rates decreased during the period observed. If we put cyclical factors to one side, these figures may be interpreted as implying that wage policies reacted in a cooperative way when confronted with more restrictive monetary policies in 1995 compared to 1991. A credible monetary policy limits the room for manoeuvre for wage bargainers to pursue redistribution objectives. The ECB cannot accommodate aggressive wage policies without endangering price stability. In the face of perfect integration of capital and goods markets in Europe, aggressive wage policies would also lead to a loss of international competitiveness. Therefore, a European central bank that has to achieve price stability, at the same time supports international competitiveness and ensures stable economic growth. An improvement in the level of employment, however, does not necessarily follow.

Wage Bargaining and Sectoral Adjustment Requirements

Membership of the European Monetary Union can be interpreted as an institutionalized import of credibility. When confronted with a credible monetary policy, there will be some influence on wage policy at least in some EU countries. In countries where foreign trade is to a large extent intra-industry trade, there will be no additional pressure on wage policy. These industries together with their foreign trading partners are able to exploit increasing returns to scale. Thus temporary monopoly profits should at least enable wages to be maintained. If, on the other hand, we look to inter-industry trade, a real shock in a monetary union induces additional pressures on wage flexibility.

Assuming that wage flexibility has to increase in some sectors, one can ask about the importance of institutional designs in wage-bargaining processes. The question is, given the requirement of price stability in EMU, what degree of centralization in wage bargaining is the best? Calmfors and Driffill (1988) show in an empirical analysis that different degrees of centralization in wage

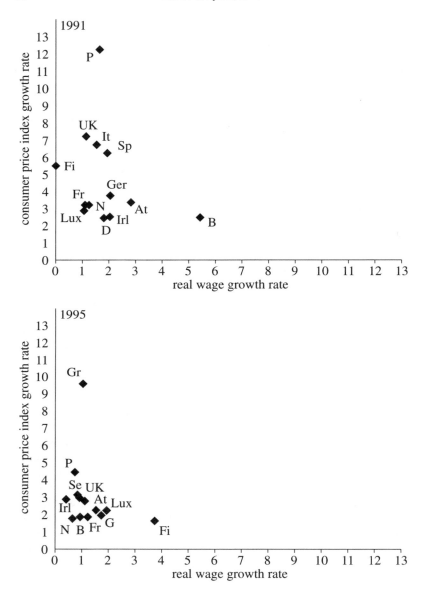

Source: CEC (1995).

Figure 4.1   Inflation and real wage growth, 1991 and 1995

policy result in different levels of employment in a closed economy. They conclude that fully decentralized and highly centralized wage-bargaining processes perform best, with regard to the level of employment and the flexibility of wages.

What influence does a credible monetary policy in EMU exert on national wage policies? The discussion about this question is dominated by two extreme conclusions. On the one hand, pressure to increase the flexibility of wage policies will give rise to a tendency towards decentralized wage bargaining and rising real wage flexibility. On the other hand, however, a tendency towards supranational wage-bargaining processes has been noted. This would result in an equalization of nominal wages, although the regional levels and rates of productivity growth differ.

In decentralized wage bargaining, the possibility of adjusting to enterprise-specific requirements is quite high. This flexibility seems to depend on the degree of substitutability for goods produced. On the other hand, empirical studies show that workers demand rather high wages in times when enterprises yield satisfactory earnings (Franz 1995). This bargaining habit restricts the effect on the levels of employment. The wage bargaining is guided mainly by the competitiveness of firms, less by the macroeconomic performance. In centralized wage-bargaining processes, there is a special focus on the macroeconomic outcome. In particular, one can find a strong relationship between bargained wages and the price level. This relationship can be characterized as a strong one, because centralized wage bargaining shows a tendency to equalization of the wage level in the considered region or country. Therefore, a rational wage policy on this level tends to be cooperative, being confronted with a credible monetary policy. By contrast, wage-bargaining processes at the industry level are judged to be inferior compared to decentralized and centralized wage policies. It is assumed that the degree of product substitutability is of less importance to this bargaining, because all enterprises in the industry are affected similarly. An important component of the strategy of a trade union at the industry level is to imitate the wage policies of other trade unions in the economy. The chosen wage policy will be aggressive, if the trade union can expect that rising wages in this industry have small effects on the general price level.

With a closer economic integration the degree of centralization in wage bargaining loses its importance. The model of Danthine and Hunt (1994) shows the effects of closer economic integration by an increase of the elasticity of substitution between two countries' aggregate goods. The competitiveness on the international markets for goods increasingly dominates strategies of wage policy. The authors conclude from their analysis, which is based on the Calmfors–Driffill model, that the relative degree of centralization in wage bargaining decreases in the European internal market. Trade unions, at the industry level, are forced to recognize the relevant rise in international competition in markets for goods. In the internal market, these trade unions seem to be in a comparable situation to those pursuing a decentralized wage policy in a closed economy. Therefore, some of the trade unions at the industry level consider wage policy cooperation at the interregional level in order to regain bargaining power.

Countries where centralized wage bargaining dominates are pushed by the competitive effects of the internal market into an inferior situation concerning employment. The decreasing relative degree of wage bargaining may lead them to a loss of employment. One has to be cautious at this point of the analysis, however, because the situation of centralized wage bargaining in an open economy cannot be compared to the wage policy at the industry level in a closed economy. The wage policy at a centralized level, when confronted with an increase of international competition, forces trade unions to choose cooperative strategies. Aggressive wage policies cannot be enforced, except in a non-credible monetary regime, since otherwise they would generate falling employment and a loss of trade union power.

What does the analysis of the decreasing relative degree of centralization in wage bargaining imply for real wage behaviour in the EMU? Two lines of argument should be distinguished. On the one hand there is the rise of substitutability in goods markets, which depends on the degree of openness of the economies in international trade and on the degree of product diversification. On the other hand, the integration of the markets for goods and capital in the European Union has already restricted opportunities for aggressive strategies in wage policy.

The abolition of national monetary and exchange rate policies in EMU will cause monetary convergence by reducing interest rates and inflation in at least some member states. The disappearance of real interest rate differentials in EMU will stimulate investment. In recent years, smaller and declining differences between national real interest rates have been observed, indicating that most EU countries have already been rather successful in harmonizing inflation rates. Therefore, the pressure on wage policies in the monetary union will not be too severe, because the degree of substitutability in goods markets will not change and capital costs will decrease.

The pressure on real wages in EMU is increased for those trade unions that do not utilize the additional cost advantages caused by a credible monetary policy. Trade unions that do not profit from decreasing capital costs by demanding higher wages gain competitiveness in the goods markets and thereby may cooperate without being forced to react to further pressure in a credible monetary regime. Trade unions which try to avoid a loss of power in wage bargaining by generating cooperation on the supranational level will lose out. Even if we assume converging economic development throughout

EMU, this strategy is misleading and merely results in a contrary situation, namely a decrease in trade union power. At least, this effect will occur if centralized wage-bargaining processes generate a tendency to wage level parity. This tendency weakens the countries' competitiveness. The requirement to generate a catching-up process in the periphery of the European Union will be hampered by interregional coordinated wage policies. These kinds of wage policies curtail the wage-cost advantages of the periphery and, therefore, create an additional competitive disadvantage in these countries. Consequently, employment will decrease and the power of trade unions will diminish. Therefore, rational centralized wage bargaining in EMU has to prevent supranational wage policies and has to avoid the tendency to equalise wage levels.

Conclusion

Is the flexibility in labour markets increased by shifting the monetary regime towards a currency union? According to the NAIRU model, monetary policy has only an indirect influence on the bargaining behaviour in labour markets, which is largely determined by the market structure. With a changed market structure the threat from a restrictive monetary policy may increase in a monetary union. Experience within the EMS during the 1980s provides evidence that the opportunity costs of a European monetary policy are rather low, because a credible monetary regime induces wage bargainers to act more cooperatively, since the danger of an unexpected inflation is reduced.

As to the changed market structure, transparency has increased in EMU and so has the competitive pressure in the internal market. At the same time, the degree of centralization of wage bargaining is less important for bargaining behaviour. On the other hand, by improving investment opportunities through lower real interest rates, a monetary union may also have favourable effects on labour markets. Trades unions may find themselves in a better position to enforce real wage claims. So it is an open question whether they strive for an institutionalization of wage bargaining on an EU level. In any case, this would be to the disadvantage of the peripheral regions.

4 CONCLUSIONS

This chapter argues that the traditional criteria for delimiting an optimal currency area – noted in Chapter 3 – are not relevant in the modern context. In particular it has been argued that the size of the currency area is endogenous to the integration process. As integration proceeds then the size of the optimal currency area will increase. The economic gains are expected to

come through greater monetary policy credibility combined with lower information and transaction costs. The degree of centralization of wage bargaining
is therefore less important for bargaining behaviour, since by improving
investment opportunities a monetary union may also have favourable effects
on labour markets. If greater investment enhances productivity, trades unions
may find themselves in a better position to enforce real wage claims. It is
therefore an open question whether they should strive for an institutionalization of wage bargaining on a European level. The wage-bargaining process
that emerges, however, is of vital importance to the ultimate success of EMU.
This is considered further in Chapter 7.

NOTE

1.   In the short run a change of real exchange rates can be based on speculative attacks.

PART II

Present Issues for EMU

5. Monetary policy in EMU

Hubert Kempf

1 INTRODUCTION

European Monetary Union (EMU) was officially introduced on 1 January 1999. After more than a decade of discussions, controversies, doubts and delays, a single currency officially and 'irreversibly' replaced the various currencies used in 12 countries of the European Union (EU). Only 3 countries either refused to or could not join EMU[1]. It is difficult to underestimate EMU's originality: it is the first currency area linking advanced economies to have been set up at the same time as 'dematerialized' money, and which is to be regulated by modern banking techniques.[2] That is, the new currency, the euro, is a fiat money, whose issuance is controlled solely by central banks.

The architects and the authorities of EMU and the EU had to anticipate the challenge of any modern central banker: they had to face the difficulty of setting rules so that the money supply is set in accordance with the needs of non-financial agents throughout the economic area covered by the eurozone, and to establish a flexible yet safe and reliable system of means of payment.

This is a daunting task within national barriers as our understanding of the workings of monetary policy is shallow at best.[3] Within a multicountry monetary union, this is aggravated by two factors:

- The extent, diversity and complexity of EMU: this union is formed by 12 countries, populated by some 300 million inhabitants, differing in wealth, customs, and economic specialization, hence with different needs, accustomed to conducting business according to different rules. In particular, the diversity of financial systems and financing activities in EMU is immense.
- The lack of precedent: the founders of EMU and the various governmental authorities involved in its creation could not refer to any similar organization, nor did they take time either to reach agreement on a set of pragmatic rules or to gain knowledge of the financial sector's reaction.

Because there is no precedent and because EMU is so new, there are as yet no detailed records on European monetary policy on which to base a sound evaluation. To understand European monetary policy, we have to develop two areas. First, we shall describe the institutional framework of EMU, since this sets the constraints placed on policy makers. Second, given this framework, the various issues linked to the conduct of monetary policy will be made explicit.

2   THE INSTITUTIONAL FRAMEWORK

The institutional design of EMU was defined in the Maastricht Treaty, and later complemented by various articles of the Amsterdam Treaty. This implies that EMU and its founding principles have been agreed by all members of the EU (15 countries) and not just by the countries participating in EMU at its creation.

EMU is based on the European System of Central Banks (ESCB). This is a two-stage system: the existing national central banks have not disappeared but rather have been used as the building blocks of EMU. This principle is of course in line with the main characteristics of the EU, which is a union of sovereign nations. Hence the national central banks are closely associated with European monetary policy, both in its design and in its implementation. In addition to these banks, the European Central Bank (ECB) has been created, located in Frankfurt (FRG). Its capital belongs to member states and part of the foreign reserves of the national central banks have been transferred to the ECB.

The European System of Central Banks (ESCB)

There are two major councils involved in monetary policy:[4]

1. *The Executive Board* comprises the president of the ESCB, its vice-president and four additional members. These members are nominated by the Council of Ministers of the European Union. They are in office for eight years, with overlapping mandates, and cannot be re-elected to the Executive Board. They cannot be dismissed, except for gross misconduct or incapacity. Decisions are taken by majority rule. In the case of a deadlock, the president has the decisive vote.
2. *The Council of Governors* comprises the six members of the Executive Board and all the governors of central banks of countries participating in EMU. Decisions regarding monetary policy are taken according to majority rule, given that each member in the council has one vote, and

hence carries equal weight. This is to say that Ireland is on a par with Germany in any decision made by the Council of Governors. Again, in the case of a deadlock, the president has the decisive vote.[5]

These two councils have differing responsibilities:

- The Executive Board heads the ECB. It is in charge of the centralized control and assessment of the daily implementation of decisions taken by the Council of Governors. It monitors the centralized system of international financial transfers between banks and financial intermediaries within EMU (the TARGET system). Moreover, the president is responsible for representing the ECSB and explaining to other European centres of power for European monetary policy under way. Finally, each member has a special administrative task regarding the management of the ECB.
- The Council of Governors meets every two weeks (on Thursdays). It defines the orientation of monetary policy to be followed over the next period, and makes strategic decisions concerning intervention instruments such that policies can be implemented efficiently. Moreover, it controls the management of the ECB and its internal organization and makes decisions about the international cooperation within the ESCB.

Given the decisions reached by the Council of Governors, it is the task of the national central banks to put them into effect: each intervenes daily on its short-term financial market(s) so as to implement the decisions taken by the Council of Governors. Guidelines have been issued and constraints placed on the operations that can be effected by a national central bank so as to guarantee consistency throughout the eurozone.

In other words, the design of monetary policy is centralized according to an equitable decision mechanism (one country, one vote), but is implementation is decentralized and unequal, reflecting the disproportions between member countries.

Independence of the ESCB

An important characteristic stressed by the negotiators of the Maastricht Treaty is the 'independence' of the ESCB, implicitly from outside pressures, mostly from other public or government agencies, and in particular from national governments and legislative bodies. The independence of a central bank is a disputed notion, difficult to assess with precision. Even its merits are questionable. In fact, it is commonly agreed that there is no such thing as 'full independence', because a non-elected public institution like a central bank has to be accountable for its actions. Hence, independence is a question of degree, that is, how much autonomy or independence can be given to a central bank. It is useful to distinguish between goal independence and instrument independence.[6] Goal independence refers to the ability of the governing board of a central bank to set the monetary policy goal independently from pressures exerted by political authorities; instrument independence refers to its ability to choose independently the strategy to be followed so as to attain these objectives.

In practice, two main issues regarding central bank independence are at stake. The first concerns the position of the policy committee of a central bank and its degree of independence from other elected centres of power. Critically, it depends on the nomination and replacement process of the members of the governing board: how they are appointed, controlled and reappointed; the length of their mandate; the restrictions imposed. But independence also depends on the existence of a veto power from government: its ability to give orders to the executive unit in charge of implementing the monetary policy. The second issue refers to the legal obligations of the central bank regarding public administration. It may be obliged to fulfil certain statutory obligations, such as the financing of public deficits, or of special public expenditures.

In the case of the ESCB, strong emphasis was put on independence. Following the model of the German Bundesbank, it is said to be the most independent central bank in the world. It is both highly goal dependent and instrument independent. The negotiators of the Maastricht Treaty were greatly concerned about pressure being brought to bear on the system and various provisions made clear that it should be as independent as possible.

- Each national central bank of countries participating in EMU must be independent. It must neither by law nor in practice be accountable to the political authorities governing the country. There must be no possibility that a government will issue orders or give advice to the national governor who sits on the ESCB Council of Governors.
- Members of the Executive Board should be immune from political pressures because of their long (eight years) non-renewable mandates.

This raises the question of the accountability of the ESCB. Being immune to undesirable political pressure, is it not therefore also immune to criticism which can be justified? Who judges the 'undesirable' political pressure and the 'normal' pressure on political actors and agencies which arise from healthy debate in democratic countries? Can we not claim that too much power without sufficient restraint and balance is corrupting? This raises a difficult issue to which we shall return in the last section of this chapter.

This concern has been voiced repeatedly throughout Europe during the ratification process of the Maastricht Treaty and partly explains the British reluctance to adhere to and initially to join EMU. It is surely premature to criticize the ESCB for its lack of accountability since detailed records are not yet available, but it is surely an issue which will be subject to intense scrutiny in the coming years.

The Operational Links between Banks

Given that a modern currency is nothing more than a fiduciary sign and flows of metallic specie have been replaced by electronic transfers between banks and financial institutions, a properly functioning monetary union relies on an efficient system linking these banks and institutions, allowing them to make these transfers routinely and safely. A European monetary union could not exist without such a system. The difficulty was then to develop a standardized and extensive system linking many banks which had been accustomed to function in highly different regulatory and technical environments. It was important to set up such a system rapidly in the years between the signing of the Maastricht Treaty and the launching of the euro, and thus the Trans-European Automated Real-time Gross Settlement Express Transfer (TARGET) system was developed. Despite some minor criticisms, it appears to function adequately and has not impaired the launching or the functioning of EMU.

3   INSTRUMENTS AND IMPLEMENTATION OF MONETARY POLICY

The instruments available to the ESCB are the standard ones of a modern central bank. On that account, EMU does not innovate. There are three categories of instruments.

1.   Permanent facilities offered by the ESCB are available 'through the window' to selected correspondents in each country. Lending facilities are available to agreed correspondents in each country, at a fixed interest rate. At the end of each day, a bank with a negative position towards its national central bank will be presumed to require such a facility. The lending interest rate will set a higher limit on short-term interest rates within EMU. Borrowing facilities are also available to these correspondents, who will be able to leave deposits in their national central bank account, remunerated at an interest rate also fixed by the ESCB. This interest rate will set a lower limit on short-term interest rates in EMU.

2. Intervention on the open market. In addition, the ESCB can make daily
    interventions on the national 'open' money markets, through national
    central banks. It is de facto the main instrument of monetary policy.
    Intervention on the open market is a flexible, quick and efficient way for
    a central bank to influence the lending behaviour of commercial banks.
    The principle is simple: a central bank takes a position in the short-term
    money market, so as to provide or absorb liquidity, with the effect of
    altering the asset position of commercial banks. The main mechanism
    will be through weekly tenders on temporary cession of eligible assets
    decided by the ESCB and applied by every national central bank ('repos').
    There is also the possibility of collateralized loans, whereby a bank will
    use eligible assets as a guarantee for the loans obtained from its central
    bank. The normal length of a contract will be two weeks. A financial
    intermediary will contract with the national central bank under the con-
    trol of which it depends.
3. Compulsory reserves. The use of compulsory reserves raised a difficult
    issue at the design stage of EMU. Some countries imposed such a device
    and others did not. Among those that used compulsory reserves, some
    countries did not offer any compensation for the holding of these re-
    serves by commercial banks. A reserve requirement is a useful tool for
    controlling money creation by commercial banks as it allows a better
    stabilization of the interest rate over short periods. It also allows a rapid
    modification of the debt position of commercial banks relative to the
    central bank. But experience shows that banks operating in a financial
    system without such a regulation still hold large idle reserves to meet
    unexpectedly large swings in outflows. Moreover non-interest-bearing
    reserves act as an implicit tax on banks. Therefore the merits of such a
    regulation are not compelling. Hence the negotiators of the Maastricht
    Treaty reached a compromise: reserve requirements would be imposed
    on all banks operating in the eurozone. But the requirement would be
    minimal, with a maximum of 2.5 per cent of deposits, and such reserves
    would bear an interest equal to the average over a period of a month of
    the interest rate charged by a national central bank for its intervention.
    This interest rate, known as the main refinancing operations (MRO) rate,
    is fixed by the Council of Governors.

Given these regulations on monetary policy, de facto, four interest rates are
manipulated by the ESCB, three of them being fixed at regular intervals and
defining a steady corridor within which the fourth one (on the open market)
varies according to daily requirements. (See Figure 5.1.)

The actual operations on markets are left to the national central banks, to
which targets and guidelines are supplied, and controls are exerted. Two

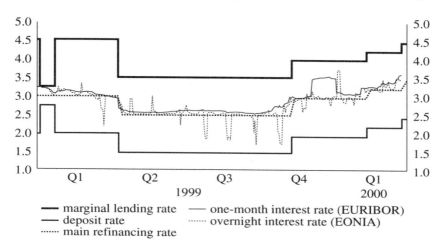

Source: European Central Bank, *Annual Report* 1999.

Figure 5.1 ECB interest and money market rates (percentages per annum; daily data)

reasons explain this two-stage process. First, the heterogeneity of national financial systems and actors, because of their history and existing legal regulations, could not be negated or discarded. Intervention requires extensive local market knowledge, which is held by the national central banks. Second, for obvious political and symbolic reasons, it was impossible to abolish large and old and often prestigious institutions such as these national central banks. Lastly, such a two-stage process exemplified the subsidiarity principle which is supposed to be enforced through the European Union. Of course, the daily operations of the national central banks are coordinated by the ECB in order to avoid any inconsistency between the actual operations performed by these banks which could be exploited by commercial banks, and jeopardize the conduct of a common monetary policy valid for the entire eurozone. It is clear that the same conditions have to be made to financial intermediaries and banks in any EMU country. Three reasons explain the necessity for coordinating the operations of national central banks: (a) there must be no distortion of competition; (b) any bias in favour of a given country, even if completely unintentional, would immediately be denounced and suspected of reflecting some political favouritism, contrary to the aims and objectives assigned to the ESCB; and (c) granting the same facilities at the same price for any operator in Europe will foster a tendency towards the homogenization of financial markets within EMU and will contribute to the establishment of a truly European financial market.

4   THE CONDUCT OF MONETARY POLICY

Within this legal framework, the issue is now to understand the principles which should, or actually do, guide the conduct of monetary policy. Of course, the Maastricht Treaty could not provide a provision for every possible contingency that the ESCB could face. In economic terms, the Maastricht Treaty represents an incomplete contract.

A Broad Consensus

One factor, often underestimated, that has contributed to the creation of EMU is the existing consensus shared by practitioners of monetary policy, and supported by a theoretical perspective widely dominant among monetary economists and macroeconomists. To put it briefly, all shared a minimalist post-Friedman view about monetary policy, no matter how ambiguous or disputable. Hence, it was relatively easy to form a consensus about some broad monetary policy propositions in EMU. Four tenets constitute this 'middle-of-the-road' consensus:

- There is no permanent trade-off between unemployment and inflation, but monetary policy can have an impact on the real economy in the short run, even though the precise channels and quantitative effects of monetary policy are not yet clearly known.
- As a consequence, price stability is the sole long-term objective.
- It is possible to devote monetary policy to that end.
- There is, however, still scope for an active monetary stabilization policy, able to avoid traps, accommodate both real and nominal shocks and redress imbalances.

This consensus was nurtured by the success of the German Bundesbank's policy in fighting inflation without experiencing a lower growth rate than equivalent economies over some 30 years. Without that consensus among economists and policy makers, it is unlikely that monetary integration would have taken place in Europe. This does not meant that there is no place for uncertainty and disagreements over monetary policy in the eurozone. In addition to the uncertainties about the workings of monetary policy, there is an additional complexity in EMU due to the diversity of its member economies: even though there is a single currency and a unique monetary policy, monetary policy operations are decentralized, as national financial systems are still very different; EMU covers a vast diversity of national prudential regulations; several authorities are involved in the definition of monetary policy, which raises the issue of the bargaining process which will take place in the ESCB. These fragmented characteristics of EMU will be felt in every aspect of monetary policy, as we shall see.

Objectives of European Monetary Policy

Assigned objectives

Three final macroeconomic objectives can commonly be assigned to monetary policy: it may have to (loosely speaking) control inflation; it may contribute to a full-employment goal over a certain time interval (again with some ambiguities over the precise meaning of full employment); finally, it may be given an objective linked to the external position of the particular currency zone, such as a balance-of-payments objective or the defence of a certain parity of the currency relative to another currency, or a basket of currencies.

The Maastricht Treaty specifies the objectives of European monetary policy in broad terms which leave enough room for the ESCB to actually set its own agenda, making it largely goal independent. According to Article 105 of the treaty, priority is to be given to the control of European inflation: 'The primary objective of the ESCB shall be to maintain price stability'. However, this is not the sole objective given to the ESCB. A secondary objective is 'to support the general policies in the (European) Community' in so far as they do not compromise the primary objective and are not prejudicial to the control of inflation. This cautious and imprecise wording suggests that the ESCB can act so as to foster growth in Europe and fight unemployment, but that its main task remains the control of inflationary pressures. This balanced view is again an expression of a compromise reached by the Maastricht negotiations over differing views about what can and should be achieved by monetary policy.

This impression can be viewed as beneficial to the ESCB as it leaves it with more room to manoeuvre and does not 'tie it to the mast'. There is no precise definition of price stability or of the other ESCB objectives, it is de facto largely goal independent. On the other hand, it could be argued that it weakens the ESCB; that the ESCB is left without sufficient guidelines. Therefore, it will be open to criticism and vulnerable in the event of failure.

Another factor of potential weakness is that the definition of the international monetary arrangements of the eurozone and more generally the assessment and control of EMU's external position is not the responsibility of the ESCB, but of the Council of the EU. De facto, the exchange rate policy of

EMU is in the hands of EMU ministers of finance, but it is clear that monetary policy cannot be followed without an eye to existing or potential external imbalances. Again the ESCB's role in dealing with that aspect is subsidiary and imprecise. Its independence is hampered by European government involvement in exchange rate matters.

Bargaining over actual objectives

Given these imprecisions, it is clear that there will be ample room for disagreements and possible implicit bargaining within the Council of Governors. The most important issue will be taking into account the economic heterogeneity within the eurozone. Let us take the example of 'price stability'. There will be different inflationary pressures in the various regions of the eurozone as different countries or regions or industries will experience different shocks and different evolutions. It has been estimated that even in an environment characterized by a tendency to low nominal increases, the differences across countries in the rates of inflation for non-tradable goods could represent 2.5 per cent per year.[7] It is not known whether the advent of EMU will modify this estimate but it is likely that large discrepancies in nominal evolutions will be observed in the eurozone. Faced with this problem, what will be the actual objectives of the ECB? Will it only take into consideration a 'common' nominal evolution, based on an EMU-wide price index, or will it also consider the discrepancies in regional evolutions, trying to minimize them even at a cost of a higher overall inflation?

We should expect the EMU objectives to be the subject of much discussion. In some ways, this is exactly why EMU has been created. We should remember the precedent of German reunification: the Bundesbank at that time was regularly accused of caring only about German interests at the expense of its neighbouring countries tied to German monetary policy through the EMS, and compelled to accept high real and nominal interest rates which led to soaring unemployment rates. At that time, the protest did not convince the Bundesbank to alter its policy as it was a sovereign central bank. Within EMU, it is not yet known how the ESCB will react to a similar asymmetrical situation, creating discord in all or part of the eurozone. It is likely that even without receiving 'orders' or 'recommendations' from their national governments or having a 'national' bias, the members of the Council of Governors will have differing views about what is to be done. The Council's decision-making procedures are not yet known, as not enough time has elapsed. But it is clear that a compromise will have to be reached in a council whose members are more independent and more on a par with the president than is the case with the American equivalent, the Federal Open Market Committee (FOMC).

Dealing with national governments

Moreover, monetary policy is not the only tool for stabilizing European economies. European countries still have control of various instruments which could either help or impair the ability of the ESCB to reach its actual objectives. The ESCB will not be able to ignore the behaviour and strategies followed by the various governments of the eurozone.

National governments of the eurozone adopt different positions, which are explained by two main factors: size and level of wealth. Some European economies are large and well diversified whereas others are small or extra small; some countries are rich and affluent while others are poor and less well developed. Their ability to constrain the ESCB will vary according to these two factors. Nevertheless it is likely that governments heading large and affluent economies will aim to constrain the ESCB or at least to influence it in various ways. Through fiscal policy or through other more indirect ways such as their influence over financial matters and actors or over the wage-setting process, they will try to 'bend' the ESCB towards their view or even their goals. It is unlikely that they will form a coalition, their interests being diverse if not contradictory. But this increases the difficulties linked to non-coordination of stabilization policies. Hence, the ESCB will have to deal with 12 governments. Whether it will then be induced to adopt rather accommodative policies or on the contrary very rigid measures, at the expense of its ability to stabilize the European economies effectively, remains to be seen.

For these reasons, the conduct of monetary policy by the ESCB will be a compromise between opposite views concerning the objectives of monetary policy. This explains the past reluctance of the German authorities and the Bundesbank in particular towards European monetary integration. Compared to the asymmetrical EMS, which de facto functioned as a D-Mark zone, not constraining German monetary policy, they could fear that they would lose their dominance and would have to compromise with less-disciplined partners. On the other hand, this necessity to bargain and reach a compromise regarding monetary policy explains the positive attitude of the French authorities towards EMU: they saw it as a way of reducing their disadvantage over actual monetary policy! Of course, the ESCB as a whole will aim to increase as much as possible its ability to act without too many constraints from the other players involved in stabilizing the European economy – commonly referred to as its 'credibility'. Whether it will succeed or not is not yet known but it is a major element of the assessment of the system as a whole and will be closely scrutinized in the coming years.

The Issue of Policy Strategy

When dealing with practical monetary policy, the possibilities are rather limited. A central bank nowadays may adopt strategies linked either to 'final' or 'intermediate' objectives. 'Final' objectives may be exchange rate stabilization, inflation stabilization, known as 'inflation targeting', or growth or unemployment. 'Intermediate' objectives may be the stabilization of interest rates or of monetary aggregates.

Given their history, credibility record and political background, the various European national central banks have followed diverse strategies. In recent years, the Banque de France has followed a policy aimed at anchoring the franc to the Deutschmark the *'franc fort'* policy. This corresponded to an exchange rate stabilization strategy. In contrast, the German Bundesbank claimed to follow a policy of money supply targeting, aimed at stabilizing some monetary aggregates around a target value. In effect, it followed a much more pragmatic policy.[8]

Hence various strategies are available to the ESCB. The Maastricht Treaty is mute on this subject: the ESCB is instrument independent. Indeed the controversy is over two options: money supply targeting or inflation targeting,[9] both of which have their advantages and disadvantages.[10]

Money supply targeting

A first possible monetary strategy is to set an 'intermediate' quantitative objective for the growth of a monetary aggregate over a given time interval (typically one year) and to manipulate monetary instruments so as to be as close as possible to this objective. Such a policy is commonly associated with German monetary policy and was originally advocated by monetarists.

A central bank closely controls only a very narrow monetary aggregate called the 'money base' (that is, interbank liquidity). But a central bank cannot control the means of payment used by non-financial agents. A money supply targeting policy aims to control the evolution of some larger monetary aggregate as much as possible, by taking advantage of the empirical proportional relations existing between different monetary aggregates, and in particular between the money base and some monetary aggregate related to the payment behaviour of non-financial agents.[11]

It is commonly argued that money supply targeting has three advantages:

- It is an objective easily controlled by a central bank, given the needs of interbank liquidity by all financial institutions.
- It is easily checked by observers and economic agents. This allows them to have a good understanding of the capacity of a central bank to implement an announced policy, nurturing its credibility.

- By means of a good medium-term relation between the monetary aggregate (an intermediate objective) and inflation (a final objective), it represents a good check on inflation, even though inflation can be affected in the short run by other real or monetary factors.

The main issue, then, is to know how robust (and hence how much confidence can we have in it) are the links between the monetary base and a larger monetary aggregate such as M3. Recently, a striking weakening of this link has been observed, giving rise to doubts that a central bank can control such a large aggregate. This weakening results from the variability of the aggregate money demand function, mainly because of financial innovations. Equally dubious or unstable is the link between the monetary aggregate and inflation which according to monetarism is implicitly the ultimate goal of such a policy. It can theoretically be claimed and empirically observed that minimizing the variability of a monetary aggregate does not imply de factor minimizing inflation variability.[12] Hence, money supply targeting appears to many economists to be weakly supported both by theory and evidence. In particular, the Bundesbank itself was not a rigid adherent to such a strategy and it was able to manipulate interest rates in ways that conflicted with a proper control over the officially targeted monetary aggregate.

Inflation targeting in EMU
The other candidate policy is inflation targeting. According to its supporters, the aim of a central bank should be to check carefully the evolution of the inflation rate, so that it comes as close as possible over time to a target value fixed by the central bank. A variety of monetary instruments could be used for that purpose, either the control of the money base or of the short-term interest rate.
   The advantages of inflation targeting are twofold:

- The first advantage derives from the defects of money supply targeting, that is, the difficulty of controlling monetary aggregates: it is no longer true that a large monetary aggregate is easily controllable. So why not immediately chase the right fox, the inflation rate, rather than an indirect beast hoping that it will lead us to the foxhole? The central bank will be able to use more information than just the evolution of monetary aggregates when formulating its decision.
- It is a policy easily understandable by non-financial agents. Hence it can affect their inflationary expectations directly and efficiently, and put them in line with inflation targets. This is particularly true when the central bank adopts a fully developed communication policy, as is the case in New Zealand, Sweden and the United Kingdom. This

adds a crucial tool to the achievement of keeping inflation under control.

But it also has its disadvantages or difficulties:

- First, inflation targeting makes it difficult to keep track of a central bank's record: if the target is reached, it will be impossible to tell whether this is due to an efficient monetary policy or to a lucky sequence of events. No one will be able to fully understand and explain what happened. Moreover, inflation targeting may make monetary policy difficult to redirect. The paradox is that the closer inflation is to its target value, the more difficult it is to orientate monetary policy in a restrictive or accommodative sense.
- Second, it is difficult to define the 'right' inflation rate. Should the goal be full price stability or is it preferable to tolerate a 'small' but positive inflation rate? If yes, how small is 'small'? Moreover, given the various lags involved with monetary policy, one objective should be to forecast the inflation rate. What then is the proper forecasting interval? How reliable are our forecasts of inflation?[13]
- It may be difficult or impossible to distinguish clearly between nonimal causes of inflation, which can be addressed, and adjustments of relative prices, reflecting necessary and beneficial adjustments to real shocks. More generally, inflation targeting amounts to incorporating in the economy an element of nominal rigidity, in the expectation that it will generate some desirable real price flexibility. Nothing allows us to conclude yet that it is a safe bet, valid in any circumstances, for any country.

These difficulties are heightened in the case of EMU because of the diversity between countries and regions within EMU.

- A first difficulty deals with the choice of the right price index. Inflation targeting implies the definition of an appropriate inflation index on which to base the whole strategy. In the case of EMU, divergences are to be expected between 'European' average inflation and 'national' inflation rates, as we have seen. This raises the issue of the control of inflation variability within the eurozone. If inflation targeting is adopted by the ESCB, should it be defined over the entire zone, or should the ESCB take into account the variability of 'regional' inflation rates within EMU?[14]
- Inflation targeting in EMU is likely to raise important distributional issues, which could jeopardize its desirability. In particular, we are not

sure that the required real price flexibility necessary to accommodate shocks within the nominal 'strait-jacket' of inflation targeting will be achieved through the adjustment of the appropriate price. In short, inflation targeting may have important distributional consequences which cannot be dismissed. A simple example should allow us to understand the problem.

Consider two countries A and B forming a monetary union. The price index of union P_{ut} is an average of the national price indices P_{At} and P_{Bt}:

$$P_{ut} = (1-\alpha)P_{at} + \alpha P_{bt}$$

which amounts to:

$$\pi_{ut} = \pi_{at} + \alpha q_t$$

with q_t representing the variation of 'terms of trade' between B and A.[15] We shall now develop two simple cases of inflationary pressures in the union.

1. *The case of wage (income) inflation*   Suppose that A is the leading country in wage formation: the representative trade union in country A is first mover and is able to set π_{at} independently of the inflation target for the union set by its central bank. Suppose that this leading wage process implies an inflation rate in country A equal to $\bar{\pi}_a > 0$. Then if the inflation target of the central bank is zero (implying a full stabilization of the 'European' price level), it implies:

$$q_t = -\frac{\bar{\pi}_a}{\alpha} < 0.$$

In words, inflation targeting implies a deterioration in terms of trade detrimental to country B! This is not a palatable result for B's workers and citizens and we should expect political difficulties to arise before long. Clearly, inflation targeting will have real effects within the union and no one knows how they will be handled. Inflation targeting within the union will imply diverging nominal evolutions among countries or regions. These divergences will not be redressed by a modification of parity able to restore the terms of trade, that is, the real relative prices between the two countries!

2. *The case of real idiosyncratic shocks*   Suppose now that a real idiosyncratic shock occurs which modifies the terms of trade be-

tween A and B: namely, there is an appreciation of the real price of goods produced in B compared with the price of goods produced in A. This corresponds to a positive value of q_t. If the goal of the ECB is stabilization of the 'European' price level, this implies that:

$$\pi_{at} = -\alpha q_t < 0.$$

In words, if the ESCB sets a 'European' goal of price stability, it is possible that there will be deflationary evolutions of nominal prices in country A and an inflationary process in country B! Again, this is likely to generate politico-economical difficulties.

It may be counterargued that these imbalances will trigger a change in behaviour in the wage-setting process, because of competitiveness effects. This may be true but is by no means certain. However, this is a good example of the uncertainties surrounding EMU.

In brief, neither candidate policy can be adopted easily by the ESCB. Both suffer from the difficulties of defining the right quantitative objectives and the fact that the transmission channels at work in EMU are as yet uncertain and largely unknown. This dilemma highlights the crucial trade-off facing European central bankers: they need to set a tight target for credibility reasons. However, this is likely to generate difficult distributional issues between countries or regions within EMU, which could undermine the political standing of the ESCB.

De facto, a pragmatic course followed by realistic central bankers

The previous discussion is important in so far as it lists difficulties faced by the members of the Council of Governors of the ESCB. However, it presents a slightly distorted view of the actual practice of central bankers, as it is highly theoretical and conjectural. In any modern monetary system, central bankers appear to be pragmatic-but-principled people. They do not act haphazardly, reacting in an unpredictable way, but nor do they single-mindedly follow a unique objective or disregard the weight of evidence and of circumstances when taking their bimonthly, weekly or even daily decisions.

The best proof of this common-sense approach to monetary policy is the famous 'Taylor rule'.[16] Taylor suggested that the US monetary authorities followed a simple yet balanced rule, aiming at stabilizing both the interest and the inflation rates. The US monetary policy followed since 1982 appears to have largely contributed to the exceptionally durable and strong expansion of the US economy. This success in turn is largely attributed to the pragmatism of the FOMC, which takes into account a large variety of indicators, either real or financial, and does not hesitate to alternate accommodative and restrictive measures, depending on the state of the economy.

The same pragmatism is to be expected from the Council of Governors, because of the complexity and the lack of precedent in EMU. Of course, it is too early to understand the actual pattern of policy decisions adopted by the Governing Board. Yet at the end of 1998 the ESCB issued a statement announcing the policy stance that the Governing Board would follow at least in the early years of EMU.[17] Even though this statement is still incomplete, and on some crucial points much too vague, it allows observers to form a rough idea of the Governing Board's strategy.

1. Price stability should be based on the 'Harmonized Index of Consumer Prices'. It is likely that the inflation target will be 1.5 per cent, with a tolerance interval between 1 per cent and 2 per cent[18].
2. The monetary strategy will take account of both the evolution of monetary aggregates in the eurozone, and 'the outlook for price developments and the risks to price stability'. It is therefore clear that no dogmatic rule will be followed, especially not monetary targeting. However, inflation forecasts by the ESCB will not be made public, whereas the target values for the monetary aggregates will be known.
3. The assessment of future price developments will be broadly based. Again, this reinforces the intended pragmatism of the ESCB. More surely, it acknowledges the fact that governors of national central banks sitting on the Governing Board are not likely to ignore their own (national) sources of information.

However, this pragmatism will be checked by the necessity of establishing its credibility as an efficient and autonomous policy maker, especially in its infancy. After more than a year, the Council of Governors modified the leading interest rate five times (see Table 5.1). The justifications offered on these occasions show an attempt to react to events rather than blindly follow a dogmatic course. But again, it is too early to distinguish a clear pattern in the decisions taken by the Council of Governors. That being said, one can add two remarks.

● In Europe, it is increasingly clear that inflation targeting was in fact the true common objective of the various central banks, and more and more so during the transition phase towards EMU. It is reasonable to conjecture that the Council of Governors will follow this trend and give high priority to the direct control of inflationary pressures, in line with its legal obligations.

Table 5.1 *Main decisions on monetary policy by the Council of Governors,*
December 1998 to April 2000

Date	Marginal lending facility interest rate (%)	Marginal deposit facility interest rate (%)	Main refinancing operations interest rate (%)
22/12/1998	4.50	2.00	–
07/01/1999	–	–	3.00
08/04/1999	3.50	1.50	2.50
04/11/1999	4.00	2.00	3.00
03/02/2000	4.25	2.25	3.25
16/03/2000	4.50	2.50	3.50
27/04/2000	4.75	2.75	3.75

- One of the reasons for the high reputation achieved by the US Federal Reserve System ('Fed') as an efficient and credible policy maker derives from the fact that 'Fed-watchers' were able to check the claims and achievements of the US central bank. The ESCB is facing the same requirement. Obviously this is easier to regard to inflation than to monetary aggregates, when there is no homogeneity in monetary aggregates in Europe, because of the differences in national financial systems and differences in the use of these aggregates. Hence, it is realistic to forecast that the ESCB will put more emphasis on inflation targeting and inflation control in Europe than on any other objective (final or intermediary) if only because it is easier to assess its performances and therefore to acquire credibility.

5 MONETARY POLICY, REGULATIONS AND FINANCE

Monetary policy understood as the proper regulation of means of payment within a currency zone necessarily interacts with financial arrangements and institutions, for obvious reasons: monetary aggregates are defined by means of aggregating various (short-term) financial assets; non-financial agents manage their demand of money partly by diversifying their asset portfolios; flows of payment are managed by financial institutions which intervene on several different financial markets at once. For these reasons, monetary authorities are aware that their actions necessarily influence the evolution and soundness of the financial sector as a whole, which in turn can facilitate or harm their ability to manage the currency.

As far as EMU is concerned, this raises (at least) three issues:

1. How will monetary policy influence European financial integration?
2. How can the regulatory powers over the banking and the financial industries in Europe be organized?
3. How will monetary policy contribute to financial stability in Europe?

Monetary policy and financial integration

Financial integration refers to the interdependence between various financial systems and markets within the eurozone. There is full integration when this interdependence is complete and it is impossible to distinguish economically between financial systems: financial institutions (firms and markets) cover the whole zone; legal regulations apply uniformly throughout the zone. In contrast, there is no integration when firms and markets are constrained by national borders, and cannot extend over these borders, and each national authority defines its own regulations, without trying to coordinate with other national regulation authorities. Of course, these are extreme cases and cannot realistically be envisaged for Europe. The reality is mixed and financial integration is therefore incomplete. It is generally agreed that the advent of the euro will foster the forces currently at work towards greater financial integration in Europe, leading eventually to a large and efficient single financial market.[19]

The extent of financial integration interacts with monetary policy. That is, it affects the 'regional' impacts of shocks between countries belonging to EMU, and the quality of regional management of shocks.[20] Even if there is a unique monetary policy set up by the ECB, because of its decentralized implementation its success will hinge on the extent of financial integration. There are 'pass-through' or spillover effects due to the existing financial integration. For example, a strengthening of lending conditions in one country will not have the same effect in every country when there is incomplete integration; it can be bypassed by means of operations on other markets or other countries when financial intermediaries are able to intervene on several markets or countries. On the whole, the control of the money supply in EMU by the ECB can be weakened in relation to incomplete financial integration.[21]

From these results, we clearly see that the regional impacts of the monetary policy covering EMU depend strongly both on the degree of EMU central bank involvement in national markets, and on the extent of interdependence between financial markets. We can then make three claims:

● The degree of financial integration interferes systematically with monetary policy whatever policy the union's central bank aims to implement, or whatever control it is able to exert upon national central banks' policies and reserves.

- The process of financial integration is likely to increase the crossover effects of monetary policy, leading to a greater variability in national money demands. It is then unlikely that EMU's monetary authorities can avoid an examination of monetary evolutions in regions of the union, when they cannot normalize the conditions of access to reserves for the whole banking industry.

- Contrary to what is frequently thought, a high degree of centralized money market operations does not guarantee maximum market efficiency, leading to the best scenario in an expected-welfare sense. This avoids the likely interference between centralized monetary operations and the handling of 'regional' financial shocks. These shocks are likely to have pronounced distorting effects when combined with a central bank whose targets will be union-wide rather than regional. On the whole, it is likely that the ESCB will try to harmonize as much as it can the lending conditions in any EMU country, by making the same requirements on each central bank. Whether that will be enough is as yet not known.

The Issue of Banking and Financial Regulation

This problem is complicated by the fact that the ECB was not given the power of supervision of banking and financial activities in the eurozone. This has been left to national authorities. According to the Maastricht Treaty, the euro system must 'contribute' to the policies followed by national authorities with respect to prudential regulations and control of financial intermediaries. A *Comité de surveillance bancaire* has been established, which includes executives from the national central banks and regulatory authorities, so as to allow cooperation and information exchanges between these institutions. This committee publishes reports and has started to assess the strength of the financial and banking sector in Europe, using information gathered from the national central banks. At the level of the European Union, a directive has relaxed the legal obstacles to the exchange of confidential information between regulatory authorities. Hence the idea is that the existing national authorities should cooperate more fully with respect to prudential control but not be overridden by a supranational authority linked to the ECB. Various reasons can explain this, as we shall see. But it is certain that the most compelling reason has been political: the designers of the Maastricht Treaty anticipated the probable resistance to EMU, viewed by many as an encroachment of national sovereignties, and tried to minimize as much as they could the transfer of competence to a supranational European body like the ECB.

We have to distinguish between the design of regulations and their enforcement, which implies supervisory controls over banks and financial firms. The legal regulatory power is that held by national public authorities to impose rules and constraints on financial firms and banks in order to foster any public or political objectives. This being said, we have to distinguish between banking and financial regulations. The aim of banking regulations is to protect banks' private depositors and to guarantee the whole non-financial sector from the systemic risks created by the possible bankruptcy of a single bank.[22] The aim of financial regulation is slightly different: it is to protect investors and redress the imperfect information characteristics of financial markets.[23] The enforcement of regulation implies a supervisory power, that is, the power to inspect and audit financial firms and banks, so as to check that they fulfil their legal obligations. This power is exerted mainly for prudential reasons, that is, to make sure that these firms are sound and financially strong, are able to resist an adverse financial shock, and do not exploit an informational advantage to the detriment of their customers. Up to now in Europe, both elements have been left in the hands of national authorities, reflecting the wide diversity of financial and banking systems and customs. Thus there is a large diversity of supervisory designs in the eurozone.

This leaves open a potential weakness of the eurozone, both in terms of regulation and in terms of supervision. There is evidently a major inconsistency, at least theoretically. Whereas private institutions will be more and more able to cover the whole zone, directly or indirectly intervening in several countries, the regulatory and supervisory authorities will remain uncoordinated and fragmented, if not divided. It may be that the fragmentation of the regulatory and supervision process will lead to an inadequate response by national authorities, exemplifying an obvious prisoner's dilemma. This danger will increase along with the deepening of financial integration in Europe, due to the single currency.

With respect to regulations, no authority will have a sufficiently broad view of the financial system and interactions in the eurozone. It may be unaware of certain crucial aspects of this system or may be unwilling to adopt painful measures, fearing that this will induce financial firms and banks to favour less-stringent countries, in an attempt to avoid their own severe regulations. Because of both ignorance and the strategic behaviour of regulatory authorities, there may be an inadequate level of regulation in the eurozone.

The same is true when banking supervision is considered. Having a partial view of the risks incurred globally by a bank or a financial institution in the eurozone, national supervisory authorities may be slow to react to a deterioration in the position of the bank. It may also prefer not to intervene, fearing that its intervention will only lead to more misuse of funds by the bank. A financially distressed bank may then take advantage of this fragmented supervisory process and try to cover up its loss by borrowing more and more throughout Europe. This may be a cause of financial fragility in Europe and lead to a major breakdown of the whole network of financial markets throughout the eurozone.

Of course, this reasoning is wholly theoretical and it is fair to add that these risks should not be exaggerated. Existing safeguards may prevent such problems occurring. First, it may be argued that the characteristics of existing national regulations are similar across Europe, that their differences mainly express the diversities of financial systems and customs and that they are sufficiently complex and adapted to modern banking firms and financial intermediaries to be able to address properly the prudential hazards associated with banking and finance. Similarly, it may be countered that the supervisory process is adequate. The recent cases of unsound banking management (Crédit Lyonnais in France, Barings Bank in the United Kingdom) are proof that either public intervention or takeover of the ailing bank by private institutions are able to limit the negative consequences of such mismanagement. It may also be countered that a proper control of the banking and finance industry requires a close relationship between regulators and regulated firms, and a detailed understanding of the existing management principles and policies followed by a bank. In brief, a complex body of information is needed to be able to regulate and supervise this industry, and to leave it to an inexperienced supranational authority is not necessarily adequate.

Finally, it may be hoped that the process of financial integration will be slow enough to allow the national authorities sufficient time to coordinate their regulations and their supervisory procedures.

All this may be true. Nevertheless, the possibility of a regulatory structural defect in Europe cannot be ignored and is a major concern of European monetary authorities. The present situation is probably unstable and is likely to change rapidly once the euro is widely used by non-financial agents.

The Issue of Crisis Management

Bank runs and lender of last resort

The aim of banking regulations is to control the lending and borrowing policy adopted by commercial banks so as to ensure that a bank can always meet its liquidity needs. Indeed, if a bank cannot meet its obligations, then a chain reaction will be triggered, which in turn can lead to a 'bank run' by non-financial agents and a major crisis in the whole economy. A 'bank run' is the sudden panic of non-financial agents who all want to liquidate their financial assets relative to a financial intermediary and convert them into a 'safe' monetary asset or currency. As a consequence, no financial intermediary can meet its obligation and a systemic crisis occurs: the spiral of credit emission can lead to a sudden collapse of the whole banking system. It has long been recognized that a way to avoid these dire consequences of unsound banking practices in a world of fiat money is to invest a public authority, often the central bank, with the role of 'lender of last resort'. This lender is able to supply the needed liquidity to a financial intermediary which cannot find it elsewhere. As such, it assures non-financial agents that their own financial intermediary is sound and able to face its obligations. Anticipating this, no agent makes a run on his or her bank and the system avoids the systemic risk associated with unwise credit policies. In other words, the existence of a lender of last resort is a major responsibility in a modern financial system based on fiat money to avoid banking panics and bank runs.

But this creates a moral hazard problem: a commercial bank has an incentive to adopt unwise risky lending strategies in order to gain market shares and profits. It knows that it will not bear the full costs of this strategy as it is de facto insured by the lender of last resort at no cost. The existence of a lender of last resort generates the risk against which it is supposed to insure the economy! The solution to this dilemma lies in the prudential regulations of banks, which constrain them to adopt sound and careful lending policies. Nevertheless, the regulatory and supervisory process may have its defects, and it is crucial to establish a lender of last resort in a modern monetary economy.

Systemic risk and EMU
How then can we analyse the risk of systemic banking crisis within EMU? In fact, there is not one but *two* moral hazard problems in EMU. This arises because there is an additional level in the banking system compared to a fully integrated monetary economy, that is, the national central banks, which together form the ESCB. One moral hazard problem is the conventional one between commercial banks and the public lender of last resort that we have just summarized; the other one is played between members of the ESCB: a national central bank could exploit the facilities granted to it in the case of a systemic risk by the ESCB as a whole to ease the liquidity facilities of its national commercial banks and give them an undesirable competitive advantage compared to their foreign competing banks.

There are two problems related to a liquidity crisis: the assessment of the coming crisis (the quicker the detection of a serious liquidity problem in a particular bank, the better, since public authorities can intervene before the problem spreads to other financial intermediaries), and the problem of defining who is responsible for a risk of default, so as to solve it as soon and as credibly as possible. We shall analyse these problems in turn with respect to EMU. We shall see that for both problems, the existence of the additional layer of national public authorities creates moral hazard problems within the set of public authorities.

1. The liquidity flows within EMU are managed by the TARGET system, which has been criticized as opaque and slow, leading to a less than optimal reactive capacity.[24] The TARGET system is very rigid, depending on almost immediate coverage of positions by commercial banks. This is explained by the desire to offer similar competitive conditions to all EMU banks, and not let them exploit the moral hazard loopholes by which they would force their national central bank to ease their liquidity position, and offer them extra liquidity facilities. But this is exactly what is required when there is a risk of systemic crisis! TARGET is therefore very reliable, except in a period of systemic crisis when banks need extra liquidity from their national central bank, which implies that they are indebted to it. As the development of a minor default into a major systemic crisis is a matter of hours, it requires an immediate reaction from the national central banker, which can be forbidden to act because of TARGET regulations. It will have to ask the ESCB for exceptional clearance – and clearly the ESCB is not renowned for its ability to react quickly.

2. There is a responsibility problem. The underlying cause of a bank run is an irresponsible lending policy by a commercial bank, which tries to recoup its loss on previous unsound loans by additional runaway lending. That is why the supervision of commercial banks is of utmost importance. It is the responsibility of the national central banks, but banks expand and may be covered by several national authorities. It is possible that they will disagree and argue both about the proper action to be taken in the case of an imprudent commercial bank and about their respective responsibility. Again, this row will take time to be resolved, during which period nothing will be done and the once circumscribed crisis will develop, possibly into a systemic crisis. This fragmentation of responsibility will nurture the double moral hazard loopholes mentioned above.

The European solution has been to leave the existing national regulatory and supervisory procedures in place, and not to introduce a supplementary supranational lender of last resort. Another solution could have been to integrate fully both the regulatory process and the leader-of-last-resort capacity and grant them to a supranational, European authority. This authority could have been the ECB or another European regulatory agency. This is the American solution: in the US, since the 1930s, there has been a national coverage of the default risk plus a national legal framework. But this would have required a much more detailed body of information than will be available to the ECB, and would imply a stunningly high level of power centralization in supranational hands. As noted at the beginning of this section, this was politically impossible.

The rationale behind the European solution is that the national central banks are responsible and competent public authorities and will act in good faith. Moreover, the regular contacts between them within the ESCB will deter a national central bank from acting irresponsibly, fearful of jeopardizing its long-term standing and influence by behaving improperly. The future will tell us whether it was a sound policy. But its success depends on the answers to three questions:

1. Are all the national central banks rigorous and disciplined?
2. The cost of their bail-out policy will be borne by all members of EMU, even though it is decided by a national central bank, because the supply of funds to a (quasi) defaulting bank will ultimately come from the ESCB as a whole. This causes a free-riding problem. Will it soften the attitude of the ESCB regarding exceptional bail-out?
3. Financial integration in Europe will surely lead to the development of multinational banks. Will the control of these financial intermediaries be tight enough, given the existing fragmentation of the regulatory process?

A failure of the solution chosen by the European governmental authorities will lead to the adoption of the 'American' solution: the creation of additional supranational powers, probably given to the ECB. Currently, the regulatory and disciplinary powers of the system are decentralized, which is likely to be a source of difficulty in the future. On the other hand, the advent of EMU is likely to foster financial homogenization within EMU, because of integration and increased competition. This will create more transparency and thus ease the coordination of the collective crisis management by the national central banks. It will then be difficult to state that the European solution is inadequate or suboptimal. But, given the short history of EMU, judgement on the correctness of the chosen solution is still pending.

6 ACCOUNTABILITY

The most important dimension for assessing the behaviour of the ESCB will clearly be political and not technical. What is at stake is the political position of the ESCB within the system of European political authorities. More precisely, the issue is about its independence, since we know that the concept of independence is unclear and poses certain difficulties. This uncovers two problems.

1. We have noted that the ESCB, legally at least, is largely independent from other political powers, be they national or 'European'. The political decision makers can still influence the ESCB, through the nomination processes for the governors and members of the Executive Board, or by exerting pressure (through the media or 'behind the scenes'). This raises the issue of the 'real' as opposed to 'formal' independence of the ESCB: will it be de facto independent and able to resist political pressures?

2. Even though it is probably a sound policy that a central bank is free from political influence when it adopts its short-term decisions and tries to stabilize the behaviour of money markets and expectations, it is less evident that it should be left free from any political interference. Ultimately, central bankers are non-elected experts, and in democratic societies power can be delegated by the people, but not abandoned. In short, clearly there is the question of the accountability of the ESCB. We may fear that too little political control is exerted on the ESCB. No (monetary) policy can be continued over the long run if it is not understood and approved by the majority of the people. There is clearly the necessity for a dialogue. Central bankers are not demi-gods, but cautious civil servants, who must deliver a good policy, ultimately convincing the electorate of their wisdom and usefulness. They must resist untimely pressures but understand their fellow citizens and their needs. But EMU may lack adequate mechanisms to ensure proper ESCB accountability.

The provisions of the Maastricht Treaty are very undemanding. According to Article 109, the ECB must present an annual report to the European Parliament, the European Commission and the Council of the European Union. There is no requirement that this report must be discussed or approved by any authority. Moreover, there is no obligation with regard to its content. The Governor of the ECB can address committees of the European Parliament at their or his request. But no vote of approval is required.

Finally, there is no obligation of publication with respect to the internal debates of the Governing Council. This may be seen as a way of protecting them from outside pressures, or alternatively as a way of avoiding any control. There are very few obligations imposed on the euro system which would represent a check on its policy. This does not imply that the people in charge of European monetary policy will not be mindful of the consequences of their actions or the general sentiment it gives rise to. Only the future will tell us how responsive and acceptable to public opinion the system will be.

7 CONCLUSION

EMU is still in its infancy. The experiment is too short for observers to be able to evaluate and assess the course of monetary policy followed by the European system of central banks. This chapter attempts to make such an evaluation possible, by making explicit the various dilemmas confronted by the ESCB when making its decisions, on objectives, on strategies, on crisis management.

On the whole, judgement of the ESCB and its design will be based on the credibility of both the institution and the policy makers. The first months of EMU have without doubt been beneficial for the ESCB. Public discussion about its decisions has abated since the resignation of the German Minister of Finance, Oskar Lafontaine in March 1999. Growth has resumed in the eurozone, even though it has been uneven. No major adverse macroeconomic shock has occurred. Finally, private agents seem to have adapted cautiously to the new system and no inflationary pressures have been recorded which without doubt would have generated fierce discussion both inside and outside the Council of Governors of the ESCB. Therefore, a very provisional judgement may be: 'so far, so good'.

NOTES

1. In January 1999 there were 11 members of EMU, but Greece joined two years later having subsequently met the conditions for membership.
2. A number of books are devoted to a presentation of EMU. See, in particular, Gros and Thygesen (1998), Kenen (1995) and Buti and Sapir (1998).
3. See Blinder (1997).
4. There exists a third council, the General Council, which consists of the president and the vice-president of the Executive Board and the governors of all central banks of the EU countries, including those not belonging to EMU. Its function is mainly to disseminate information, but it is also responsible for preparing non-participating countries for admission into EMU.
5. National decisions (for example, regarding capital) are made with weighted votes. The weight attached to each governor's vote is equal to the weight of that country's ECB capital. The majority rule is qualified (two-thirds of the weighted votes, and at least one-half of the owners of ECB capital).
6. See Fischer (1995).
7. See Artis and Kontolemis (1998).
8. See Clarida and Gertler (1998); Clarida et al. (1998); Bernanke et al. (1999).
9. A preliminary study by the European Monetary Institute, the institution which preceded the ECB, had previously narrowed the various possibilities to these two alternatives (European Monetary Institute 1997).
10. A detailed discussion of these alternatives is offered by Svensson (1999).
11. A sufficiently large monetary aggregate such as M3 is generally chosen.
12. See Rudesbusch and Svensson (1999).
13. This issue is addressed in Svensson (1997).

14. On the contrary, we should expect steady divergences in real wage growth and compensation since EMU should foster convergences in productivity and standards of living.
15. We can write:

$$P_{ut} = (1-\alpha)P_{at} + \alpha P_{bt}$$
$$= P_{at}[1 + \alpha(Q_t - 1)]$$

defining $Q_t \equiv P_{bt}/P_{at}$. Hence:

$$\pi_{ut} \cong \log P_{ut} - \log P_{ut-1} = \pi_{at} + \alpha(Q_t - Q_{t-1}) = \pi_{at} + \alpha q_t$$

with: $q_t \equiv Q_t - Q_{t-1}$.
16. See Taylor (1993).
17. European Central Bank (1998).
18. The ECB has more recently announced its inflation target to be two percent per annum.
19. See McCauley and White (1997).
20. Asdrubali et al. (1996) studying the US economy show that financial markets play a major role in managing interstate risk sharing, more important than the role played by the Federal government.
21. A theoretical example is developed in the appendix to this chapter.
22. See Diamond and Dybvig (1983).
23. See Meyer and Neven (1991).
24. See Begg et al. (1998).

APPENDIX 5A MONETARY POLICY AND FINANCIAL INTEGRATION

We want to assess the importance of financial integration for monetary policy and its impact within a monetary union (MU). We shall consider an MU with two countries, A and B. MU's money supply is equal to:

$$M = M_A + M_B$$

with M_A the money quantity in circulation in A and M_B the money quantity in circulation in B. The total quantity of central bank reserves R is equal to:

$$R = R_A + R_B$$

with R_A the quantity of reserves held at A's central bank and R_B the quantity of reserves held at B's central bank.

It is assumed that under national laws, sustained by the subsidiarity principle, a commercial bank must obtain reserves only from the central bank of the country to which it belongs.

The demand for reserves from the banking system in country A is given by the following equation:

$$R_A = R_A \left(\underset{+}{M_A}, \underset{-}{r}, \underset{+}{i_A}, \underset{-}{i_B} \right)$$

Where the signs under the variables denote the signs of the corresponding partial derivatives. r denotes the short-term interest rate of the MU's money market, i_X denotes a synthetic variable summarizing the conditions of lending in country X (interest rates on X's financial market, financial regulations enforced in X, risk factors and so on). A similar equation holds for country B:

$$R_B = R_B \left(\underset{+}{M_B}, \underset{-}{r}, \underset{+}{i_B}, \underset{-}{i_A} \right)$$

We may assume that both equations are identical.[1] We shall dispense with the reserve requirement issue by assuming that the desired level of reserves for the banking system as a whole in each country is higher than the minimum level imposed by law. The extent of financial integration within the MU can be characterized by the impact of the lending conditions in one country on the demand for reserves in the other country. The more national financial markets are integrated, the larger will be the impact of lending conditions in country A on the demand for reserves in country B. Suppose an increase in i_A:

if markets are integrated, then commercial banks in country B are induced to increase their lending to inhabitants in country B, which increases their desired level of reserve holding. There is complete financial integration if B's (A's) bank is indifferent between lending in A or in B, that is, if:

$$\left|\frac{\partial R_B}{\partial i_A}\right| = \left|\frac{\partial R_B}{\partial i_B}\right| \quad \left|\frac{\partial R_A}{\partial i_A}\right| = \left|\frac{\partial R_A}{\partial i_B}\right|$$

and no financial integration if:

$$\left|\frac{\partial R_B}{\partial i_A}\right| = \left|\frac{\partial R_A}{\partial i_B}\right| = 0.$$

We shall assume that the 'short-term' money market is fully integrated over the MU and that it is perfectly efficient, that is, without any adjustment frictions. This means that 'changes in the local composition of money balances leaving the total MU money supply ... have no consequences for the demand for bank reserves, and therefore the interest rate'.[2] In other words, the local distribution of money holdings has no effect on the money market interest rate as long as the total quantity of money is constant.

We shall now compare two types of monetary policy:

1. a '*hands-off*' policy, whereby the MU's central bank sets only the total amount of reserves it is willing to supply to the whole MU's banking system. Such a policy allows the national central banks to trade for reserves according to the needs of their own banking system. In other words, the MU's central bank limits its intervention to the national central banks to a minimum, leaving them autonomy when dealing with their banking system; and
2. a '*hands-on*' policy, whereby the MU's central bank not only sets the amount of reserves it is willing to supply to the whole banking system, but also the precise sum it will supply to each national central bank. Each central bank is then on a short leash, and cannot lend or borrow reserves from any other one. It has no autonomy and can merely pass on the conditions set by the MU's central bank to its banking community.

Now suppose that the MU's central bank tries to stabilize the union's price level by means of a stable reserve level. There is a proportional link between the total quantity of money in circulation in the MU and the total level of reserves supplied by the MU's central bank. An idiosyncratic shock occurs in country A, namely a variation di_A in the lending conditions to non-banking agents in country A.

First, let us consider the *hands-off* policy and suppose that the MU's central bank decides not to increase the total amount of reserves, despite this shock. This implies that:

$$dR_A = -dR_B.$$

Given the demand equations for reserves, and the proportional relationship between money and reserves, given the efficiency assumption on the money market, such a policy implies that:

$$\frac{dM_A}{di_A} = \left(\frac{\partial R_B}{\partial i_A} - \frac{\partial R_A}{\partial i_A} \right) \Big/ \left(\frac{\partial R_A}{\partial M_A} + \frac{\partial R_B}{\partial M_B} \right)$$

which is negative, given the signs of partial derivatives of the reserve demand functions.

Note first that the idiosyncratic shock occurring in A has an impact on the money quantity in circulation in B. The hands-off policy does not insulate country B's monetary conditions from the shock in A. Second, note that the impact of the shock on both countries depend on the integration of financial markets.

We now turn to the impact of financial integration. With no financial integration, the impact of the idiosyncratic shock on the quantity of money in circulation in country A is equal to:

$$\frac{dM_A}{di_A} = -\frac{1}{2} \left(\frac{\partial R_A}{\partial i_A} \right) \Big/ \left(\frac{\partial R_A}{\partial M_A} \right)$$

whereas with financial integration, it is equal to:

$$\frac{dM_A}{di_A} = -\left(\frac{\partial R_A}{\partial i_A} \right) \Big/ \left(\frac{\partial R_A}{\partial M_A} \right).$$

Hence, rather counterintuitively, it appears that no financial integration mitigates the regional discrepancies arising from the union's monetary policy. This is because there is no effect in addition to the mechanical effect of compensating moves in national money demands. In country B, money demand decreases when money demand increases in A because of full efficiency of the money market. This decreases the demand for reserves in B from its banking community, without any amplifying effect from the idiosyncratic shock on this demand, due to the absence of financial integration. Financial integration would add such an effect, and by so doing would increase the diverging paths of national money demands.

Consider now the *hands-on* policy. Now the MU's central bank, still willing to stabilize the union's price level, decides not to increase any level of reserve supplied to any country.[3] This implies that:

$$dR_A = dR_B = 0.$$

Whatever the level of financial integration, the short-term interest rate must vary, since money demands will vary without compensation through a flow of reserves from one country to the other. When the MU's central bank follows such a policy, in the case of full financial integration, the impact of an idiosyncratic shock to country A on the quantity of money in circulation in A is:

$$\begin{cases} \dfrac{\partial R_B}{\partial M_B} dM_B + \dfrac{\partial R_B}{\partial r} dr + \dfrac{\partial R_B}{\partial i_A} di_A = 0 \\ \dfrac{\partial R_A}{\partial M_A} dM_A + \dfrac{\partial R_A}{\partial r} dr + \dfrac{\partial R_A}{\partial i_A} di_A = 0. \end{cases}$$

When there is no financial integration, the short-term interest rate must vary, because money supplies vary, even though total reserves do not vary. We therefore have a set of simultaneous equations:

$$\begin{cases} \dfrac{\partial R_B}{\partial M_B} dM_B + \dfrac{\partial R_B}{\partial r} dr = 0 \\ \dfrac{\partial R_A}{\partial M_A} dM_A + \dfrac{\partial R_A}{\partial r} dr + \dfrac{\partial R_A}{\partial i_A} di_A = 0. \end{cases}$$

The comparison of the net effect of the idiosyncratic shock on the money demands is then unclear. Linearizing around the steady state, and assuming strict identity of the reserve demand functions, one can show that no financial integration dampens the diverging variations of national money demands. This is because in such a case the impact of the idiosyncratic shock on the short-term interest rate is decreased, which leads to a larger national money demand, and an increase in the gap between these two variables, compared to the no financial integration case.

NOTES

1. Von Hagen and Fratianni (1994) use a slightly more complex equation.
2. Von Hagen and Fratianni (1994, p. 132).
3. It is most likely that neither this policy nor the previous one is optimal. However, we focus not on the optimal design of monetary policy in an MU, but on its differentiated effectiveness.

6. Fiscal policy in EMU

Frank Barry*

---

1 INTRODUCTION

The adoption of a single currency removes a number of macroeconomic instruments from the control of national authorities. Exchange rate policy clearly becomes redundant while monetary policy, formerly determined by national central banks, becomes the preserve of the European Central Bank in Frankfurt. Fiscal policy, representing government expenditure and taxation, is one of the few macroeconomic instruments over which national authorities retain control. Yet even with the reduced set of instruments at their disposal, governments have willingly accepted important constraints on its operation. These constraints are embodied in the 'Maastricht criteria' which countries have been required to satisfy in order to qualify for participation in the single currency, and in the 'Stability and Growth Pact' which membership of the Economic Monetary Union (EMU) entails.

This chapter explores the motivation for, and likely consequences of, these fiscal constraints, as well as the impact of monetary union (and increasing integration) on the role of fiscal policy.

We begin with an analysis of the general role of fiscal policy in the economy. Government expenditure and taxation decisions have implications for long-term economic growth as well as medium-term stability. These issues are discussed in turn. High government consumption is generally found to be detrimental to growth, while government investment up to some point is generally agreed to be beneficial. Yet government consumption has been climbing inexorably. This has led in recent times to the study of circumstances under which fiscal consolidation can be effected with least adverse short-term consequences. These review sections provide us with the analytical tools needed to analyse how fiscal policy will operate within EMU.

The debate over whether or not the fiscal constraints associated with EMU are appropriate is reviewed in Section 3. The proponents of the Stability Pact hope that its provisions will assist national governments in withstanding interest-group pressures; the fiscal constraints, viewed in this light, represent government's contribution to a new social contract that proponents hope will lead to greater labour market flexibility. On several grounds however, this is likely to be overoptimistic. Rather, it is our view that the shrinking of national budgets that will arise from the combination of increased tax competition and the terms of the Stability Pact will leave a vacuum that must ultimately be filled by an expansion of the central European Union (EU) budget.

2   ECONOMIC EFFECTS OF FISCAL POLICIES

Fiscal Policy and Growth

Most textbook discussions of fiscal policy focus on the effects of fiscal actions on aggregate demand. These effects are left until the next section. Here the focus is on the impact of government spending on the long-run productive potential of the economy.

The literature distinguishes between the effects of government consumption and public capital spending. The overlap with the current and capital accounts of the public authorities is not, however, exact. For example, Barro (1991) excludes government spending on defence and education from government consumption, arguing that these items are more like public investment in their effects on property rights and private sector productivity. Government consumption on the other hand, he argues, has no direct effect on private productivity; rather it reduces growth through distortions associated with the expenditure programmes themselves or with the taxation required to finance it.

There is fairly widespread agreement that government consumption so defined has an adverse effect on economic growth. Crafts and Toniolo (1996) find that the rising share of government consumption in GDP in post-1973 Europe helps explain the reduction in average European growth experienced in this period, while the very large public sectors of the Scandinavian countries reduced Scandinavian growth relative to the European average.[1]

Economic theory would suggest that high rates of taxation should have adverse effects on growth. The fact that Easterly and Rebelo's (1993) results are less decisive on this issue than might have been expected could partly be explained by their use of average rather than marginal tax rates. A more intriguing possibility though is suggested by Eichengreen (1996) who argues that, in the immediate post-war decades at least, wage moderation, which is conducive to investment and growth, may have required high welfare spending and associated higher taxes as part of government's contribution to the social contract.

The impact of public capital investment on growth is not viewed in nearly as negative a light as that of government consumption. Here the important questions are whether public capital affects private sector productivity, and the extent to which it simply replaces or 'crowds out' private investment expenditure.

Aschauer (1989a) found public capital to have significant positive effects on private sector productivity. Of the various subcategories of public capital he found the greatest explanatory power coming from 'core infrastructure', including streets and highways, airports, electricity and gas facilities, mass transit, and water and sewerage systems. On his finding that categories of public capital spending such as public hospitals and the stock of educational buildings had statistically insignificant effects, Aschauer points out that long lags would come between the construction phase and their ultimate productivity effects.[2]

Aschauer (1989b) explores the substitutability of public for private capital spending. Controlling for the separate influence of public capital on the return to private capital, he finds an almost one-for-one crowding-out effect, reflecting strong substitutability. The effect on the rate of return to private capital is strongly positive, however (reflecting externality effects), so that taking both channels into account an increase in public capital is found to lead to a higher long-run stock of private capital.

Levine and Renelt (1992) and Easterly and Rebelo (1993) also affirm that various categories of public infrastructure have positive effects on economic growth.

Fiscal Policy and Stabilization: Old and New Views

Notwithstanding the overriding importance of factors that impact on growth, most textbooks still discuss fiscal policy primarily in terms of stabilization, and more specifically in terms of its impact on economies in recession. In focusing on the mechanisms through which fiscal policy is thought to raise aggregate demand, textbooks fail to emphasize sufficiently strongly that stabilization requires that policy be countercyclical, with increased deficits during the recession compensated for by deficit reductions during the boom.

The Keynesian view of how fiscal policy stabilizes the economy is based on the idea that prices and wages are less flexible downwards in the face of adverse shocks requiring wage and price reductions, than they are in an upwards direction when a fully employed economy is hit by positive shocks. A fall in aggregate demand under these circumstances reduces output as firms cannot sell all they desire to produce at existing prices. A fiscal expansion, whether effected through discretionary expenditure increases or tax reductions, or through the impact of automatic stabilizers (such as social welfare payments and income taxes) on the size of the deficit, raises aggregate spending back towards its initial level and therefore stabilizes output and employment. This is the traditional view enshrined in textbooks.

A new and influential line of argument has emerged recently, however, which holds that this link between fiscal expansion and output recovery may no longer apply. It suggests that mechanisms not recognized in the Keynesian literature may now have come to the fore, and that non-Keynesian short-run effects can arise in certain circumstances. This view, termed the 'expansionary fiscal contraction (EFC) hypothesis', was developed in the wake of two episodes of fiscal contraction in the 1980s, when Ireland and Denmark while undergoing strongly contractionary fiscal policies actually boomed. Giavazzi and Pagano (1990) identified non-Keynesian responses of private consumption and investment, though their results have frequently been extrapolated to suggest that domestic absorption (that is, consumption plus investment plus government spending) rose.

A number of theoretical models consistent with the notion of an expansionary fiscal contraction have appeared in the literature. These focus for the most part on circumstances under which aggregate demand can expand. Barry and Devereux (1995) argue, however, that the demand-side effects of fiscal consolidation are unlikely to generate employment increases, particularly in the tradable sectors of the economy, unless associated with beneficial supply-side developments (that is, improvements in cost competitiveness). As far as the two forms of controlling deficits are concerned, however, improved cost competitiveness is more likely to result from expenditure cuts, which will be associated with the expectation of future tax reductions, than from tax increases.

Alesina and Perotti (1995) draw similar conclusions from a large cross-country data set. Focusing on episodes of 'very tight' fiscal stance, they define as successful those contractions that lead to a long-run consolidation of the budget, as opposed to episodes that have soon been reversed. They find that successful and unsuccessful contractions differ little in terms of size but differ strongly in terms of composition.[3] Successful adjustments entail expenditure cuts (particularly in transfers and the public sector wage bill), while unsuccessful episodes are generally based on tax increases. Crucially, they find that successful adjustments are associated with a fall in unemployment, improved competitiveness and more rapid growth, with the opposite applying to unsuccessful adjustments.

This debate between aggregate-supply (or cost competitiveness) and aggregate-demand interpretations cropped up in the analysis of the successful Irish fiscal stabilization of 1987–90. In contrast to Giavazzi and Pagano (1990), Barry and Devereux (1995, pp. 260–61) argued that the fiscal contraction depressed aggregate demand, but that these effects were outweighed by other factors working in the direction of recovery. These included 'buoyant world demand, improvements in cost competitiveness and an inflow of foreign investment in the lead-up to the Single European Market'. What is interesting about the episode though is the link between fiscal stabilization and the improvement in cost competitiveness. Cost competitiveness was consolidated by the social partnership programmes that followed the cutbacks; these saw unions moderating their wage demands in return for promised future income tax reductions.

As Bean (1989), Barry and Devereux (1995) and Alesina and Ardagna (1998) argue, wage moderation is the *sine qua non* for fiscal contractions to have expansionary aggregate effects (with the expansionary rightward shift of the aggregate supply curve offsetting the contractionary leftward shift of aggregate demand). Furthermore, Alesina and Ardagna (1998) point out the role played by earlier exchange rate depreciations in facilitating the wage moderation associated with successful fiscal contractions. The significance of this point will become clearer below.

3   FISCAL POLICY WITHIN EMU

Having set the stage by discussing the various channels through which fiscal policy operates, we now move on to issues related specifically to EMU. We begin with a brief discussion of the fiscal constraints represented by the Maastricht criteria and the Stability Pact, and ask why governments have been so willing to adopt these constraints. We then discuss how the European economy is likely to function under EMU when fiscal policy is constrained in this way.

Fiscal Constraints and EMU: The Maastricht Criteria and the Stability Pact

The Maastricht Treaty signed in December 1991 set out the criteria by which the various candidate countries for monetary union were to be judged. The criteria specified boundaries on exchange rate movements, interest rates, inflation rates, budget deficits and debt-to-GDP ratios. The fiscal constraints were tightened further in 1996 with the signing of the Stability Pact. This allows for the levying of fines on countries whose budget deficits exceed 3 per cent of GDP for a certain period of time in other than exceptional circumstances.

Several arguments have been advanced as to why explicit fiscal constraints are required within a monetary union. Fiscal profligacy could lead to pressure being exerted on the European Central Bank to inflate away part of a country's debt burden, or could involve pressures on other national governments to bail out the country with the debt problem (*European Economy*, CEC, 1990). Furthermore, since fixed exchange rates increase the potency of fiscal policy (the Mundell–Fleming result), the incentive for fiscal activism may be stronger under EMU, and the resulting effect on the euro could have negative externalities for other member states.

These arguments have been strenuously debated. Does monetary union lead to looser fiscal policy? Agell et al. (1996) argue that it does. They point out that in the seven years after 1979, the countries cooperating monetarily with Germany through the exchange rate mechanism (ERM) experienced larger increases in their budget deficits than did OECD countries remaining outside the ERM. De Grauwe (1997a) argues though that since budget deficits cannot be financed by money creation, monetary union represents a strengthening of the budget constraint. In support of this he provides evidence that average budget deficits of states and provinces in existing monetary unions are lower than for those not in such unions.

Would the absence of fiscal constraints necessarily lead to greater pressures being exerted on the Central Bank? Sceptics argue to the contrary that the inability of governments to engage in fiscal expansion will encourage them to lobby for monetary expansion instead. In response to the bail-out problem, Buiter et al. (1993) argue that this is exactly why the 'no bail-out' clause was explicitly incorporated into the Maastricht Treaty.

Focusing on the implications for fiscal policy of the increased integration of the European economy, Krugman (1989) argues that this will also tighten rather than loosen fiscal policy. The more integrated the European economy the less impact aggregate-demand management will have on domestic output, since more of it will go towards imports. The incentives facing national authorities will therefore be suboptimally low since the gains to the overall EU are not taken into account.[4]

Since these arguments question the need for fiscal constraints, it remains to be answered as to why governments have so readily agreed to their adoption. Buiter et al. (1993) suggest that the adoption of external fiscal commitments could provide a way around the domestic factors that systematically induce excessive deficits and ratchet up current spending. The European Commission, in *One Market One Money* (CEC 1990), appears to agree in arguing that wages are likely to be set closer to equilibrium levels if these fiscal constraints are present.

Much of the material presented above, on both the long-term and medium-term effects of fiscal policy, can be read as supporting this perspective. We noted the general presumption that increases in government consumption (as a proportion of GDP) adversely affect long-term growth. The 'new view of fiscal contraction' can also be read as indicating that government spending is currently above the level deemed optimal by the private sector as a whole. We mentioned above Eichengreen's (1996) argument that the European social consensus initiated in the 1960s purchased wage moderation at the cost of a large role for the public sector.[5] If this still represented the social consensus, wage moderation could not be guaranteed in the face of contractions in government spending. We see currently though that wage moderation appears more likely in the face of a reduction in the size of government, suggesting that the public sector is now perceived by the private sector as being too large.

It is no surprise, given the extent of government participation in the Swedish economy, that economists from Sweden were the first to point out that as the public sector grew, the social contract of the 1960s could prove self-defeating. Rather than promoting wage moderation, 'excessive government' bolstered wage demands (Calmfors and Forslund, 1990; Henrekson et al. 1996). Rather than helping maintain a high-growth trajectory the expansion of the public sector and the welfare state beyond some optimal size appears to have reduced growth. Accordingly a cut in the public sector might now be read primarily as an indication of future tax cuts, which could trigger off an expansionary phase of wage moderation.[6]

With powerful internal constituencies arrayed against the rollback of government, faster growth can only be achieved, according to this view, if the national authorities insulate themselves by 'tying their hands' on fiscal policy.[7]

Adjustment in EMU When Fiscal Policy is Constrained

According to the analysis in the previous section, the fiscal constraints are seen by governments as a means of keeping domestic interest groups at bay, with beneficial long-term growth consequences in mind. Critics of the Stability Pact are sceptical that these arguments have any relevance, in the short term at least. The Pact, they argue, will leave governments with insufficient flexibility to adjust to the types of shocks that buffet economies continuously.

Buti et al. (1997) analyse how binding a constraint the Stability Pact is likely to be by considering developments in EU over the 1951–96 period. They identify 24 severe recessionary episodes over this period, bunched around the years 1974–75, 1980–82 and 1991–93.[8] In each case the deficit rose, driven by the automatic stabilizers. Surprisingly, however, there was no systematic tendency for budgetary policy to be loosened during these severe recessions; in only half the cases was an expansionary countercyclical discretionary stance adopted.

This fiscal conservatism increased over time, driven by the worsening of pre-recession debt and deficit levels. With average deficits of 3.5 per cent of GDP in 1990 compared to less than 1 per cent in 1973, for example, EU governments were much more reluctant to adopt expansionary stances when hit by recession. Member states with debt and deficit ratios above the EU average in the year preceding the recession conducted a less-accommodating policy than states in more desirable fiscal positions. Such states actually tended to tighten their fiscal stance during recessions, in contrast to the countercyclical stance recommended by the textbook analysis. This suggests that some of the restrictions nominally associated with the Stability Pact had been internalized already.

On the other hand the Pact forces EMU participants to move towards fiscal balance immediately, because the room for manoeuvre will be severely constrained in the event of recession. Buti et al. (1997) show that 16 of the 24 recessionary periods would have led to violation of the excessive deficits procedure if countries had deficits of 2 per cent of GDP before the onset of recession, compared to only five out of the 24 if countries had begun with deficits of zero. These five cases are of course important, though, since they indicate that even starting out with sound budgetary positions, contractionary policies would be required during recessions to stay within the limits of the Pact.

Eichengreen and Wyplosz (1998) carry the exercise further, evaluating a counterfactual in which governments carry out the fiscal actions necessary to remain within the limits of the Pact. They conclude that the cumulative output losses for France, Italy and the UK would lie somewhere between 5 and 9 per cent of GDP, which is equivalent to a loss of between a quarter and a half per cent of GDP per annum. They emphasize also the requirement for continued fiscal tightening as countries move beyond the Maastricht criteria (requiring that budget deficits not exceed 3 per cent of GDP) towards implementation of the cyclically-adjusted budget balances implied by the Stability Pact. This will imply a particularly harsh regime for highly indebted countries such as Italy and Belgium. One analysis cited by Alesina and Ardagna (1998) suggests that Italy will have to maintain primary budget surpluses of 5 to 6 per cent for more than a decade.

These prognoses are gloomy of course only to the extent that the EMU economies continue to operate in traditional textbook fashion. Two arguments can be advanced to explain why their structural responses may in fact change. The European Commission (CEC 1990, p. 149) suggests that 'wage adjustments are likely to come faster than otherwise' when domestic fiscal policy is no longer available to bail out regions which have been hit by adverse shocks. In contrast, though, Blanchard and Muet (1993) found little evidence of increased wage flexibility in France as the franc-DM peg gained in credibility.

The second argument derives from the 'new view' of fiscal stabilization, which suggests that the response can be expansionary rather than contractionary if the stabilization is effected through expenditure reductions rather than through tax increases. This view may also be deemed to be overoptimistic, however. We have already seen that successful bouts of fiscal stabilization tend to be preceded by exchange rate devaluations, which are of course ruled out within EMU. It is likely to remain easier to cut real wages through inflationary policies such as devaluation than through deflationary aggregate-demand management (Akerlof et al. 1996).[9] Another reason why this view appears overoptimistic is that there is clearly a limit to how low tax rates can fall, and it may be difficult to reduce them in recessionary times when aggregate revenues are falling in any case.

A third criticism that can be levelled at Eichengreen and Wyplosz (1998), though, is that they ignore the growth premium associated with lower average ratios of government consumption spending. Such a premium would offset, to some extent at least, the accumulated output losses that their analysis implies.

Fiscal Policy in EMU: The Argument for Greater Centralization of Fiscal Powers

Those who are optimistic about the EMU project draw succour from the 'new view' of fiscal stabilization which holds that fiscal contractions effected through expenditure reductions can have expansionary effects. With tax competition likely to increase in importance in EMU, fiscal stabilization is indeed more likely to take the form of expenditure reductions. We warned, however, that successful fiscal stabilizations have tended to be preceded by exchange rate devaluation, an option that is clearly not possible under EMU.

The ultimate implication, of course, of reducing both expenditure and tax rates is a diminution of the welfare state, as recognized by Alesina and Ardagna (1998). Notwithstanding the current ascendancy of left-of-centre EU governments and the emphasis of the Commission (CEC 1993, pp. 128–9) on a specifically European (as opposed to American) model of development, the diminution of the welfare state appears inevitable unless the central EU budget expands as national budgets shrink.

Even if the welfare state is to be rolled back, there are other factors suggesting that a greater centralization of fiscal power is required. One is that, as Krugman (1989) points out, economic integration exacerbates the problems associated with uncoordinated national policies; centralization clearly makes coordination easier. More important though is the fiscal-federalist argument, which holds that centralized budgets are necessary to offset the effects of 'asymmetric' (or region-specific) shocks. Consider the extent of such structures in existing monetary unions such as the US and Canada, where regional adjustment is in any event easier than in the EU because of greater interregional labour mobility. Sala-i-Martin and Sachs (1992) show that in the US every $1 decline in regional income relative to the national average induces a fall of 25 cents in federal tax liabilities and an increase in inward transfers of 10 cents; thus over one-third of a fall in regional income is offset by the federal budget. The equivalent figure for Canada is about one-fifth. There is no such system in place in the EU.[10]

For a severe recession that caused a 10 per cent decline in the incomes of one-half of the EU, transfers to depressed regions on a scale equivalent to that available in the US would amount to 0.5 per cent of EU GDP. This would entail a massive 50 per cent increase in total spending on EU programmes (Eichengreen 1990). Could monetary union survive if such aid were not forthcoming from a federal EU budget? While political scientists warn that the political fabric does not exist to deliver a significantly larger EU budget, and that 'subsidiarity' in any case militates against the transfer of welfare state functions to Brussels, Costa and De Grauwe (1999) have warned recently that the 'failure [to create a European government with similar responsibilities to present national ones] creates the risk of the break-up of the monetary union'.

4   CONCLUDING COMMENTS

There is an important distinction between public consumption and public investment as components of overall government spending. Public consumption appears to affect growth adversely while public investment, up to a point, appears to be growth enhancing. The fiscal restrictions associated with EMU, we argue, are designed to strengthen the hand of European governments in resisting pressures to continually raise government spending. The fiscal restrictions, however, ignore the distinction between public consumption and investment, and some analysts accordingly worry about the long-term consequences of the restrictions, particularly since cutbacks frequently fall on infrastructure and educational expenditure.

The problem is that the borrowing restrictions apply equally to items for which it makes sense to borrow; these include public investment expenditures, the alleviation of crises that require a local lender of last resort, and the financing of pension reform.[11]

The restrictions on borrowing for public investment purposes could have particularly adverse consequences for the cohesion economies of Greece, Portugal, Spain and Ireland. Consistent with the findings of Psacharopoulos (1994) and Baffes and Shah (1998) that social rates of return to education are higher in poorer countries, and Khan and Kumar (1997) who report similar findings on rates of return to public investment, infrastructure levels appear to be below the optimum in all four cohesion countries.[12] The scaling back of the Community Support Framework programmes for these countries as enlargement proceeds will throw them back onto their own resources, and it makes good economic sense for them to borrow for these purposes.

Bean, in his comments on Eichengreen and Wyplosz (1998), makes a similar point with respect to necessary pension reform. Since switching from a pay-as-you-go system to a fully funded pension system involves at least one generation having to save for their own pensions as well as paying for those of their parents, equity dictates that governments should borrow to spread this burden across several generations. Again this is largely excluded by the Stability Pact.

While the underlying motivation behind the fiscal restrictions may make strategic sense, then they are much too blunt an instrument to make economic sense. It is no surprise that even at this early stage of EMU the provisions of the Stability Pact appear to be being watered down.

NOTES

* Helpful discussions with Carla Costa, Edgar Morgenroth, Martin Stewart and Brigid Laffan are gratefully acknowledged.
1. Aschauer (1989a) presents results broadly in line with these, though controlling for aggregate-demand effects through the inclusion of the capacity utilization rate. Kormendi and Meguire (1985) also find some evidence, though stemming from the variation in unanticipated money, that demand stability is important for growth.
2. Although Aschauer's analysis is incapable of picking up the growth effects of public spending on health and education, the literature is unambiguous in finding that human capital, accumulated through education, is a key stimulus to growth; see, for example, Mankiw et al. (1992).
3. They also find that contractions are more likely to be successful when imposed during business-cycle booms.
4. Increased labour mobility further reduces the incentive for fiscal expansion since part of any employment increase will be accounted for by immigration.
5. Eichengreen (1996) argues that rapid post-war European growth was based on a social contract whereby governments purchased wage moderation via the guarantee (a) of a wel-fare state, and (b) that wage moderation would result in high investment. As Europe caught up to US living standards in the late 1960s, however, the pact broke down. Governments tried to resurrect the contract by expanding the public sector and by intervening directly in wage bargaining. This strategy does not appear to have been successful, however.
6. Calmfors and Horn (1985) sketch out a model that works along these lines.
7. The fact that the rise in debt-to-GDP ratios among EU economies over recent decades has resulted primarily from public finance imbalances in non-recessionary rather than recessionary periods, as evidenced by Buti et al. (1997), points to the presence of this constituency.
8. Mild recessions, they find, do not lead to excessive deficits unless strongly expansionary policies are followed and are not reversed after the recession.
9. A possible explanation for this is that workers are concerned with relative as well as real wage levels. When wage contracts are staggered, each group of workers is reluctant to be the first to accept nominal wage cuts.
10. For comparison purposes consider Eichengreen's (1993) calculation that the Delors-1 Structural Funds package provided about 1 cent for every \$1 that a region lagged behind the EU average.

11. Lane (1998) considers the eventuality of a local financial crisis, with national central banks unable to act as lenders of last resort and the fiscal authorities prevented from borrowing to do so. He suggests that national authorities should accumulate fiscal reserve funds to cover this, and that these funds should remain distinct from the general government budget.

12. I am grateful to Edgar Morgenroth for demonstrating that this is implied by the results of Bougheas and Demetriades (1997).

7. EMU and European unemployment

André van Poeck and Alain Borghijs

1 EUROPEAN UNEMPLOYMENT AT THE START OF EMU

Is Economic and Monetary Union the long expected cure for European unemployment as has often been proclaimed, or does EMU stand for Even More Unemployment? This chapter attempts to shed some light on the effect that monetary union is likely to have on European unemployment. The issue is not only relevant from a theoretical perspective but it is also of utmost social importance. Many European countries struggle with high and persistent unemployment. As Table 7.1 shows equilibrium unemployment[1] in the EMU countries is on average almost twice as high as in the non-EMU countries. Moreover in seven out of the 11 EMU countries (among which Germany, France and Italy) equilibrium unemployment has increased in the 1990s while the other EMU countries experienced stable or decreasing equilibrium unemployment rates. In the non-EMU group only three out of 11 countries saw their equilibrium unemployment rates increase in the 1990s. The other countries (for example, the US and the UK) registered stable or falling equilibrium unemployment rates.

The European unemployment problem has a number of common features. The first is the high share of long-term unemployment. This is illustrated in Table 7.2. About half of the people in the European unemployment pool have been continuously without a job for more than a year. This is not only remarkably high compared to the US (about 10 per cent) or Japan (about 20 per cent), but this figure has remained fairly stable, indicating that long-term unemployment has grown in line with total unemployment. Note that countries with high unemployment rates are also characterized by higher proportions of long-term unemployed (data for 1997 in Table 7.2). In so far as long-term unemployment can be considered an indicator for the amount of equilibrium unemployment, this confirms the information from Table 7.1. Second, the rise in European (long-term) unemployment is largely due to a decline in the outflow rates out of unemployment, whereas the inflow rates remained more or less stable. This suggests that the problem is situated at the hiring side of the unemployment

Table 7.1   Equilibrium unemployment in the OECD countries[a]

EMU countries	1986	1990	1997	Non-EMU countries	1986	1990	1997
Increasing NAWRU							
Austria	4.1	4.9	5.4	Iceland	0.8	1.5	4.0
Belgium	11.7	11.0	11.6	Sweden	2.1	3.2	6.7
Finland	5.5	7.0	12.8	Switzerland	0.7	1.3	3.0
France	8.9	9.3	10.2				
Germany	7.3	6.9	9.6				
Greece	7.8	8.2	9.8				
Italy	8.4	9.7	10.6				
Stable NAWRU							
Portugal	7.8	5.9	5.8	Canada	8.3	9.0	8.5
Spain	19.1	19.8	19.9	Japan	2.5	2.5	2.8
				Norway	3.1	4.2	4.5
				US	6.2	5.8	5.6
Decreasing NAWRU							
Netherlands	8.0	7.0	5.5	Australia	7.9	8.3	7.5
Ireland	14.6	14.6	11.0	Denmark	8.6	9.2	8.6
				New Zealand	4.7	7.3	6.0
				UK	9.5	8.5	7.2
Average equilibrium unemployment rate[b]							
	9.5	9.7	10.8		5.7	5.5	5.4

Notes:
a.   As a percentage of the labour force. Equilibrium unemployment data are based on esti-
     mates of the NAWRU (non-accelerating wage rate of unemployment) made for OECD,
     Economic Outlook, No. 63, 1998. An increase or decrease is considered significant (in
     absolute terms) if it exceeds one standard deviation. The latter was calculated for each
     series and country during the 1986–97 period.
b.   Weighted average of country unemployment rates using the labour force as weight.

Source: Elmeskov et al. (1998) based on OECD secretariat.

pool (OECD 1993). Finally, European unemployment is unequally dispersed
over the different professions. Low-skilled and manual workers are affected
more than high-skilled and white-collar workers (Layard et al. 1991).

However, it would be a mistake to consider EU15 or even EU12 as a
homogeneous region. Although Viñals and Jimeno (1996) detect a non-negli-
gible common component in European unemployment, a brief look at the

Table 7.2 Long-term unemployment

	1983		1990		1997	
	Total	Long term[a]	Total	Long term	Total	Long term
Austria	3.8	–	4.7	–	6.1	29
Belgium	13.3	65	8.8	69	12.7	61
Denmark	10.4	44	9.6	30	7.9	27
Finland	5.4	19	7.6[b]	9	14.6	31
France	8.3	42	8.9	38	12.4	41
Germany	7.9	42	6.2	47	10.3[c]	48
Greece	7.9	33	7.0	50	10.5	56
Ireland	13.5	37	12.9	66	10.3	57
Italy	7.7	58	9.1	70	12.3	66
Luxembourg	1.6	35	1.3	43	3.3[c]	28
Netherlands	11.0	49	6.0	49	5.8	49
Portugal	7.9	–	4.7	45	6.8	56
Spain	17.7	52	15.7	54	21.0	56
Sweden	3.5	10	1.6	5	8.1	30
UK	11.3	46	5.9	34	6.9	39
EU 15	9.1	–	7.7	49	10.7	50
US	9.6	13	5.6	6	5.0	9
Japan	2.7	13	2.1	20	3.4	22

Notes:
a. Unemployment longer than 1 year as a percentage of total unemployment.
b. Figure for 1991.
c. Figure for 1996.

Source: OECD Statistical Compendium and Eurostat (for EU15).

figures in Tables 7.1 and 7.2 shows that large disparities in (equilibrium) unemployment rates exist between the different member states. As Nickell (1997) indicated, there is much more difference within Europe than between the European average and the US. European equilibrium unemployment rates range from 5.4 per cent in Austria up to about 20 per cent in Spain, with an average of 10.8 per cent. Layard et al. (1991) found that these disparities are mostly accounted for by differences in youth and female unemployment, rather than in male unemployment.

The above observations lead us to conclude that the beginning of EMU coincides with a negative balance on the employment side. This stands in sharp contrast to the monetary side of the economies involved. Under the impetus of the Maastricht Treaty, the EMU candidates have significantly improved their records on inflation and ultimately also on government deficits in the 1990s in order to be eligible for entry. These efforts were effective but turned the attention away from structural measures directed to the labour market and have even worsened the unemployment picture.

2   THE CAUSES OF EUROPEAN UNEMPLOYMENT

The causes of the above-described evolutions in the European labour market have been the object of extensive empirical and theoretical research. Two factors have been found to contribute to poor labour market performance in Europe. On the one hand, a number of authors[2] stress the importance of adverse shocks that have hit Europe. Others[3] point to a number of inflexible labour market institutions. However, it is the interaction of shocks and labour market institutions that has been advocated as the cause for high and divergent unemployment throughout Europe.[4]

In order to get a better understanding of how the interaction of shocks and labour market institutions lead to poor labour market performance, we shall first briefly recall the theoretical model that lies behind this explanation. This will enable us to evaluate how the introduction of the single currency is likely to influence labour market performance.

The Theoretical Model

The framework used can be positioned in the new-Keynesian literature and builds on the 'competing claims' model that has been developed by, among others, Layard et al. (1991). The central idea of this model is the fact that there exists a unique level of equilibrium (un)employment[5] for which the competing claims on national output of trade unions/workers (wage-setters) on the one hand, and firms (price-setters) on the other hand are compatible. Incompatible claims can lead either to rising wages and prices (in the case where the sum of the claims exceeds national output) or to falling wages and prices.

Figure 7.1 illustrates the basic idea. At first sight, this graph looks much like a simple demand and supply framework in the labour market, with the real wage (W/P) on the vertical axis and employment on the horizontal axis. It is, however, fundamentally different in the underlying assumptions. Most importantly, it assumes that both product and labour markets are characterized by imperfect competition, which fits well with the reality in Europe. Price-setters, as well as wage-setters possess a certain amount of market power. Apart from that, the equilibrium level of (un)employment for which the claims are compatible is not market clearing.

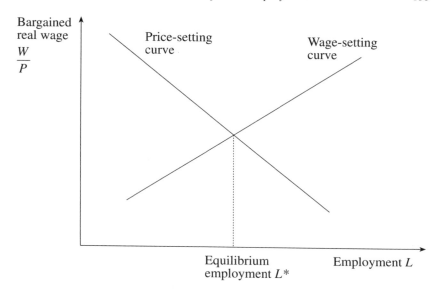

Figure 7.1   Equilibrium employment in a competing claims framework

The equilibrium level of employment, denoted by L^*, lies at the intersection of the wage-setting curve (henceforth WS curve) and the price-setting curve (henceforth PS curve). The WS curve reflects the positive relationship between employment and the bargained real wage. Higher levels of employment strengthen the bargaining position of workers and reduce the availability of outside options for the firm. As a consequence, higher wages will be bargained. The slope of the WS curve depends on the degree of real wage rigidity. The higher the rigidity of the bargained real wage, the lower the responsiveness of the real wage to changes in unemployment and the flatter the WS curve.

The relationship between the bargained real wage and the level of equilibrium unemployment is, however, more complex. A number of additional factors determine the precise position of the WS curve. An increase in labour productivity exerts an upward pressure on wages. More productive workers generate a higher surplus, of which unions claim a share. Higher employee contributions reduce purchasing power, which unions attempt to compensate by higher real wage demands. An autonomous increase in union power caused, for example, by an increase in union density – or a shift in union preferences from employment to wages – also increases wage demands for every level of employment. A downward pressure on wages is exerted if the unemployed become a more valuable alternative for workers. This can among others be achieved by an active re-employment policy.

The PS curve, also referred to as the labour demand curve, reflects the price-setting behaviour of firms in the product market. The basic idea is that firms in imperfectly competitive markets set the price of their products by determining a mark-up over nominal wage costs. With respect to the relationship between the mark-up and economic activity, there exists some controversy. Some authors assume that the mark-up is increasing in relation to the degree of economic activity. Firms tend to increase margins when the economy is buoyant. Rising mark-ups for a given nominal wage result in lower real wages as output/employment is rising. This gives rise to a negative relationship between the real wage and employment. Another hypothesis is that prices fluctuate very little due to changes in demand. This results in a horizontal PS curve. Thus it is clear that the slope of the PS curve depends on the flexibility with which prices react to changes in output. Low price flexibility leads to a flat PS curve.

Again, the precise position of the PS curve is determined by a number of additional factors. Higher labour productivity enables a higher real wage for a given mark-up and thus shifts the PS curve upwards. A downward shift is caused by a rise in employer contributions, by an increase in the non-wage production costs (such as, for example, energy costs, the cost of raw materials, transaction costs) and an autonomous increase in the mark-up.

European Unemployment Explained

Using the above framework, economists have linked the rise in European equilibrium unemployment to the interaction of adverse shocks and inflexible labour market institutions.[6] For that purpose, it is useful to keep in mind that from the model in the previous section, equilibrium employment L^* can be adversely influenced by the following:

1. An increase in labour taxes can either shift the WS curve upwards (employee contributions) or shift the PS curve downwards (employer contributions).
2. An increase in the price of non-wage costs shifts the PS curve downwards.
3. An increase in the bargaining power of trade unions shifts the WS curve upwards, as does an autonomous increase in the wage preference of unions.
4. A decrease in the effectiveness of the average unemployed shifts the WS curve upwards.
5. An autonomous increase in the mark-up shifts the PS curve downwards.
6. A decrease in labour productivity shifts both WS and PS curve downwards and therefore leaves the effect on L^* inconclusive.

Moreover, recall that the flat slopes of both WS and PS curves indicate that wages and prices, respectively, respond little to changes in unemployment and therefore contribute to an aggravation of unemployment. The slopes and shifts of WS and PS curves can readily be linked to a number of labour market institutions and shocks.

Institutions

Among the possible labour market institutions that affect equilibrium unemployment we count the degree of coordination in the wage-bargaining process (see 3 above), unemployment protection legislation (so-called hiring and firing costs) (see 4 above), the level and duration of unemployment benefits (see 4 above), a high share of passive (unconditional payment of benefits) versus active (education, mediation) labour market policy (see 4 above) and last, but not least, the tax burden on labour (see 1 above).

Recent empirical research by Scarpetta (1996), Nickell (1997) and Elmeskov et al. (1998) confirms the relevance of these institutions for labour market performance. One institution significantly influencing equilibrium unemployment is the organization of wage bargaining. Both Scarpetta and Nickell conclude that a high degree of unionization, combined with poor coordination among employers is detrimental for unemployment. This is confirmed by Elmeskov et al., who find that a high degree of bargaining coordination between the employer and the employee reduces equilibrium unemployment by increasing real wage flexibility. Moreover, Scarpetta (1996) confirms the Calmfors–Driffill hypothesis, according to which centralized and firm-level bargaining arrangements outperform sector-level bargaining arrangements (Calmfors and Driffill 1988). In terms of the competing claims model, this means that increased bargaining coordination shifts the WS curve downwards and steepens its slope.

Generous unemployment benefits are in general also found to have a negative impact on employment and on the adaptability of the labour market to shocks by shifting the WS curve upwards and flattening its slope. Unconditional benefits reduce the downward pressure on wages and sustain (partially voluntary) unemployment. Nickell (1997), however, finds that high benefits combined with an active labour market policy can be beneficial. If benefits are limited in time and conditional upon the willingness of the unemployed to follow retraining or other re-employment programmes, positive employment effects are noted as the effectiveness of the average unemployed is increased.

According to Scarpetta (1996) and Elmeskov et al. (1998), employment protection legislation contributes to high youth and long-term unemployment. This can be explained by the fact that high hiring and firing costs decrease job turnover and make firms reluctant to hire new and inexperienced workers. This makes it especially hard to find a job for young people and long-term unemployed who may have lost some of their skills.

A last significant determinant of high unemployment in European labour markets can be found in the non-wage component of labour costs. In particular, young and low-skilled workers are affected. High minimum wages combined with high payroll taxes make labour costs for these categories expensive for employers compared to their expected productivity. However, as both Nickell (1997) and van Poeck et al. (1998) point out, reducing payroll taxes would shift rather than solve the problem, since tight government budget constraints make lower payroll taxes without compensation unlikely. Only a decrease in the overall tax burden could have positive employment effects.

Shocks

Although a number of (country-specific) labour market institutions have contributed to high and divergent equilibrium unemployment, they are not the sole cause of poor labour market performance in the European Union (EU) member states. An equally important factor is adverse fluctuations in economic activity. To understand the effect of economic fluctuations or shocks, the competing-claims model is supplemented by an aggregate demand–aggregate supply (AD–AS) frameworks (see Figure 7.2). The theoretical underpinnings for the AS curve were laid in the previous section. Its positive slope reflects that firms and unions are willing to expand production only at a

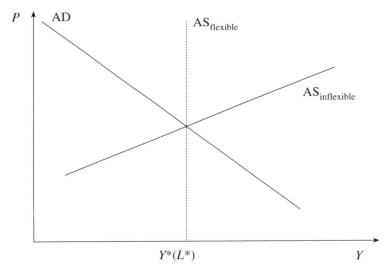

Figure 7.2   A simple AD–AS framework

higher market price and real wage. The higher the degree of price and wage flexibility, the steeper the slope of the AS curve. Perfect flexibility of prices and wages (often assumed to occur in the long run) results in a vertical AS curve. The standard negative slope of the AD curve 'is explained by the negative effect of price increases on aggregate demand, due to an increase in the real interest rate (at a given money supply), a decrease in real wealth and a decrease in international competitiveness.

Economic shocks can be represented by shifts of the AS curve (supply shocks) or the AD curve (demand shocks). The former can be further unravelled into a shift in the WS or PS curve. The importance of the interaction between shocks and labour market institutions is straightforward. For a given AD curve, adverse supply shocks have greater (equilibrium) unemployment effects, the flatter the AS curve, that is, the more rigid prices and real wages react to unemployment. Demand shocks are considered less damaging than supply shocks, as they shift actual unemployment away from its equilibrium value only temporarily. Persistent low demand however, can have supply-side effects, causing the equilibrium unemployment rate to follow the path of the actual unemployment rate (hysteresis). A possible channel through which temporarily reduced demand negatively influences equilibrium unemployment is the fact that people who become unemployed are no longer represented by the workers. Unions are not inclined to reduce wage demands to re-employ the unemployed. Another possible channel is the skill loss from which the unemployed may suffer as they remain out of work for a longer period. This reduces their effectiveness. Yet another possibility is the permanent loss of market share if a persistent appreciation reduces the competitiveness of the domestic firms and gives foreign firms the opportunity to establish themselves in the market. This allows us to add another cause to the list of factors that determine L^*, namely:

7.   A combination of prolonged restrictive monetary and fiscal policy reduces equilibrium employment due to hysteresis effects.

The interaction of shocks and institutions can also account for the diversity in national unemployment rates. First, it is possible that only one or a limited number of member states are hit by an asymmetric shock. This can, for example, be the case when shocks are caused by divergences in the rate of productivity growth, or by differences in the stance of macroeconomic policy. Even with identical labour market institutions, national labour markets will obviously diverge. Second, when shocks hit the entire eurozone, they do not necessarily have to work out symmetrically for every individual member state, as labour market institutions are very different over countries. Every country then reacts idiosyncratically to the identical shock, causing divergent unemployment rates.

Rising unemployment in the 1970s was largely caused by a number of adverse supply-side shocks. The two oil shocks are notorious for their damaging effect on employment. They influenced the supply side of the economy negatively through the sharp increase in energy prices. This period was additionally characterized by a sharp decrease in labour productivity and rising payroll taxes. These shocks can be represented by a downward shift of the PS curve (in Figure 7.1) and an upward shift of the AS curve (in Figure 7.2), resulting in a decrease in L^*. The size of the employment decrease, however, depended crucially on the slope of the WS curve. Countries in which real wages reacted in a flexible way to unemployment changes (low degree of real wage rigidity) witnessed a downward adjustment of the real wage level, which limited the negative unemployment consequences. Many European countries, however, were characterized by labour market institutions that were not favourable to a high degree of real wage flexibility.

In contrast to the supply shocks of the 1970s and the beginning of the 1980s, a series of adverse demand shocks hit Europe throughout a large part of the 1990s. The combination of a restrictive monetary and fiscal policy that was pursued by the EU members in order to fulfil the Maastricht criteria, had a negative impact on European unemployment. Although it was expected that only the demand side – and hence cyclical unemployment – would be negatively affected, the concerted nature of the monetary and fiscal restriction throughout the EU turned cyclical unemployment into equilibrium unemployment.

The importance of the policy mix for unemployment can be illustrated by the figures in Table 7.3, in which the stance of monetary and fiscal policy and the evolution of unemployment in the US and the EU members is compared for the 1990s.[7] The figures in the first column show us that the yearly average change in structural deficit over the 1992–97 period has been positive, both in the US and in Europe. This points to an intended fiscal tightening by both governments, since the figures are adjusted for business-cycle effects. The second column points far less in the same direction. Whereas inflation in the US has dropped only marginally over the period considered, the European figures show a far more restrictive monetary policy in the majority of the member states. Especially in the beginning of the 1990s, US monetary policy was far more expansionary than European. The explanation is fairly obvious. As a consequence of German unification in 1989, the German Bundesbank maintained a very strict monetary policy to prevent inflationary pressures from developing. And since the European Monetary System (EMS) in fact was a leader–follower situation, most EMS countries – with Italy and the UK as notorious exceptions – had no choice but to follow the deflationary movement to preserve the fixed exchange rate mechanism.[8] It should be stressed, however, that apart from German unification the determination to fulfil the

Table 7.3   *Fiscal consolidation, inflation reduction and unemployment costs, 1992–1997*

Country	Average change in structural balance[a]	Inflation reduction[b]	Cumulative unemployment change [c]	Unemployment increase $(u_{97}-u_{92})$	$u_{97}-u^*$
Austria	−0.02	2.8	3.8	0.8	0.7
Belgium	1.16	1.8	11.8	2.3	1.6
Denmark	0.18	−0.2	−5.0	−3.4	3.0[d]
Finland	−0.12	−0.4	18.9	1.5	12.5[d]
France	0.36	1.1	8.6	2.1	2.7
Germany	0.44	4.7	11.1	3.7	1.6
Greece	1.66	8.4	6.6	1.8	–
Ireland	0.20	2.0	−10.8	−4.8	−0.2[d]
Italy	1.46	2.1	13.9	3.5	1.7
Netherlands	0.48	−0.3	6.7	0.4	−0.8[d]
Portugal	0.50	7.6	12.8	2.6	1.0
Spain	0.62	5.0	22.3	3.1	7.8[d]
Sweden	1.42	−0.7	13.5	2.8	6.8[d]
UK	0.50	2.3	−7.8	−3.3	0.8[d]
EU	0.66	2.7	8.5	1.7	1.3
US	0.74	0.7	−8.5	−2.5	−0.9[d]
Japan	−0.50	0.6	4.3	1.2	1.0[d]

Notes:
a.   A positive number indicates that on average the structural deficit has decreased.
b.   A minus sign means an increase in the inflation rate.
c. $= \sum_{i=93}^{97} u_i - u_{92}$, which gives an indication of the total cost in terms of unemployment.
d. u^* (equilibrium level of unemployment) calculated over 1980–88 (Source: Layard et al. 1991).

Source: OECD *Economic Outlook*, No. 62, December 1997 and OECD *Economic Outlook*, No. 61, June 1997 for u^*.

Maastricht criteria was an equally important determinant for the restrictive monetary policy.

The relevance of the policy mix for the unemployment performance is documented in the next columns of Table 7.3. Whereas the European Union underwent a cumulative increase in unemployment of 8.5 per cent, the US benefited from an identical unemployment decrease over the same period. The other indicators in the remaining columns also point in the same direction. European unemployment is 1.7 per cent higher in 1997 than in

1992 and exceeds the estimated equilibrium unemployment figure by 1.3 per cent. The figures for the US on the other hand show the opposite evolution.

European Unemployment Solved?

Having identified to a large extent the causes of high and divergent unemployment in Europe, we have offered part of the answer that should solve the problem. In broad lines, it boils down to the following: reform the labour market institutions that have a negative impact on employment, reduce the number of (asymmetric) shocks and limit the effect of shocks on employment. Referring back to the previous section, these general principles can be translated into a number of concrete guidelines.

Reform labour market institutions
As it was concluded that uncoordinated bargaining contributes to the rise in equilibrium unemployment, progress could be achieved when there was more consensus between firms and unions. Moreover, sector-level bargaining does not lead to optimum labour market performance. The generosity of unemployment benefits should be reduced or at least be combined with active labour market policy and employment protection legislation should be relaxed. Finally, a reduction of the overall tax burden could reduce equilibrium unemployment. However, it should be stressed that the above are only a number of general guidelines. A unique set of institutions that minimize equilibrium unemployment probably does not exist.

Reduce the number of (asymmetric) shocks
An absolute reduction in the number of shocks would probably be hard to achieve, as the causes of shocks are often external to the economy. This was, for example, the case for the oil shocks. Asymmetric unemployment evolutions may be easier to avoid. One source of asymmetry could lie in diverging wage developments between member states, which could be avoided by European-wide wage-bargaining cooperation. There is, however, also a trade-off that occurs: European sector-level bargaining could be the cause of poor labour market performance.

Large differences in other labour market institutions can also be a source of asymmetric consequences of shocks. Although Eichengreen (1990) has shown that a certain degree of institutional divergence can be allowed, this is probably more true for the US than for Europe, as interstate migration and horizontal redistribution mechanism are more extended in the former (Ehrenberg 1994). More coordination of labour market policy would therefore be desirable.

Another source of asymmetry lies in uncoordinated stabilization policy decisions. Convergence in the stance of monetary and fiscal policy could potentially lead to more symmetry in the reaction to shocks. This fact has been empirically confirmed by Hochreiter and Winckler (1995). They found that although Austria did not form an optimum currency area with Germany in the 1970s, credibly pegging to the Deutschmark triggered off an adjustment process so that eventually Austria lined up with Germany and the number of asymmetric shocks decreased. Crucial factors in the adjustment process were a sufficient degree of real wage flexibility and an increase in intraindustry trade.

Limit the effect of shocks on unemployment

One instrument limiting the damaging effect of shocks on labour markets is the use of monetary and fiscal policy. As we shall discuss further, this option has been largely limited in EMU. More flexibility is thus needed from prices and wages.

3   THE IMPACT OF EMU ON EUROPEAN LABOUR MARKETS

In the previous section, we have linked the level of equilibrium unemployment to its determinants. This allowed us to determine that high European unemployment is caused by the interaction of adverse (demand and supply) shocks and a set of inflexible and adverse labour market institutions. A number of (tentative) policy conclusions were drawn. We shall now investigate to what extent the introduction of the single currency could influence the determinants of equilibrium unemployment, which will allow us to evaluate whether EMU might contribute to lower or higher equilibrium unemployment.

Although the above overview has indicated the importance of labour market institutions for explaining the European unemployment problem, thinking in terms of labour market institutions hides the economic agents who operate behind them. The majority of the above-mentioned institutions are the responsibility of the government. Firms and trade unions also play an important role through the wage-formation process. This makes it highly relevant to investigate what impact the introduction of the single currency will have on the behaviour of these three players on the labour market.

Before analysing the likely impact of the introduction of the single currency on labour market performance in the member states, it is important to stress that the effects will predominantly be of an indirect nature. These indirect effects are complex and therefore hard to identify, particularly because they depend on how economic agents will react and adapt to the new economic environment. Among the most important channels through which the single currency might influence labour market outcomes are:

- the impact of EMU on price-setting and competitive behaviour of firms;
- the reaction of trade unions, notably concerning the degree of coordination in the wage-bargaining process and the consequences for the evolution of wages and labour costs;
- the stance of macroeconomic policy in EMU; and
- the incentives for governments to implement labour market reform.

The notion that the impact of EMU largely depends on the (re)actions of the economic players, refers to the so-called 'Lucas critique', which states that economic agents do not act passively when new policy measures are introduced, but that they respond strategically to take advantage of these measures. In the light of this finding, it is crucial to endogenize the behavioural changes of firms, unions and national governments as a result of the introduction of EMU.

Firms, Price-Setting and Competitive Behaviour

In this section, we analyse the EMU impact on product markets and their spillover effects on the labour market. Three effects can be distinguished: a cost effect, a competition effect and a location effect.

The cost effect follows from the two direct gains from the adoption of the single currency. The first gain for firms operating on the European product market comes from the elimination of exchange rate uncertainty. It is a well-documented fact that exchange rate variability leads to profit losses.[9] Especially longer-period swings in intra-European exchange rates appeared hard to hedge against. In order to benefit from the elimination of exchange rate risks, it is sufficient to have a monetary system with fixed exchange rates, a condition that has been fulfilled in the eurozone since the beginning of 1999. The second gain additionally requires the adoption of a common currency. With the introduction of the euro, the eurozone will benefit from the replacement of the national currencies of the member states with one single currency. All trade within EMU then takes place in one currency. This lowers transaction costs that previously arose from foreign exchange operations.

Within the above-sketched competing claims model, a decrease in transaction costs reduces the non-wage production costs. This causes an upward shift of the PS curve. As a consequence, the real wage and equilibrium employment increase. The size of the net employment effect depends on the behaviour of the trade unions. The shift in the PS curve allows unions to raise wage claims, which reduces the employment effect compared to a constant-wage scenario. This is reflected in the positive slope of the WS curve. A high degree of (upward) real wage rigidity dampens wage rises and increases the positive employment effect.

The competition effect follows from the fact that firms become more directed towards the international market. The reduction in transaction costs enlarges the relevant market for firms and fosters competition through a larger number of direct competitors. Increased product market competition would then lead to lower mark-ups to the advantage of consumers.

Within the competing claims model, an increase in product market competition has two effects. On the one hand, a decrease in concentration in the industry increases the price elasticity of product demand with which the firms are confronted. As the mark-up is inversely related to the price elasticity, the former declines for every level of activity. Graphically, this means that the PS curve will shift upwards, thus increasing employment and the bargained real wage. On the other hand, a concentration decrease in the industry increases the number of agents on the labour demand side. In other words, the bargaining power of the firms declines in favour of the trade unions. This will put an upward pressure on wage demands by the unions, which is translated into an upward shift of the WS curve.

Adding the two effects clearly indicates that – still according to the competing claims model – more competition in the product market raises the bargained real wage whereas the effect on employment is ambiguous.

However, it is not entirely sure that the future will be characterized by an increase in product market competition. We observe nowadays that firms try to counterbalance the increased competitive pressure by mergers and other forms of acquisitions in order to maintain or even increase their market power. It is thus not unthinkable that we end up with even more concentrated product markets. A good example of this evolution can be found in the banking sector, although the single currency is not the only driving force behind the concentration movement. Technological and demographic developments are equally important and might have led to the current outcome anyway (White 1998).

Concerning the impact of product market competition on labour market outcomes, there exists another strand of literature.[10] The theoretical conclusions are the following: the lower the degree of product market competition, the higher the wage and the lower employment. The intuitive explanation is twofold. On the one hand price-setting power allows producers to raise the price above marginal cost, generating a surplus. Unions on the other hand use their bargaining power to claim a share of this surplus. Product market collusion thus leads to higher wages and lower employment than a perfectly competitive industry. Although the conclusions from these microeconomic models do not correspond with the ones from the competing claims model, they are not inconsistent. At the micro level, the increase in concentration is translated into a rise of prices and profits, of which a part is shared with the workers in the form of higher (nominal) wages. At the macro level, however, an overall rise in the level of prices reduces the purchasing power of the workers, which is only partially compensated by a nominal wage increase. As a consequence, the bargained real wage falls.

The location effect describes the relocation of activity to take advantage of the single currency. Krugman (1993) argues that the eurozone is bound to go the same way as the US, with states/countries becoming more and more specialized as firms concentrate their means of production more at a limited number of locations to benefit from spatial economics of scale. Again these cost-saving measures are likely to have positive effects on employment and the bargained real wage. However, a disadvantage lies in the fact that this geographical concentration movement renders countries more vulnerable to asymmetric shocks. Alternatively, as Krugman argues: 'A common market may mean exactly the opposite of a common destiny'.

Summarizing this section, two (tentative) conclusions can be drawn. On the one hand, positive employment effects are to be expected from the microeconomic benefits of introducing the euro. The elimination of exchange rate uncertainty and the reduction in transaction costs are supply-side factors that can decrease equilibrium unemployment. A factor potentially counter-balancing these positive effects is the risk of increased wage demands in the light of the rent-sharing hypothesis.

Moreover, if the trend towards geographic clustering of sectors continues, these positive employment effects could be spread unevenly over the member states. This would shift the need of labour market policy away from reducing equilibrium unemployment towards protecting the labour market against asymmetric evolutions in the different member states.

Unions and Wage Formation

From the competing claims model, we have concluded that wage costs, wages and wage flexibility on the one hand, and employment on the other hand, are closely related. In this section, we therefore discuss how EMU might influence the WS curve through the behaviour of trade unions.

In the period before the start of EMU, wage costs[11] have remained constant or have even declined in the participating countries. The first explanation for this evolution is the downward adjustment of inflation expectations. In some countries, nominal wage claims rose more slowly than the price index. Another reason is the amount of labour market reform that has been undertaken in several member states. One of the achievements in this respect is that real economic variables such as productivity growth, the situation in the labour market or the evolution of profits are increasingly taken into account in the wage-bargaining process (CEC 1998b).

Let us now turn to the future evolution of wage costs in EMU. The payroll tax component of the wage cost is not likely to alter significantly in the near future. On the one hand, considerable reductions in the non-wage component are not to be expected as the fiscal austerity that has been required to meet the Maastricht criteria will have to be prolonged in the near future. On the other hand, a further increase in labour taxes is not very likely either, since the Maastricht criteria have been met by most countries and since the excessive rise of public debt has been brought to a halt. Given a fairly stable payroll tax component, the question remains how wages will evolve from 1999 onwards. Arguments can be found for wage decreases, as well as for wage increases.

A first incentive for moderate wage demands is the fact that competitive devaluations to correct excessive wage claims are henceforth impossible. This knowledge may incite unions to evaluate carefully the effect of their wage claims. This is especially important for bargaining arrangements made at the industry and national levels. The second argument is the elimination of exchange rate uncertainty. Andersen and Sørensen (1988) conclude that anticipated exchange rate variability is totally accounted for in wage claims. However, unanticipated exchange rate fluctuations are by nature impossible to include without contingent contracts. Therefore, risk-averse unions raise wage claims to account for unpredictable exchange rate movements. In their framework, EMU would thus lead to lower wage claims and higher equilibrium employment.

Increasing wage demands can be expected if wages are bargained at industry level throughout the entire eurozone. As this region is a fairly closed economy compared to the openness of every individual member state, this evolution would significantly strengthen the bargaining position of the unions. An increase in bargaining strength can be translated into an upward shift of the WS curve, causing rising wages and decreasing employment. The evidence about what direction future wage developments will take is thus mixed. In favour of reduced wage demands are the absence of the *ex post* correction mechanism and the certainty about exchange rates. Rising wages on the other hand could be expected if wages were bargained at the industry level.

What remains to be determined is how the degree of wage flexibility as a substitute for national monetary policy will evolve under EMU. Rephrasing the question, we actually ask to what extent wage policy will become available as a policy tool for national governments. This is determined by the degree of coordination in the wage-bargaining process. If wages are set at the national level, as is the case in some member states, it is easier for national governments to influence the bargaining process, especially compared to the situation in which bargaining arrangements are made at the European level. It is thus necessary to have a closer look at the impact EMU could have on the degree of wage-bargaining coordination.

EMU both increases the incentives and lowers the costs for coordination. The increase in coordination incentives can be explained as follows. Due to the competitive pressure on the product market, unions are forced to set lower nominal wages. This in turn increases the gap between what could be considered the non-cooperative wage on the one hand, and the wage outcome that could potentially be negotiated by a monopolistic union on the other hand. Therefore, increasing economic integration makes it more interesting for unions to cooperate. EMU on the other hand fosters integration not only in the product market, but also in the labour market. Through increased transparency, reduced uncertainty and a convergence of the institutional environment EMU lowers the barriers for European coordination among trade unions.

However, empirical confirmation for the (theoretically) expected European trade union cooperation is very limited nowadays. Although the European Trade Union Confederation (ETUC) offers the platform for international coordination for more qualitative labour conditions, there are only limited signs of a similar cooperation regarding the macroeconomic key variables, wages and employment.[12] Further empirical evidence for inertia in labour market institutions in general was found by Wallerstein et al. (1997), who investigated the influence of globalization on national labour market institutions. Their main finding was that countries, characterized by corporatist labour relations, changed very little under the globalization process. One of the causes of the inertia in the coordination of wage bargaining across countries could lie in the fact that both employer associations and trade unions have to come to an agreement on the institutional setting.

The Future of Economic Policy in EMU

The last player in the labour market is the government, by which in this case we mean both national and European governing bodies. Government influence on labour markets is twofold. On the one hand, stabilization policy (both monetary and fiscal policy) – although primarily directed towards demand-side variables – may influence equilibrium unemployment indirectly. On the other hand, the labour market institutions mentioned in the first section are also determinants of equilibrium unemployment. In this section, we therefore analyse how EMU affects economic policy in the European member states.

Monetary and fiscal policy

Stabilization policy is important for European equilibrium employment in three respects. First, a prolonged restrictive policy mix can potentially decrease equilibrium employment. Second, a restrictive monetary policy may moreover reduce real wage flexibility. Third, stabilization policy should be sufficiently available to national authorities to limit unemployment divergence within the eurozone.

The stance of monetary and fiscal policy is to a large extent institutionally determined. According to its statutes the primary goal of the European Central Bank (ECB) is to preserve price stability. It is only in second order that the ECB is required to target output growth and stabilization. As the ECB appears to be primarily concerned about building up a reputation as an inflation fighter, it should not be expected to be a forerunner in the fight against unemployment. The risk of supply-side effects therefore remains. Large systematic budget deficits are not allowed either. The Stability and Growth Pact imposes severe penalties if national governments systematically exploit deficit spending. Theoretically, it seems thus fairly unlikely that this will happen. However, as Sutter (1999) points out, sanctions have to be voted for. He calculates that the majority-voting rule reduces in practice the likelihood of actual sanctions.

A second issue concerns the stance of monetary policy and its effect on real wage flexibility. When inflation is very low, cuts in real wages can only be achieved by nominal wage cuts, which are usually even more resisted than real wage cuts. High inflation allows real wage cuts by slowing down nominal wage growth below the level of price rises.[13] Given the policy of the ECB, increases in real wage flexibility are not to be expected.

A third issue concerns the availability of policy instruments to prevent (asymmetric) shocks from affecting the labour market. The above discussion has made clear that monetary and fiscal policy – if not entirely unavailable – is seriously restricted. This explains why a large literature has been devoted to the likelihood of asymmetric shocks in the eurozone. A decrease in the number and size of idiosyncratic shocks could be expected once the European economy becomes more integrated and once national economic policies become more coordinated.

Labour market policy

We have already formulated a number of measures that could be taken to reduce equilibrium unemployment. A considerable role was reserved for labour market reform in order to bring down unemployment and to increase the flexibility of wages. Unresolved so far has remained the question whether EMU influences the incentives to take the necessary measure to reform the labour market. Calmfors (1998a) develops a number of arguments that show how EMU could influence labour market reform.

In general, countries have an incentive for labour market reform not only because it decreases equilibrium unemployment, but also because it brings down the inflation bias (Barro and Gordon 1983). For countries inside the monetary union, the link between national labour market reform and inflation bias is much weaker. Since reform in a single member state brings down equilibrium unemployment in the union by only a small amount, the benefits of a reduced inflation bias are only marginal. The incentives for labour market reform are therefore smaller for countries in EMU.

A second argument why policy makers are more reluctant to carry out labour market reform in EMU could be the lag between the reform and the positive employment effects. This occurs in the case where nominal wages are rigid. Rigid nominal wages prevent the wage level from falling and the employment level from rising immediately after the reform. This effect could be mitigated by combining labour market reform with a (temporary) monetary expansion, which in combination with rigid nominal wages would decrease the real wage level and increase equilibrium employment. However, it is less likely that the ECB will cooperate in this policy mix than a national central bank.

A third argument (Calmfors 1998b) results in more labour market reform inside EMU. The argument is that unemployment will be more volatile in EMU, as monetary policy is no longer available to stabilize asymmetric shocks. In so far as governments are especially averse towards very bad unemployment outcomes, they will anticipate the problem and carry out precautionary labour market reform.

Summing up the three arguments, it remains inconclusive whether EMU will reduce or increase the incentives for labour market reform.

4   CONCLUSION

Will EMU cause or cure European unemployment? The question remains largely unanswered, but we have nevertheless been able to distinguish some trends.

European unemployment has been identified as a common European problem with national differences. Its causes have been the interaction of adverse shocks and inflexible and adverse labour market institutions. The oil shocks in the 1970s and the restrictive policy mix in the 1990s caused especially high unemployment in the member states with adverse labour market institutions, such as uncoordinated wage bargaining, generous and unconditional unemployment benefits, strict employment protection legislation and high payroll taxes. Better labour market performance could thus be achieved by reforming these institutions and by limiting the number of (asymmetric) shocks.

It remains to be seen whether EMU will promote or prohibit the necessary (and often unpopular) measures to be taken to reform the labour market. We have identified arguments in both directions. Wage bargaining could potentially evolve in a more unfavourable direction. We found (theoretical) support for increased European sector-level bargaining. This evolution reduces the number of instruments to accommodate (asymmetric) shocks and could potentially weaken overall labour market performance. Moreover, as we concluded that monetary and fiscal policy would be restricted, we devoted some attention to the likelihood of asymmetric developments in the eurozone. Again, arguments in both directions were found. A reduction in the number of asymmetric shocks could be achieved by coordinated wage bargaining, monetary and fiscal policy coordination and a greater degree of openness. International relocation of industries could potentially reduce these positive effects.

Finally, a number of channels were identified through which European equilibrium unemployment could be positively influenced. Among these we count the reduction in transaction costs for international trade and the elimination of exchange rate uncertainty with positive effects for prices and wages.

NOTES

1. Equilibrium unemployment is used to correct for differences in the business cycles among countries.
2. Bayoumi and Eichengreen (1993); Burgess and Knetter (1998).
3. Scarpetta (1996); Nickell (1997); Elmeskov et al. (1998).
4. Bean (1994); Blanchard and Wolfers (2000).
5. As we assume that labour supply does not depend on the real wage, we can use employment and unemployment in their mirror meanings.
6. See van Poeck et al. (1999) for an overview.
7. The figures for Japan are included for informative purposes only and will not be discussed in the example.
8. Applying the Taylor rule, Morin and Thibault (1998) calculated that the short-term nominal interest rate was indeed optimal for Germany. However, according to them the rate for France was 3.5 percentage points too high.
9. However, De Grauwe (1997a) argues that risk-neutral firms can benefit from exchange rate variability in the form of higher expected profits if the exchange rate fluctuates randomly around a certain stable value.
10. See, for example, Sørensen (1993); Huizinga (1993); Naylor (1998 and 1999).
11. Measured by the real unit labour cost.
12. A notable exception would be the recent intentions of Belgian, Dutch and German unions to cooperate in the metal industry.
13. Note that this argument assumes a certain degree of money illusion.

PART III

The Future: Beyond 2000

8. ERM-II: problems for the 'outs' and their relationship with the 'ins'

Heather D. Gibson and Euclid Tsakalotos

1 INTRODUCTION

March 1998 saw the publication by the European Commission and the European Monetary Institute (EMI) of two independent reports on convergence of European Union (EU) countries (in relation to the provisions laid down in the Maastricht Treaty). On the basis of these reports on the extent to which individual EU countries met with the convergence criteria, ECOFIN (the Council of EU Finance Ministers) decided in May 1998 which countries were eligible to join the European Monetary Union (EMU). At the same time, the exchange rates for EMU entry were also announced.

As a consequence of this decision, the situation in the EU has been very different since 1 January 1999. Most member states participate in the eurozone and the common monetary and exchange rate policy (the 'ins') but there are those which do not (the 'outs'). The purpose of this chapter is to examine the relationship between the 'ins' and the 'outs' and, on the basis of past EU experience, suggest the kinds of problems which the 'outs' in particular might be expected to face.

Our account here will, by necessity, touch upon many well-known debates and controversies concerning how best to arrive at monetary union. For instance, take the issues at stake between the so-called 'economists' and 'monetarists'. The former have usually argued that monetary integration should be preceded by economic and economic policy integration, with financial integration – the removal of all capital controls and completely fixed exchange rates – as the final act. Without such an approach, the 'economists' feared that economies risked destabilization (for instance, through unsustainable exchange rate targets) or real economic divergence (the result of, amongst other things, high interest rates, necessary to keep within the exchange rate target, leading to lower investment and growth), making their final participation in the monetary union that much more difficult. On the other hand, 'monetarists' argued that measures of financial integration should be adopted

quickly to force economies, and economic policy, to converge. Without such
financial 'rigour', it was feared that national economic policy makers would
always postpone making the difficult economic choices that were entailed in
joining a monetary union. Any pain that had to be borne was better done so
quickly. In this way, it can be seen that the debate between 'economists' and
'monetarists' overlaps with that between 'gradualists' and the promoters of
'shock therapy' (see, for example, Chapter 2).

Of course, many more nuanced positions were possible and academic and
policy-making opinion has tended to shift quite frequently on these matters
over recent years. Thus, in the late 1980s when the exchange rate mechanism
(ERM) was considerably tightened – there were no realignments between
1987 and 1992 and countries such as France and Italy removed their remaining capital controls – most economic analysts in Europe were quite upbeat
about the prospects for the ERM leading fairly painlessly into monetary
union (Giavazzi and Spaventa 1990; Gros and Thygesen 1992). Those who
were unconvinced about this sanguine conclusion (Gibson and Tsakalotos
1991, 1993), either because they feared that the overall economic environment could change or because they felt that what held for some of the
stronger economies (Germany, France, Italy) might not hold for the weaker
southern European economies, were proved partially right when the ERM
crises of 1992 and 1993 erupted. Among the lessons that seemed to be worth
learning from those crises was that the best-run institutional system is vulnerable to a major shock to the overall economic environment (German
unification) and that the lack of cooperation or policy disagreements between
member countries (for instance, the dispute after 1990 over whether inflation
or unemployment should be prioritized) could severely undermine any system.[1] The crises led to a much looser ERM with 15 per cent fluctuation
bands[2] – although this was partly balanced by the Maastricht criteria which
did impose strictness elsewhere (inflation, fiscal deficits and debt). In the
event, therefore, the road to monetary union for the 11 first members relied
on a mixture of institutions, rules and policies from both 'monetarist' and
'economist' cookbooks. There is much to be learned from this experience on
a number of important questions such as how gradual the transition period
should be, the importance or otherwise of cooperation between member
states, and the appropriate sequencing of economic liberalization (for example, should external liberalization only be concluded once macroeconomic
stability is ensured?).

On the other hand, while learning as much as possible from previous
experience, it is also important that the new participants do not concentrate
on 'fighting the last war'. That is to say, in some ways the new participants in
ERM-II face different conditions. First, for these aspiring members, EMU
already exists and so the nature of the end-point is now much clearer than it

was for the older members. As we shall see, it is not clear that this necessarily constitutes a source only of advantage. Second, there is the fact that on the whole the new members will have weaker economies than the original members of the old ERM had when it began in 1979. This clearly is a source of disadvantage. In what follows, we hope to shed light on all these aspects.

The chapter is divided into three main sections. First, we discuss the extent to which member states fulfilled the Maastricht criteria. We also consider the prospective EU members (both the fast- and slow-track countries) and investigate some of the relevant characteristics of their economies. Second, we consider one aspect of the new institutional framework of the EU, namely, ERM-II which replaced the old ERM in January 1999. So far, only Denmark and Greece are members but there is every expectation that others will join. Finally, we analyse the environment in which the 'outs' or prospective 'outs' find themselves and ask whether the institutional structure of ERM-II will facilitate their successful convergence on the eurozone. Our argument here is that there are good reasons, based on past experience, for thinking that the 'outs' are likely to have a bumpy ride on the way to monetary union. We examine one way in which this bumpy ride could materialize, namely, by the 'outs' finding themselves between the Scylla of excess credibility and the Charybdis of speculative crises. We focus in the chapter on macroeconomic convergence since that is what the Maastricht criteria focus on and because, as the southern European countries show, a country can join a monetary union without real convergence. However, it can be noted that implicit in our argument is the view that this bumpy ride will not be the best framework for the promotion of real convergence between the 'outs' and the eurozone.

2 THE EUROZONE: 'INS', 'OUTS' AND NEW MEMBERS

Table 8.1 provides a summary of the status of the EU countries and various prospective members as of May 1999. It is important to include the latter as potential 'outs' since their convergence process to EMU will most likely take place within ERM-II. Of the current 15 EU members, 11 were admitted to monetary union in the first wave. Four countries, Denmark, Greece, Sweden and the UK, remain outside.

Figures 8.1 and 8.2 along with Table 8.2 provide evidence on the degree of nominal convergence which had occurred among EU countries by the time the assessment took place.[3] Figure 8.1 shows government deficits (as a percentage of GDP) for 1994 and 1997. Considerable convergence had occurred in all countries and estimates for 1998 suggested that consolidation would continue. France just met the 3 per cent reference value. Greece was the only country not to meet the criteria with a deficit of 4 per cent although consider-

Table 8.1   The eurozone: 'ins', 'outs' and new members

Existing EU members	Ins	Austria, Belgium, Finland, France, Germany, Ireland, Italy, Luxembourg, Netherlands, Portugal, Spain
	Outs	Denmark, Greece*, Sweden, UK
Prospective EU members	Fast track	Cyprus, Czech Republic, Estonia, Hungary, Poland, Slovenia
	Slow track	Bulgaria, Latvia, Lithuania, Malta, Romania, Slovak Republic

Note: * Greece joined the 'ins' in January 2001.

able progress had been made. Figure 8.2 shows debt/GDP ratios for the same years. Among high debtors, there was some consolidation over the 1994–97 period. However, a number of countries were still above the 60 per cent reference value and it is clear that the subclause to the debt criterion was invoked. That is, the relevant question was whether the ratio was diminishing sufficiently. This has a backward aspect (what progress has been made) and a forward-looking aspect (how quickly the 60 per cent would be met).[4] Italy

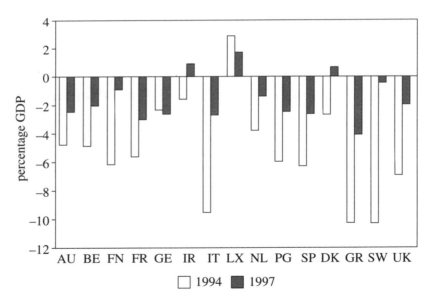

Figure 8.1   Budget surpluses (+)/deficits (–) in EU countries

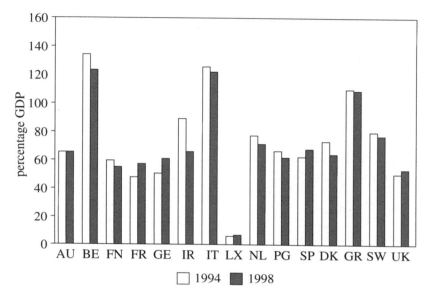

Source: EMI, *Convergence Report*, various years.

Figure 8.2 Debt/GDP ratios in EU countries

and Belgium were problematic in these respects because of the very high debt ratios with which they began. Greece was also a country significantly outside of the convergence criteria, although again reductions had been occurring.

Table 8.2 provides information on the other criteria: inflation, interest rates and membership of the ERM (with no realignments over the past two years). The data refer to annual percentage changes between January 1997 and January 1998. The table shows that all countries except Greece met the interest rate and inflation criteria. With respect to the exchange rate criterion, those countries who wanted to join were all members of the old ERM, although Finland and Italy had not been members for two years at the time of assessment and Greece had joined only on 16 March 1998.[5]

Thus, it was on the basis of these figures that the initial 11 participants were chosen.[6] Of the four countries outside the monetary union, Denmark and the UK have derogations, Sweden declared that it did not want to be among the first wave and Greece wanted to join but was judged not to have met the criteria. Greece, however, was reassessed in mid-2000 and joined EMU in January 2001. Therefore, only one of three 'outs' is at present a member of ERM-II – Denmark and Greece. However, in the future, with the

Table 8.2   Inflation and interest rate performance in EU countries

	HICP inflation[1] (Jan. 1997–Jan. 1998) reference rate: 2.7 (AU, FR, IR are the 3 lowest – add 1.5% to average)	Long-term interest rates (Jan. 1997– Jan. 1998) reference rate: 7.8 (countries are as in inflation criteria – add 2% to average)	ERM membership plus no realignment for 2 years
Austria (AU)	1.1	5.6	yes
Belgium	1.4	5.7	yes
Finland	1.3	5.9	no (< 2 years)[2]
France (FR)	1.2	5.5	yes
Germany	1.4	5.6	yes
Ireland (IR)	1.2	6.2	yes
Italy	1.8	6.7	no (< 2 years)[2]
Luxembourg	1.4	5.6	yes
Netherlands	1.8	5.5	yes
Portugal	1.8	6.2	yes
Spain	1.8	6.3	yes
Denmark	1.9	6.2	yes
Greece	5.2	9.8	no (joined 16.3.98)
Sweden	1.9	6.5	no
UK	1.8	7.0	no

Notes:
1. HICP is the harmonized consumer price index used by the EU.
2. Finland joined the ERM in October 1996; Italy rejoined from November 1996. It was
    judged that these two countries met the criteria since by 1 January 1999 they would have
    two years in the system without realignment.

Source: EMI, *Convergence Report* (March 1998).

planned widening of the EU, it is likely that other countries will participate in
ERM-II. Table 8.1 provides a list of these countries divided into fast-track
countries and slow-track countries as defined by the European Commission.

Tables 8.3–5 present some information about the exchange rate systems,
the nature and existence of capital controls as well as selected macroeconomic indicators for these countries. From Table 8.3, it is clear that a variety
of exchange rate arrangements exist. The fast-track countries generally have
some kind of exchange rate peg which for those countries with inflation
problems sometimes includes an element of preannounced crawling depre-

Table 8.3   Exchange rate systems of prospective EU members

Country	Exchange rate arrangements
Fast-track countries	
Cyprus (Cyprus pound)	Pegged to ECU at ECU1.706 per Cyprus pound within margins of 2.25% from January 1999 pegged to Euro at 1.7066 Euro per Cyprus pound A forward exchange market exists but margins in the market cannot be greater than those set by the central bank
Czech Republic (Czech koruna)	Until May 1997, pegged to basket of currencies (DM and US$) with margins of 7.5% Since May 1997, managed float (intervention occurs to reduce volatility) A forward market exists
Estonia (Estonian kroon)	Pegged to DM at EEK8 per DM A forward market exists
Hungary (Hungarian forint)	Preannounced crawl against a currency basket (70%Euro; 30%$). The rate of deprecia-tion was around 1% per month (and falling) in 1997 and 1998, 0.6% per month from January 1999; 0.4% from October 1999, from January 2000 a preannounced crawl against the Euro has been in operation A forward market exists
Poland (Polish zloty)	Pegged to basket of 5 currencies with the central rate adjusted according to a preannounced crawling peg. Margins of 7% held until 25.3.98; since then margins of 10% operate. From 1 January 1999 baskets changed to 55% Euro and 45% and since March the margin of 15% operates Forward cover is available through liquid swap market
Slovenia (Slovenian tolar)	Managed floating A forward market exists

161

Table 8.3 continued

Country	Exchange rate arrangements
Slow-track countries	
Bulgaria (Bulgarian lev)	From 1.7.97 a currency board has been in operation with the DM as the peg (lev1000 = DM1; from 1 January 1999 lev1955.83=1 Euro)
	There is no forward market
Latvia (Latvian lats)	Pegged to SDR at a fixed rate since February 1994
	A forward market exists
Lithuania (Lithuanian litas)	From April 1994, a currency board has been in operation with the dollar as the peg
	A forward market exists
Malta (Maltese lira)	Pegged to a weighted basket of currencies (sterling, dollar and ECU (euro)) with margins of 0.25%
	The forward market is operated by the central bank
Romania (Romanian leu)	Managed floating: the dollar is the reference exchange rate. Since August 1997, the central bank has intervened to depreciate the leu
	A forward market exists
Slovak Republic (Slovak koruna)	Managed floating
	There is no forward market

Table 8.4 Capital controls of prospective EU members

Type of capital control	Fast-track countries						Slow-track countries					
	Cyprus	Czech Republic	Estonia	Hungary	Poland	Slovenia	Bulgaria	Latvia	Lithuania	Malta	Romania	Slovak Republic
On invisible transactions	yes	no	no	no	yes	no	yes	no	no	yes	yes	yes
On proceeds from exports and/or invisible transactions	yes	yes	no	yes	yes	yes	yes	no	no	yes	yes	yes
Capital market securities	yes	yes	no	yes	yes	yes	yes	no	no	yes	yes	yes
Money market instruments	yes	yes	no	yes	yes	yes	yes	no	no	yes	yes	yes
Collective investment securities	yes	yes	no	yes	yes	yes	yes	no	no	yes	yes	yes
Derivatives and other instruments	yes	yes	no	yes	yes	yes	yes	no	no	no	yes	yes
Commercial credits	yes	no	no	yes	yes	yes	yes	no	no	no	yes	no
Financial credits	yes	yes	no	yes	yes	yes	yes	no	no	yes	yes	yes
Guarantees, sureties and backup facilities	yes	yes	no	yes	yes	no	yes	no	no	no	na	yes
Direct investment	no	no	no	yes	yes	yes	yes	yes	yes	yes	yes	yes
Liquidation of direct investment	yes	no	no	no	no	no	no	no	no	yes	no	no
Real estate transactions	yes	yes	yes	yes	yes	yes	yes	yes	yes	yes	yes	yes
Personal capital movements	yes	no	no	yes	yes	yes	yes	no	no	yes	yes	no
Provisions specific to commercial banks and other credit institutions	yes	yes	yes	yes	yes	yes	yes	yes	yes	yes	yes	yes
Provisions specific to institutional investors	yes	yes	no	yes	yes	yes	no	no	no	yes	na	yes

Source: International Monetary Fund, *Annual Report on Exchange Rate Restrictions*, Washington, DC: IMF, various issues.

163

Table 8.5 Macroeconomic indicators of prospective EU members

Indicators	Year	Fast-track countries						Slow-track countries					
		Cyprus	Czech Republic	Estonia	Hungary	Poland	Slovenia	Bulgaria	Latvia	Lithuania	Malta	Romania	Slovak Republic
CPI inflation	1995	2.6	9.1	28.80	28.3	26.8	12.60	62.00	25.00	39.70	4.00	32.20	9.90
	1996	3.0	8.8	23.10	23.5	20.1	9.70	123.00	17.60	24.60	2.60	38.80	5.80
	1997	3.6	8.4	10.60	18.3	15.9	9.10	1082.00	8.50	8.80	3.10	154.80	6.10
	1998	2.2	10.7	4.10	14.4	11.7	8.60	22.60	4.60	2.70[b]	1.90[c]	59.10	8.30
Budget deficit (% GDP)	1995	-1.0	0.5	0.04	-6.4	-2.0	-0.29	-5.25	na	-4.8	-3.25	-2.96	na
	1996	na	-0.1	-0.71	-3.1	-2.2	0.06	-15.41	-1.56	-3.60	-9.47	-4.04	na
	1997	na	-1.0	2.39	na	-1.4	-1.49	2.07	0.73	-1.90	na	na	na
Interest rates[a]	1995	6.5	9.5	4.94	28.0	25.8	14.62	53.09	22.39	26.73	5.50	41.30	9.75
	1996	7.5	10.5	3.53	23.0	20.6	11.42	119.88	13.08	20.26	5.50	35.10	8.80
	1997	7.0	13.0	6.45	20.5	22.4	13.78	66.43	3.76	9.55	5.50	45.00	8.80
	1998	7.0	7.5	11.66	19[d]	17.2[e]	8.55	2.35[e]	4.42	6.12	5.50[e]	37.90	8.80[d]
Foreign exchange reserves (excl. gold, US$m.)	1995	1,117	13,843	580	11,974	14,774	1,821	1,236	506	757	1,604	1,579	3,364
	1996	1,542	12,352	637	9,720	17,844	2,297	484	654	772	1,620	2,103	3,419
	1997	1,392	9,734	758	8,408	20,407	3,315	2,249	704	1,010	1,416[f]	3,803	3,230
	1998	1,459[e]	12,354[e]	811	8,704[e]	26,432	3,639	2,831	728	1,409	na	2,865	2,869

Notes:
a. Money market rate for Bulgaria, Estonia, Latvia, Lithuania, Poland; discount rate for Cyprus, Czech Republic, Hungary, Malta, Slovak Republic; bank rate for Romania; central bank rate for Slovenia.
b. In 12 months to November 1998.
c. In 12 months to October 1998.
d. At end of second quarter 1998.
e. At end November 1998.
f. At end of second quarter 1997.

Source: International Monetary Fund, *International Financial Statistics*, Washington, DC: IMF, various.

ciation. The exceptions are the Czech Republic (which abandoned its peg in May 1997 following a heavy speculative attack) and Slovenia. The DM or ECU/euro figure in all the pegging arrangements. A similar story can be told for the slow-track countries, although it should be noted that Bulgaria and Lithuania both operate a currency board.[7]

Table 8.4 provides an in-depth account of the extent to which these countries still retain capital controls. Of course, joining the monetary union will require a removal of capital controls in these countries at some time in the future. None the less, as we argue later in the chapter, their presence could be important to the stability of ERM-II in the transition. Table 8.4 indicates that capital controls are still widespread among the prospective members. The exception is the Baltic states which seem to be successfully pegging their currencies with almost free capital movements.

Finally, Table 8.5 presents selected macroeconomic indicators for the prospective EU members. With the exception of Cyprus and Malta, who actually met the Maastricht criteria on inflation and interest rates in 1998, the other countries, on the whole, fail to meet the criteria and/or exhibit considerable instability in these key aggregates. It is quite clear that currency pegs have been used in a number of cases to disinflate. Bulgaria perhaps offers the clearest example of this: inflation averaged over 1000 per cent in 1997 and a currency board was formed in July of that year; by 1998 inflation had fallen to 22 per cent on average. The situation with respect to budget deficits is good for those countries for which statistics exist in 1997. The picture is complicated by the fact that budget deficit data is only available with a considerable lag in some countries. If the fast- and slow-track countries do have something which distinguishes them on economic grounds, it is that the former have had better inflation experience than the latter. Additionally, budget deficits have been lower among fast-track countries. This suggests that the fast-track economies are generally more stable and this perhaps provides an economic rationale for an earlier entry into the EU and hence possibly ERM-II.

3 THE RELATIONSHIP BETWEEN THE 'OUTS' AND THE 'INS': ERM-II AND THE NEED FOR EXCHANGE RATE COORDINATION

In designing a new exchange rate system to accommodate both current and potential 'outs', it is important to bear in mind the fact that, as we have seen, the system may have to accommodate countries with very different economic conditions. This suggests the need for a flexible system. The basic framework for the setting up of ERM-II from 1 January 1999 was agreed at the Dublin

Summit in December 1996. The underlying rationale for the design of the system was twofold. First, there was a need for some framework to structure the relationship of the 'outs' to the 'ins' and to set out the broad outline of how the 'outs' will become 'ins'.[8] On the other hand, there was also a strong desire on the part of those countries who believed they would be 'in' to make sure that the new European Central Bank (ECB) keeps to its mandate of price stability. Since it was argued that in the first few years the ECB will lack a reputation (credibility needs to be earned), the negotiations surrounding the construction of the new system concentrated on ensuring institutional safeguards which protect the ECB from having to commit itself to intervention or policy coordination of a type which may lead it to abandon or compromise price stability. In this section, we provide a critical assessment of the ERM-II framework. This will entail seeing what we can learn from the experience of the old ERM for the effectiveness of ERM-II. Additionally, it will also entail examining the extent to which the desire for coordination between the 'ins' and 'outs' may create tension with the goal of price stability (among other goals, perhaps) of the 'ins'.

A prior question which needs to be addressed before looking at the principles of the new system is why a new ERM-II was needed in the first place. Indeed, some countries tried to argue that membership of ERM-II will not be a necessary condition for eventual membership of the eurozone (the UK and Sweden fall into this category[9]). The first point which can be made is that there is a legal obligation contained in the Maastricht Treaty (para. 109m) that the exchange rate of member states is a matter of common interest and that some form of coordination of exchange rate policies is useful. Furthermore, under the principle of equal treatment of all EU members, it could be argued that some form of exchange rate criterion will have to apply to those 'outs' seeking entry into EMU.

There are also a number of economic arguments which support coordination.[10] First, it can be noted that there are spillover effects from the exchange rate policy in one country on other EU countries. The incentive for any one EU country to allow depreciation of its currency to relieve some of the disinflationary pressures of convergence may be great even if this has a cost in the future in terms of higher inflation and hence some divergence. The experience of Italy and the UK on leaving the old ERM in 1992 provides an example. It appears that substantial depreciation of both currencies helped these countries to move out of recession and these benefits were achieved without great cost in terms of higher future inflation (Dornbusch 1996). However, such a strategy clearly has costs for other EU countries and, perhaps, more generally for the single market. For if a lack of coordination leads to competitive devaluations, then this could be destabilizing not only for exchange rate coordination but also for the whole project of integration between EU members.

A second possible rationale for exchange rate coordination stems from the role this can play in helping to promote disinflation through a refusal by the monetary authorities to offset wage increases through depreciation (Giavazzi and Pagano 1988). Of course, this relies on the system operating asymmetrically. The result is a real appreciation of the currency that helps to reduce inflation by dampening demand and altering expectations in labour markets.[11] Moreover, such an exchange rate policy may be useful in preparing countries for the subsequent formation of a monetary union since it allows them time to get used to not relying on the exchange rate as a means of adjustment and maintaining or improving competitiveness.

Third, exchange rate coordination can help to promote policy cooperation between the 'outs' and the 'ins'. The lessons of the experience of exchange rate coordination in general and the period of the early 1990s in the ERM in particular are clear in this respect (De Grauwe 1994). Exchange rate coordination can only be successful over an extended period if there is agreement between the parties concerned over the general course of macroeconomic policy. If exchange rate coordination can help to improve the degree of policy cooperation, then this is again an advantage in the run-up to monetary union.[12]

Indeed, an exchange rate arrangement between the 'ins' and 'outs' could help to act as an important signal to financial markets that the 'outs' are not being left behind. However, we shall argue below that it will only be a useful signal if the 'ins' are seen as being as committed to the admission of the 'outs' as the 'outs' are themselves. If the 'outs' are left to get on with convergence without help from the 'ins' then an exchange rate arrangement could actually be destabilizing since it might suffer from periods characterized by a lack of credibility.

We can identify five basic features of ERM-II as agreed following extended negotiations among the EU15 countries.[13]

'Hub and Spokes' System

The new ERM will operate with the eurozone at its centre (the 'hub') and each 'out' will tie its exchange rate to the euro bilaterally. In this sense ERM-II differs from the old ERM. The latter was a bilateral grid system where each country tied its exchange rate to the ECU which was a weighted average of all EU currencies and this tied individual currencies to one another with the fluctuation bands being around the bilateral rates). Thus, in principle, there was no centre country.

This hub and spokes set-up has two consequences. The first is that the new system will be highly asymmetric. One rationale for this is that ultimately it is the 'outs' which have to ready themselves for joining the 'ins' – they are the ones who have to converge – and asymmetry in the exchange rate system will help this process. A second and just as important rationale is the need to build and preserve ECB credibility by allowing it the independence to pursue whatever monetary policy is required in order to carry out its mandate of ensuring price stability. It cannot therefore commit itself to a system which may compromise that ability (Dornbusch et al. 1998). A possible criticism of such a framework is that the duty of the 'outs' to converge appears to receive very little help from the 'ins', in spite of the fact that the latter is a large bloc which would find it much easier to sterilize than Germany did when it was the leading country in the old ERM.[14]

A second consequence of the hub and spokes system is that the bilateral exchange rates between 'outs' could fluctuate up to twice as much as against the euro. With fluctuation bands of 15 per cent around the euro rate, the rate between two 'out' currencies could fluctuate by as much as 60 per cent if one currency moved to the top of its euro band while the other moved to the bottom. This consideration leads us to the issues surrounding the second principle.

Wide Fluctuation Margins

The desire for flexibility in order to accommodate countries at very different stages of convergence led to the adoption of wide fluctuation margins. It should be noted that the 15 per cent fluctuation bands are not designed to preclude closer bilateral cooperation between individual 'outs' and the eurozone should convergence have reached levels that warrant it. The actual details of any such arrangement are to be negotiated separately by the country concerned.[15]

These wide fluctuation bands might be considered an advantage since they allow for greater flexibility between the 'outs' themselves and hence may prevent problems of one 'out' from affecting the ability of the other 'outs' to converge. Indeed there was general agreement among EU countries that ERM-II should provide for flexibility in dealing with countries at different levels of convergence. This seems particularly important for the prospective new members of the EU which, as we have seen, exhibit widely differing degrees of convergence. In this way, the design of ERM-II follows more the 'economists' approach which, as we argued in the introduction, places more emphasis on the need to get economic and economic policy integration before moving to monetary union.

However, the argument against large fluctuation margins is that, if exchange rate stability is valued because of its contribution to the single market and economic integration within the EU generally, then the system does not help to promote this. This is particularly true of the bilateral rates between the 'outs'. If the stability of exchange rates between the 'outs' is necessary for the operation of the single market, then this argument supports a multilateral system (like the old ERM) where there is an explicit commitment to maintain exchange rate stability between the 'outs' themselves.

Realignments

Realignments will be allowed and indeed decisions on realignments should be taken quickly to avoid severe misalignments of exchange rates. Of course, it should be remembered that those who are close to joining EMU should not have realigned for two years (as is currently specified in the Maastricht Treaty). Realignments in ERM-II are to be decided jointly by the ECB and other central banks in the system. The ECB has the right to initiate realignment discussions if it feels that exchange rates are getting out of line. The latter is again designed to 'protect' the ECB from potentially undesirable threats to its independence in carrying out monetary policy.

Of course, realignments help with flexibility – and it may also be useful in this respect if new EU members whose economic conditions are quite far away from the eurozone have the opportunity of maintaining capital controls in the first instance. As we saw above, most of these countries do still maintain extensive systems of capital controls and hence the timetable for their removal would need to be carefully negotiated. New EU members should be allowed a period of experience with exchange rate targeting similar to that which was afforded to the early members of the old ERM since it is widely recognized that the early ERM owed its success to the existence of capital controls and frequent realignments (Gibson and Tsakalotos 1991). We develop this point more thoroughly in the next section.

Intervention Rules and Credit Facilities

Credit (in the form of the very short-term financing facility) is available as in the old ERM in order to help with intervention. Intervention is compulsory and automatic at the margins and both the ECB and the national central bank are required to intervene. However, there is a 'get-out' clause for the ECB: it has the right to suspend intervention unilaterally if it feels that intervention is interfering with the pursuit of price stability. This is designed to enhance the credibility of the ECB and of the system (by ensuring that it will promote convergence).

This desire to create a system which protects the independence and autonomy of the ECB may also lead to further asymmetries becoming evident as experience with operating ERM-II is gradually built up. The ECB is likely to be able to sterilize all intervention since the eurozone will be fairly big and hence the amount of intervention required is likely (at normal times) to be fairly small. By contrast, the national central banks of the 'outs' may not sterilize (either because they want to promote convergence automatically or because they do not have the foreign exchange reserves to allow them to buy up their currency continuously). Thus all the burden of adjustment may fall on the 'out' countries.

Furthermore, eligibility for continued support by the ECB may depend on the implementation of a convergence programme that the ECB judges adequate and that includes an assessment of fiscal and debt developments along with price developments. Finally, intervention could be limited (or ultimately, suspended) if the ECB judges the currency to be misaligned. Indeed, this was the reason why the ECB was keen to have the right to initiate discussions about realignments. It does not want to find itself in the position of supporting a country whose exchange rate is severely overvalued.

Conditions of these kinds attached to intervention imply only a limited responsibility on behalf of the ECB to promoting exchange rate stability with the EU as a whole (and hence only a limited role for the ECB in helping the 'outs' to become 'ins'). Moreover, unlike the old ERM, ERM-II is clearly asymmetric – there are no divergence indicators which at least sought to provide the old ERM with some symmetry even if in practice they played little part.[16] The intervention rules in ERM-II are also likely to make it more difficult for the 'outs' to maintain exchange rate stability. Evidence from intervention by the Group of Seven in the 1980s suggests that coordinated intervention is much more likely to be successful than uncoordinated intervention, since agreement between the two central banks involved can help to alter expectations in financial markets. A commitment to coordinated intervention may be important for countries which are close to convergence but whose progress is undermined by foreign exchange markets responding to political rumours in the run-up to decisions about whether certain 'outs' will be allowed to become 'ins'. If the ECB has the ability to withdraw support whenever it wishes, then this may actually help to magnify disturbances rather than dampening them.

Policy Coordination

Policy coordination is seen to be a significant part of ERM-II. However, it is important to clarify exactly what this means. As we have already seen, the agreement places most of the burden of adjustment on the 'outs'. Moreover, it is expected that intervention to support exchange rates will be supported by policy changes by the 'out' country.

Before the start of monetary union, coordination took the form of an *ex ante* exercise where economic and financial indicators were gathered for all countries (including forecasts), monetary policy intentions were submitted and an examination of the monetary policies of each member state's policies was then conducted. After monetary union, this exercise is evolving into one where information is gathered on each 'out' country and its monetary policy and the consistency of the proposed policies will be assessed in relation to the policy to be pursued by the ECB. This appears to rule out any macroeconomic policy cooperation between the 'ins' and the 'outs' of the type 'I'll change my policy a bit if you do too'.

However, it could be argued that such cooperation might be beneficial for two reasons. First, as was recognized at the time of the Basle–Nyborg agreement of 1986, at times of speculative pressure on exchange rates, reinforcing changes in short-term interest rates by *both* countries can help to relieve pressure. The experience in the ERM in the early 1990s seems to support this: changes in interest rates by only one country (the one whose currency was depreciating) were not enough to reassure the markets and the reluctance of the appreciating currency to alter its interest rates was taken as a sign of lack of commitment to the system (Buiter et al. 1998).

The second reason why macroeconomic cooperation is justified is that it is necessary for 'out' countries to gain experience with cooperation with the eurozone members to aid policy formulation once they join EMU. The old ERM showed itself to be highly vulnerable not only to a lack of cooperation over interest rate changes but also to disagreements over the objectives of policy in general. The ultimate success of EMU between EU countries will depend crucially on their ability to develop mechanisms that can help to mediate policy differences between them. There seems no reason why such mechanisms cannot be developed before individual 'outs' join the monetary union. Yet the new exchange rate arrangement excludes the 'outs' from having any say in the policy of the monetary union because of fears that the 'outs' may water down the commitment to price stability.

4   THE 'OUTS' OF EMU: BETWEEN THE SCYLLA OF EXCESS CREDIBILITY AND THE CHARYBDIS OF SPECULATIVE CRISIS

In the light of some of the problems outlined with the institutional framework of ERM-II, we now turn to examine why the 'outs' may have a bumpy ride on the route to becoming 'ins'. In many ways the problems they may face are not new to EU member states. Spain and Portugal as well as the recent experience of Greece suggest that the 'outs' may face alternating problems of excess credibility and speculative crisis. By examining Greek experience in the 1990s, we hope here to shed some fight on the problems for future 'outs' which may result from widening of the EU to include the countries of Table 8.1. The convergence of countries such as Spain, Portugal and Greece was a very different process from the convergence experience of countries such as Italy and France. The former group of countries probably have more to teach us about convergence of possible new EU members. We argue that, like the experience of Greece in the 1990s, the 'outs', instead of their economies being characterized by relatively stable conditions as convergence proceeds smoothly, are more likely to face a situation of large changes in the markets' perception of their economies. The consequence may be alternating periods of excess credibility (which can undermine monetary policy) and a lack of credibility (with associated speculative attacks).

Greece only became a member of the ERM in March 1998. However, its disinflation strategy prior to that involved the pursuit of an exchange rate target, the aim being to allow the exchange rate to depreciate in each year by less than the inflation differential (between Greece and the EU). This strategy was known as the 'hard drachma' policy. Figure 8.3 illustrates the operation of this policy between 1993 and 1998. We plot the annual rate of depreciation

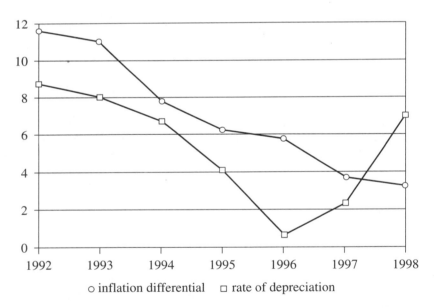

o inflation differential   □ rate of depreciation

Note: The figure for 1998 for the rate of change of the exchange rate includes the devaluation on entry into the ERM (see main text).

Figure 8.3   Drachma/ECU depreciation and differential inflation between Greece and the EU

Table 8.6   Consumer price inflation in Greece (December to December)

Year	1991	1992	1993	1994	1995	1996	1997	1998
CPI inflation	18.0	14.4	12.1	10.6	7.9	7.3	4.7	3.9

Source: National Statistical Service of Greece.

of the drachma against the ECU as well as the differential inflation (defined as Greek inflation minus average EU inflation). As can be seen from the figure, the rate of depreciation in each year was less than differential inflation with the result that there was a real appreciation of the drachma. This real appreciation continued until entry into the ERM which was associated with a corrective devaluation of 12 per cent against the ECU in 1998. The consequence of this policy for inflation is shown in Table 8.6: inflation has been falling steadily.

The policy was not, however, without difficulties. Between 1994 and 1996, the main problem encountered was one of large capital inflows which might be considered a problem of 'excess credibility' (similar to the problems encountered by Spain in the late 1980s). This was followed in late 1997 and into 1998 by problems of speculative pressure on the drachma and capital outflows (especially following the general turbulence in the world economy associated with the Asian crisis). The period of speculative pressure ended with entry into the ERM. Subsequently, the Greek experience in general has returned to one of excess credibility and the monetary authorities have allowed the drachma to appreciate in the ERM to try to moderate capital inflows.

The Scylla of Excess Credibility

The problem of excess credibility arises when the exchange rate target is highly credible, while, at the same time, the monetary authorities continue their tight monetary policy. It can be compounded further if the government has a relatively loose fiscal policy. This is exactly the situation which applied in Greece between 1994 and 1997.[17] Domestic interest rates were higher than foreign ones – and, more importantly, the domestic interest rate was greater than the foreign plus the expected depreciation of the drachma *vis-à-vis* foreign currencies. This encouraged large capital inflows.

Figure 8.4 shows the *ex post* interest rate differential between Greece and Germany. That is, we plot the Greek interest rate minus the foreign interest rate along with the actual depreciation of the drachma *vis-à-vis* the foreign currency. This clearly shows the incentive that Greek residents had to

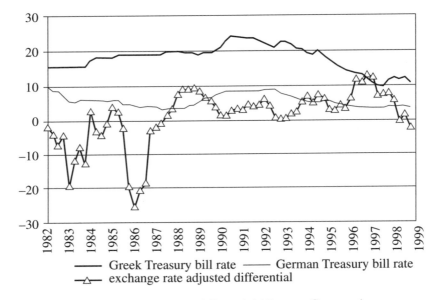

Figure 8.4   Ex post *interest rate differential (Greece–Germany)*

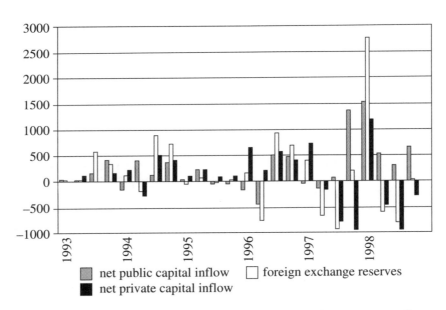

Figure 8.5   *Net capital flows and change in foreign exchange reserves (in drachmas)*

borrow funds from abroad, and following the removal of capital controls in May 1994 they did just that as Figure 8.5 shows. If we look at net capital inflows from the private sector, we can see they were sometimes quite large.

Capital inflows, however, have consequences for the domestic money market. The Bank of Greece, in order to keep its exchange rate target and prevent appreciation, had to intervene in the foreign exchange market and sell drachmas (buy up foreign exchange). This caused foreign exchange reserves to increase (shown also in Figure 8.5) and, in some periods, the increase was substantial. As a result, the monetary base increased and there was a resulting excess supply of liquidity in the interbank market at prevailing interest rates. This undermined the attempt to reduce inflation.

A number of policy solutions are available to central banks facing such conditions. However, they are not without their costs. We look at each of them in turn. First, the most common response to capital inflows is sterilization and the Bank of Greece did exactly this, that is, it absorbed the excess liquidity caused by the increase in the foreign component of the monetary base. This leads to a reduction in the domestic component of the monetary base. The central bank can do this either by selling government bonds or, more commonly since the abolition of monetary financing of government deficits by central banks in Europe, by offering to take in deposits at higher interest rates than those prevailing in the interbank market (these deposits are usually automatically reversed after some period unless they are renewed – that is, they take the form of repos). In this way, excess liquidity was removed from the interbank market, preventing interest rates in the economy from falling and the monetary stance loosening.

In Figure 8.6, we show movements in the domestic and foreign components of the monetary base in Greece. It is clear that they are the mirror image of each other – when the foreign component increases, the domestic component falls. (The correlation coefficient is –0.85 from 1993 to 1998 and is high even in various subperiods.)

However, sterilization is not without its problems. It costs the Bank of Greece. Although the increased foreign exchange reserves provide the bank with increased interest receipts, interest is paid out on the Bank of Greece deposits taken in. Since foreign interest rates are below domestic ones, the net cost is positive.

A second policy response is an increase in reserve requirements which allows the monetary base to increase when foreign exchange reserves increase, but reduces the money multiplier and hence prevents the increase in the base from reaching the broader monetary aggregates. The Bank of Greece has also used this policy: it raised reserve requirements between August and October 1995 and again in May 1996; it also broadened their coverage in

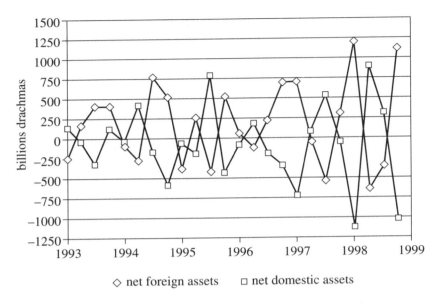

Figure 8.6   Domestic and foreign components of the monetary base
(quarter-to-quarter changes)

May 1996 to include liabilities to non-residents. This reduced the amount of intervention that was needed in the domestic money market.

The cost of this policy is partially borne by the banking system (and ultimately its customers) since reserve requirements, if they are not renumerated at a market rate, act as a tax on the banking system. This reduces the competitiveness of banks. In the context of the single financial area, this can be problematic because national banks now face competition from banks in other EU countries where reserve requirements are much lower. The Bank of Greece also bears some of the cost since reserves are remunerated to some extent.

A third policy response is the imposition of capital controls. Countries usually resort to this policy if capital inflows continue for some time – since sterilization is costly and can get more difficult. A common type of capital control is a requirement that a certain proportion of foreign inflows caused by domestic residents borrowing abroad are deposited with the central bank. This discourages capital inflows since it acts as a tax on them. Such a policy has the advantage that it is flexible because the required proportion can be changed quickly to respond to changing conditions. It also penalizes short-term foreign borrowing more severely. This can be particularly useful if the central bank is worried about the speculative nature of the capital flows.

Spain resorted to this policy in the late 1980s. The problem for Greece, however, was that this was not really an option in the mid- to late 1990s. Capital controls had already been removed and, although it is possible under the Maastricht Treaty to introduce them under exceptional circumstances (Articles 73f, 109i), to have done so may have been seen as a retrogressive step in the country's attempt to join monetary union. For the prospective members of the EU and ERM-II, the lessons are clear. It is much better that external financial liberalization be accomplished once macroeconomic conditions have stabilized and hence interest rates are closer to those in the eurozone.[18]

Fourth, the exchange rate target can be modified. If the Bank of Greece had allowed the exchange rate to float, then inflows would have resulted in an appreciation with no impact on the monetary base. However, appreciation is not a response which is possible when the aim is monetary union and a country is trying to keep its exchange rate fixed to meet the Maastricht criteria. Moreover, it could worsen the current account, which may already be showing signs of a deterioration because of the real appreciation associated with disinflation via an exchange rate target.

One way in which the exchange rate can be modified without the abandonment of the target is to allow greater volatility around the target. The advantage of this is that it introduces uncertainty, thereby increasing the risk that short-term foreign borrowing is not profitable. The disadvantage is that if the greater volatility induces uncertainty in the foreign exchange markets, it could make the target more difficult to achieve. Greece did try to indicate that greater volatility would be allowed in its exchange rate target and, of course, once it had joined the ERM it has actively used this policy by allowing the drachma to appreciate relative to its central rate. This implies both that some of the inflows simply lead to appreciation and not to excess liquidity (the Bank of Greece is not intervening to sell drachmas) and it creates expectations of a depreciation back to the central rate in the future.

Finally, if the policy mix has some part to play in the capital inflows, then improving it can help. Once again, this points to the need for macroeconomic stabilization (reduction of the budget deficit) before liberalization occurs. Otherwise, the relatively tight monetary policy combined with the fiscal deficit will continue to keep interest rates above those in the rest of the eurozone. Of course, credible fiscal consolidation requires time especially when it is often the case that the problem is related as much, if not more, to difficulties with revenue collection as it is to too high spending. It is for this reason that delaying external liberalization is a policy which may recommend itself.

The Charybdis of Speculative Crisis

Periods of excess credibility usually change, often rather quickly, to periods
where credibility is lacking and the exchange rate comes under severe pressure. In general, three possible causes are identified in the literature. We
begin here by reviewing some of the literature on these causes before return-
ing to the case of Greece once again.

The first argument is that speculative crises may arise from diverging
fundamentals. The classic reason originates from the fact that one problem of
using the exchange rate to disinflate is that it requires a period when exchange rate changes do not offset prices differentials between the country and
its trading partners. Hence the country becomes increasingly uncompetitive
and this can lead to expectations of a realignment if uncompetitiveness is
thought to be causing major problems for the tradables sector (Dornbusch
1982).

Assume we have two countries that are in a fixed exchange rate system
(Flood and Garber 1984). Country A, say, has a higher inflation rate than
country B: it is increasing the domestic component of its money supply faster
than country B. The higher inflation country will slowly lose competitiveness: its prices are rising faster than those of country B yet the nominal
exchange rate is fixed. As country A loses competitiveness, so its balance of
payments will move into an ever-increasing deficit and it has to increasingly
intervene in the foreign exchange markets, buying up its currency to prevent
depreciation. Hence the foreign component of the money supply (its foreign
exchange reserves) will be falling. In the foreign exchange markets, traders
attempt to anticipate the reaction of the authorities to this situation, asking
themselves whether or not the authorities will allow the situation to continue.
Doing nothing will lead to an exhaustion of foreign exchange reserves and
exit from the system.

However, because foreign exchange markets are forward looking in this
model, participants try to anticipate the authority's reactions and likely course
of action because anticipating correctly can lead to large profitable opportunities for speculators. Thus, if the foreign exchange markets see that the
course of action is unsustainable, then, if they are rational, they will anticipate a realignment or the abandonment of the fixed exchange rate regime.
Hence they will begin to sell assets denominated in country A's currency now
(rather than later) and this causes a large fall in foreign exchange reserves and
the fixed exchange rate system breaks down as country A is unable to defend
its parity in the face of the huge speculative attack. After the speculative
attack, the currency floats and the domestic money supply grows at the same
rate as the domestic component (since foreign exchange reserves are unchanged).

These models point to the dangers for the 'outs' either of trying to avoid convergence (an unlikely scenario in that EMU membership is desired) or of trying to converge at a reasonably slow pace (more likely). Slower convergence can offer advantages in that it allows market expectations to adjust to the new regime and it is certainly the option which has been followed by most EU countries. However, it can have the side-effect that it introduces uncertainty into the minds of market participants and hence small deviations from the convergence targets set could trigger a speculative crisis.

A second reason why inflows may turn to outflows is because of perceived policy differences. In the case of ERM-II the 'outs' could become susceptible to perceived (real or otherwise) policy differences between themselves and the centre. One of the lessons of the 1992–93 crises in the ERM was that if the exchange rate commitment implies that one country has to follow a policy which is unsuited to its economic conditions at the time, then this can call into question the credibility of the exchange rate targets/central rates. Ozkan and Sutherland (1995) develop a model where the costs to the monetary authorities of continuing to peg the exchange rate depend on the deviations of output from trend. If output is below trend and unemployment rising, then the costs of maintaining the peg may exceed the benefits and the authorities may decide to abandon it. Market participants realizing this are, of course, likely to put the peg under pressure, expecting a devaluation or abandonment of the peg.

Such a model, it could be argued, fits the experience of the old ERM in the early 1990s quite well. Countries like France began to feel that they had disinflated enough and that it was now time for the EU to think about growth and the reduction of unemployment. But this was in conflict with the German desire to curb inflationary pressure after unification. De Grauwe (1994) tries to test this hypothesis. He measures credibility by looking at long- and short-term interest rate differentials. He argues that if interest rate differentials are small, then expectations of a change in the exchange rate are also small and the ERM is more credible. Regressions suggest that there is a positive relationship between the size of the differential and the level of unemployment:

$$\text{ST diff} = -8.0 + 1.0 U_t + 1.1 P_t$$
$$(-1.8) \quad (2.5) \quad (3.3)$$

$$\text{LT diff} = -6.9 + 0.7 U_t + 1.6 P_t$$
$$(-6.4) \quad (7.0) \quad (17.8)$$

where ST diff (LT diff) is the average interest differential of each ERM country with Germany; U_t is unemployment rate in the ERM in year t; P_t is the standard deviation of inflation rates within the ERM in each year t. While these equations are rather simple and hence open to criticisms of bias because of missing variables, they do suggest that the ERM became much weaker (less credible) when unemployment increased or when inflation differentials increased. This leads De Grauwe to conclude that recessions weaken the credibility of the ERM: it is not difficult to then argue that the crisis in 1992 arose from weakened credibility due to recession, which led to policy disagreements.

Eichengreen (1993, pp. 1350–52) places more weight on the cumulative effect of policy disagreements. He argues that even though inflation differences were much more moderate by the late 1980s compared to the early 1980s, the cumulated effect of these differences on competitiveness was still large. He points to evidence which suggests that Italy and probably also the UK, Spain and Portugal all had competitiveness problems in 1992 just before the crisis.

Both De Grauwe and Eichengreen (and their arguments are not necessarily incompatible) point to the fact that policy divergences weaken exchange rate systems. This again has implications for ERM-II. In a system which is asymmetric and where the ability of the 'outs' to influence policy decisions taken by the ECB is strictly limited, the potential for future policy disagreements is probably quite large. In other words, with the entire burden of responsibility on the 'outs' in ERM-II, policy disagreements may become more acute and these will be manifested in pressure on the exchange rates of the 'outs' *vis-à-vis* the eurozone. Thus the lack of policy cooperation which we noted in the previous section was a feature of ERM-II may make for a bumpy ride for the 'outs'.

A final cause of exchange rate pressure that has been identified results from self-fulfilling attacks and contagion effects (Obstfeld 1996). In this case, the fundamentals do not suggest that the economy is doing badly with the targeting policy. Often it has been the case that disturbances in international markets spread over into selected countries. On the other hand, the 1992 crisis in the old ERM began with problems specific to Sweden which caused financial markets to question the sustainability of other central rates which had not previously been in doubt. We cannot exclude the possibility that in the future disturbances in one 'out' may spread to other 'outs' in the system.

The recent experience of Greece provides another example. The re-emergence of speculative attacks in SE Asia in late October 1997 (along with their intensification) led to large falls in Asian stock markets with the consequence that financial institutions around the world lost a lot of money in emerging markets. Greece, which is also classified as an emerging market, faced significant capital outflows (Figure 8.5, above). Financial institutions tend to lump together all countries classified as emerging markets and are concerned with their overall exposure to those countries. They do not look at countries on an individual basis. Thus even emerging markets with improving fundamentals can be affected by a generalized withdrawal from emerging markets. This is indeed what happened in Greece. Financial institutions sold their holdings of Greek government bonds (causing problems with government financing) and repatriated the funds. The latter put downward pressure on the drachma and the Bank of Greece was required to intervene.

These external pressures (external in the sense that they were not based in the performance of the Greek economy) caused speculators to question the exchange rate target and also the level of the real exchange rate and whether it was overvalued or not. As a consequence, further speculative bouts followed and there was a real danger of a self-fulfilling speculative attack. The outflows ceased only when the drachma entered the ERM in March 1998.

The problem is that these developments impose a cost on the 'out' country. The initial response to such disturbances is usually a rise in interest rates. Indeed, the Bank of Greece placed a penalty rate on the cost of banks borrowing from it (set initially at 0.4 per cent per day – this meant an annual rate of 170 per cent – the rate applied to *increases* in the overdrafts which commercial banks had with the bank). This discouraged commercial banks from borrowing large amounts of funds from the central bank, converting them to foreign currencies and waiting for the devaluation to occur when the money would be repatriated at a handsome profit. But rises in interest rates in the interbank market often spread to loan rates (on consumer credit, housing loans and so on) thus hitting the real economy. They can also have implications for the financing of the government deficit. Thus a further policy which could be useful is the maintenance of capital controls. These could help to allow necessary realignments to take place more smoothly as the experience of France and Italy in the early 1980s demonstrates (Gibson and Tsakalotos 1991). But additionally, they could help to prevent speculative attack (Wyplosz 1986) and especially those unjustified by fundamentals.

De Grauwe (1997a) argues that there are two opposing forces in ERM-II which influence the likelihood of self-fulfilling attacks. On the one hand, the wide bands reduce the probability of a speculative attack and allow realignments to occur without a jump in the exchange rate since it is highly probable that the new bands will overlap with the old. On the other hand, entry into monetary union may be strongly influenced by investor expectations. If they believe entry is likely, then interest rates will fall and this will help reduce budget deficits and debt, make the exchange rate commitment more credible and hence increase the chances of the Maastricht criteria being met. By contrast, if entry is in doubt, interest rates will have to rise, deficits and the debt position will worsen and entry becomes less likely. A speculative attack could easily follow and any lack of commitment to intervene on the part of the ECB may simply validate the attack. This, in turn, would obviously seriously impede a country's attempt to change its status from that of an 'out' to an 'in'.

5   CONCLUDING REMARKS

In many ways, the 'outs' have an institutional framework which is quite conducive to their becoming 'ins'. EMU already exists and the rules of the game for joining are quite clear. The 'outs' can also draw on the experience of the ERM in the 1980s and the 1990s. However, we have argued that over and above their own economic difficulties – and for most new aspiring members these will be more acute than the problems of, say, France and Italy in the early 1980s – the framework of ERM-II is not unproblematic. On the one hand, given what we have learned from the old ERM and the diverging nature of the 'outs', it is surely right that the system is quite flexible. This, we have argued, will allow individual countries to be treated on an individual basis and also allow the 'outs' to get used to operating under the rules of the game. On the other hand, we have argued that a possible weakness of ERM-II is the lack of any real cooperation between the 'ins' and the 'outs' – here we have made much of the distinction between cooperation and coordination – and the fuzziness of the rules surrounding the intervention obligations of the ECB. The latter stems from a perhaps exaggerated concern for price stability in the eurozone. An optimistic reading of events is that, as the ECB and other EU policy-making institutions build on their experience and grow in confidence, their fear of EU instability may recede and their willingness to contribute to the success of EU 'outs' may correspondingly grow. However, if this is too sanguine a view, and given the fact that what many of the 'outs' will be trying to achieve constitutes a difficult objective – almost irrespective of the institutional framework – then it would perhaps be more advisable for the new 'outs' to plan ahead for what is likely to be, as we have argued, a bumpy ride.

NOTES

1. See De Grauwe (1994), Kenen (1996) and Buiter et al. (1998) for various accounts of the crises.
2. On the other hand, any reimposition of capital controls was only temporary.
3. The figures which follow are taken from the EMI's *Convergence Report* of 1998 which

formed the basis for the decision on which countries would be admitted to monetary union. The Treaty stated that actual outcomes from the previous year (that is, 1997) were to be used and not estimates for the current year when the decision was taken (that is, 1998).

4. If the debt/GDP ratio is above the reference value of 60 per cent then provided it is 'sufficiently diminishing and approaching the reference value at a satisfactory pace', then the country can be admitted to monetary union (EMI 1998, p. 35).

5. Finland and Italy had joined/rejoined the old ERM in October and November 1996, respectively. This meant that by the start of EMU, they would have had two years within the ERM with no realignment.

6. It could be argued that there was a case for including all countries who wanted to join EMU from the start. First, from the point of view of the EU as a whole, the creation of 'ins' and 'outs' could be highly divisive since the European Central Bank (ECB) will be deciding on its monetary policy with no regard for the 'outs'. Second, a number of authors have questioned the relevance of the criteria themselves. The literature on the costs and benefits of monetary union focuses more on structural factors than on macroeconomic performance in determining the suitability of countries for a monetary union, yet the Maastricht criteria were solely macroeconomic. Finally, the 'outs' themselves have an interest in being included in the monetary union from its initiation so they can have a say in formulating the way in which the ECB operates and in moulding the other institutions that develop within monetary union.

7. With a currency board system, the exchange rate is tied rigidly to a currency and foreign exchange reserves usually back the domestic money supply completely. Monetary policy is thus completely and automatically linked to the exchange rate peg.

8. In fact, there are still a number of questions regarding the assessment of the 'outs' now that monetary union has gone ahead among a number of countries. For example, on the inflation and interest rate criteria, the question arises as to whether the three best performers will be taken from all EU countries (both 'ins' and 'outs') or whether the eurozone will be counted as one. There is also some confusion on the exchange rate criterion and whether it is necessary or not.

9. The UK argues that what is important is that the exchange rate should have been stable for some time before entry into monetary union.

10. We should note here that exchange rate coordination does not necessarily imply what we might term 'cooperation' where the latter involves some give and take on the part of the countries involved and hence is more symmetric. In other words, by using the term 'exchange rate coordination', we do not mean to imply any symmetry in the mechanism.

11. Whether this helps to reduce the costs of disinflation is a matter of some debate. See, for example, Giavazzi and Giovannini (1989) and De Grauwe (1990).

12. On the importance of cooperation on the path to monetary union, see Currie and Whitley (1994) and Artis (1994).

13. On ERM-II, see also De Grauwe (1997b) and Lamfalussy (1996).

14. The fact that there is evidence that Germany did manage to sterilize (Brissimis et al. 1998) strengthens this point further.

15. This could be like the bilateral agreement between Germany and the Netherlands which operated when the old ERM had wide fluctuation bands. The agreement confined movements in the DM/guilder exchange rate to within 2.5 per cent on either side of the central rate. Conceivably, the agreement could have included some arrangement between the two countries concerning joint intervention to support the narrower bands. Since the agreement was never made public, it is not clear whether this was the case. Indeed, one question which such an agreement between an 'out' and the eurozone might face is how much of it to make public. This turns on the question of the extent to which markets should be kept well-informed of central bank intervention rules. On the one hand, uncertainty can cause market participants to overreact to small items of news; on the other, central banks may feel that secrecy can strengthen their hand in any confrontation with financial markets.

16. That is, ERM-II is asymmetric *by design*. On whether the old ERM was de facto asym-

metric, see Giavazzi and Giovannini (1987), Fratianni and von Hagen (1990a) and De Grauwe (1988).

17. This section draws on some of the work in Brissimis and Gibson (1997).
18. This conclusion is one which has also been drawn by the literature on sequencing (Gibson and Tsakalotos 1994) and it is one which has been strengthened following recent problems in Southeast Asian countries.

9. Exchange rate strategies of new EU entrants

Jens Hölscher and Lúcio Vinhas de Souza

1 INTRODUCTION

The Eastern enlargement of the European Union (EU) includes a large number of countries. Official accession processes have been opened with Bulgaria, Cyprus, the Czech Republic, Estonia, Hungary, Latvia, Lithuania, Malta, Poland, Romania, Slovakia and Slovenia,[1] through the mechanism of the Accession Partnerships.[2] Substantive negotiations for accession were opened on 10 November 1998, with Cyprus,[3] the Czech Republic, Estonia, Hungary, Poland and Slovenia, the so-called 'first wave' countries. These six first-wave entrants would add over 63 million inhabitants to the current Union's population (almost two-thirds of them in Poland alone) and over 240 billion euros to its GDP (again, over half of this figure in Poland). That will mean, respectively, a 17 per cent increase in the Union population, but a mere 3 per cent increase in its GDP. The so-called second-wave entrants (Bulgaria, Latvia, Lithuania, Malta, Romania and Slovakia) would add to these figures another 57 million people and 97 billion euros. That is a 15 per cent increase in the population of the Union, but an even more marginal increase of 1.2 per cent in its GDP.

In terms of the number of countries, this will be the biggest wave of expansion of the Union since 1957, surpassing the North Sea Accession of 1973 (the Kingdom of Denmark, the Republic of Ireland and the United Kingdom), the Mediterranean Accession of 1982 (the Greek Republic), the Iberian Accession of 1986 (the Kingdom of Spain and the Portuguese Republic) and the Nordic–Central European Accession of 1995 (the Republic of Austria, the Republic of Finland and the Kingdom of Sweden). In this negotiation process, there is one major institutional difference from the previous expansion waves: namely, that the new entrants cannot benefit from the use of 'opt-out' clauses, which were used by the United Kingdom and Denmark for EMU (European and Monetary Union), and also by the UK for the Social Chapter. Therefore, the *acquis communautaire* is expected to be, in time, *taken in full* by all future new entrants, including, of course, EMU participation and all the requisite 'criteria'. All future entrants are supposed to become members of euroland.

These circumstances require an adequate exchange rate strategy to be prepared for final EMU membership. The following section presents the EMU convergence criteria and the current status of the candidate countries concerning these benchmarks. The third section presents the economic rationale behind EMU and a fourth section presents the current linkage strategies of the candidate countries. The fifth section questions what an optimal strategy could be for the new entrants. The chapter ends with the proposal for an ERM-II type of strategy.

2   TRANSITION ECONOMIES AND THE MAASTRICHT CONVERGENCE CRITERIA

How the applicant countries would currently fare regarding the Maastricht criteria[4] can be seen in Table 9.1 (values in bold indicate that they surpass the reference values used as a benchmark).

Only interest rates are above the benchmark for most of the countries, reflecting high real interest rates for these countries, underdeveloped capital markets and the fact that inflationary expectations have not yet been subdued. It must also be noted that for the long-term interest rate, proxies were used with much shorter maturity than the ten-year bond rate used for evaluating the eurozone members.[5]

On the face of it, the fiscal situation for these countries, in general terms, is even better than the average fiscal situation for either the eurozone or the whole set of EU members, especially concerning the debt-stock-to-GDP ratio. Only Bulgaria, Cyprus, Estonia, Hungary, Lithuania, Malta and Romania breach either of the two fiscal subcriteria, and only Hungary breaches both.

As a result of the surprisingly fast deflationary process of the past few years, caused in part by the introduction of tighter monetary policies, the inflation criterion is now also respected by most of the countries. The deceleration of inflation was also assisted by the emerging markets crisis which started in 1997 and reached Eastern Europe in 1998. World market prices were tempered, while an economic contraction added to the deceleration of domestic inflation. These criteria are interrelated and cannot be regarded as independent from one another. For instance, the nominal rate of interest depends on the real rate of interested plus the expected inflation rate.

Concerning the exchange rate stability criterion, none of these countries, of course, is an ERM member, but the currency board countries (Bulgaria,

Estonia and Lithuania), plus Cyprus, the Czech Republic, Slovakia and Latvia have recently had relatively stable currencies. In addition, Poland, Hungary and Slovenia have had steady and relatively moderate currency devaluations. Only Romania seems to have experienced serious exchange rate instability recently.

The actual fulfilment of the operational criterion of an independent central bank is a controversial question. As already alluded to in the previous paragraph with respect to Bulgaria, Estonia and Lithuania, a currency board is by definition an independent organ, but, also by definition, one that does not have the means to engage in open market operations. For the other accession countries it is a fact that their central banks are now assured a considerable degree of legal independence (in some cases, like Poland and Slovenia, this is even enshrined in their constitutions). The actual relationship between the central bank on the one hand and government *and* parliament on the other, however, can be one of conflict (see Radzyner and Reisinger 1998), with the last two trying, more or less systematically, to influence the first. Also, in several cases, the monetary financing of government deficits is still permitted.

As a conclusion, the interpretation of the mostly positive figures above must be cautious. The transition process is still ongoing in virtually all the former centrally planned economy countries. This implies that the twin long-run processes of transition and of catching-up with the EU average development level will imply both higher average domestic inflation and higher interest rates for the time being. Also, concerning the budgetary criteria, the apparently healthier fiscal situation masks the fact that the transition process has meant a *still incomplete shift* from government consumption towards social transfers, which reduced the GDP share of government expenditures drastically. This, added to unavoidable future financial commitments for structural reforms and coupled with still incomplete tax reforms, could indicate a future worsening of their fiscal position.

Nevertheless, a broadly positive assessment of the capacity of the accession countries to fulfil their *future* Maastricht commitments seems in order: we must remember the scepticism of most commentators about the capacity of so-called 'periphery countries' in the old ERM to achieve the Treaty benchmarks – and even more recently, the same behaviour towards Greece – which, in the end, hugely underestimated the convergence efforts undertaken by those countries.

3   WHY ECONOMIC AND MONETARY UNION?

According to the theory of optimum currency areas (OCAs)[6], the positive economic factor that arises from having an independent national currency is

Table 9.1   EMU criteria for the candidate countries (most recent official data)

Countries	Inflation rate	Long-term interest rates	Deficit or surplus as a share of GDP	Public debt as a share of GDP	Monetary authority status
EMU criteria	*2.8%* *(1.5+1.3*[HICP,E CB, 01–08/99]*)*	*7.36%* *(2.0+5.36*[Weighted Average of 10-year Government Bonds in eurozone, ECB,9/99]*)*	*–3%* *(Value for euro area:* *–2%*[Eurostat,98]*)*	*60%* *(value for euro area:* *73.7%*[Eurostat,98]*)*	*Legally independent central bank*
Cyprus	2.8[CPI,CBC] 12/98	5.5[One Year Treasury Bill,CBC, 09/99]	**–5.3**[CBC, 97]	57.7[CBC, 97]	Non-independent central bank (b)
Czech Republic	2.7[CPI,CNB,08/99]	6.8[One Year Pribor, CNB,08/99](d)	–1.4[IMF,12/98]	10.7[Central Government,IMF,12/98]	Legally independent central bank(b)
Estonia	2.8[CPI,BoE,09/99]	6.75[One Year Talibor, BoE, 09/99]	**–6.6**[CSO/MoF,06/99]	11.11[CSO/MoF,Central Government Debt plus Guaranteed Debt, 06/99]	Currency board arrangement
Hungary	**9.52**['Core' PI, MNB, 06/99]	**15.5**[Refinancing One Year Rate, MNB, 07/99]	**–4.1**[General Government, MNB,98]	**65.8**[General Government, MNB,98]	Legally independent Central bank (b)
Poland	7.2[CPI,NBP,08/99]	**22.5**[Commercial One Year Loan, NBP, 08/99]	–2.2[NBP Forecast for 1999]	50.1[General Government, IMF, 1997]	Legally independent central bank
Slovenia	**6.6**[CPI,BoSE, 10/99]	9.71[6-Months Treasury Bill, BoSE, 10/99]	–0.6[BoSE, 1998]	25.23[BoSE, QII,1999]	Legally independent central bank (b)

Malta	2.23 CPI,BoM, 98	5.29 One Year Treasury Bill, BoM, 06/99	−8.8 BoM, 98	56.3 IMF Forecast, 08/99	Non-independent central bank (b)
Bulgaria	−0.5 CPI,BNB, 07/99	5.40 Yield on Government Securities, BNB, 07/99	0.0 BNB,12/98	96.42 Domestic and Foreign Debt, BNB, 01/99	Currency board arrangement
Latvia	2.4 CPI, BoLa, 09/99	12.25 One Year Treasury Bill, BoLa, 10/99	0.1 BoLa, 12/98	12.7 Domestic and Foreign Government Debt, BoLa, 06/99	Legally independent central bank
Lithuania	1.0 CPI, BoLi,09/99	12.0 Three Months Government Securities, BoLi, 10/99	−5.8 IMF,98	17.0 IMF,98	Currency Board Arrangement (b), (c)
Romania	48.7 BCE,08/99	35.0(a) BCE,08/99	−2.6 BCE,08/99	18.0 IMF,97	Legally independent central bank (b)
Slovakia	9.4 BoSa,09/99	15.84 BRIBOR Six Months,BoSa, 08/99	−2.66 BoSa,98	20.7 BoSa98	Non-independent central bank (b)

Notes:
(a) Interbank rate;
(b) Lending to government is still permitted;
(c) Capable of engaging in some types of open market operations;
(d) Ceiling on domestic interest rate. Values in **bold** indicate a transgression of the Maastricht criteria.

Sources: International Monetary Fund, European Central Bank and respective national central banks.

related to the *conditional* ability to reduce adjustment costs caused by exogenous shocks.[7] On the other hand, the negative economic factor is related to the increase in transactions and risk costs generated by having to deal with several different currencies.

Research on the subject has concentrated in trying to develop some quantifiable results, usually through the testing of effects of the so-called 'asymmetric shocks'. This concept is linked to Mundell's original definition of an OCA as a region, and of the related notion of adjustment costs that would have to be borne by that region to face any changes in the external environment. A region would then be defined, for the purpose of testing this hypothesis, as an area where the economic structure would be so similar as to react in a homogeneous fashion to any external shocks.

The testing procedure would usually rest on the results of a vector auto regression (VAR) model (which has the known advantage of saving the researcher from defining clear structural assumptions in its model) subject to changes – 'shocks' – in some key exogenous variables.[8]

The usual conclusion of such estimations would be that the United States is an OCA, due to the existence of factors such as (i) a federal system of fiscal transfers and (ii) a high degree of labour mobility. These features would bear the costs of adjustment, thus rendering the use of the currency instrument unnecessary, while the EU, due to the lack of such features, does not seem to be an OCA (not at the start of the process, at least).[9]

The studies above tended to concentrate on the 'minus' side of a single currency area (the increase in adjustment costs), without taking into consideration the likely benefits arising from its constitution: the elimination of transaction costs (that is, without performing a cost–benefit analysis).

Another set of studies tried to systematize the estimation of the positive components, the most influential of which is the European Commission study on the 'Costs of non-Europe' (see CEC 1990). This study also presents estimates of the costs of EMU, but these losses are far outweighed by the benefits arising from the constitution of the European common currency area. Nevertheless, most of the studies in this latter set lack the conceptual and model consistency of the first group, usually resorting to a piecemeal estimation of several types of costs (currency exchange risks, interest rate differentials, impacts on trade and capital flows and so on) arising from the lack of a single currency, and then adding them up. The common currency constitution is then usually presented as a one-off gain that eliminates these costs.

Within this framework, what are the advantages, from the new entrants' point of view, of their integration in the eurozone? There have been few specific studies, to date, for the applicant countries, but we can safely assume that they would indicate that the eurozone – in itself not an OCA – would still not be one even with the new entrants added to it.[10]

We could, nevertheless, use as an initial working assumption that the pattern of benefits (and costs) would be roughly similar to those estimated for the Southern European economics.[11] Using Portugal as an example, participation in the eurozone would increase the level of GDP per capita, on a ten-year horizon, by only 1 per cent, as compared to the counterfactual scenario[12] (see Ministério das Finanças 1998).

The positive impact on Eastern European economies would probably be substantially greater, since not only are the interest rate differentials still much larger, but other channels of transmission would also have considerable effects (the increase in trade flows, lower transaction costs, larger public financial transfers from the EU, more substantial private capital flows and so on.[13]

Obviously, all those effects would happen, in varying degrees, with the maintenance of sustainable macro policies and the progress towards EU accession, with or without EMU. It is, therefore difficult to identify effects that are *exclusively* related to EMU, but we could, nevertheless, support an initial working assumption that EMU participation would have net positive effects for the new entrants.[14]

In addition, to support this an aggregate computable general equilibrium (CGE) model for the Eastern European countries as a group (see Baldwin et al. 1997) estimates huge long-run benefits arising from the *eastward* expansion of the Union (mostly from trade), for both the EU and Eastern Europe, with the gains for the Eastern European countries as a whole being three times larger than the gains in the EU countries (30.1 billion ECU and 11.2 billion ECU, respectively). Those gains are, of course, even greater for the former group, when estimated in terms of their respective GDP shares. Even more promising, gains still arise even after when the estimated costs arising from the eastward expansion are taken into consideration.

4 EMPIRICAL REVIEW OF EXCHANGE RATE REGIMES VIS-À-VIS THE EURO

Realizing the EMU macro convergence criteria for the new entrants has to be seen as a set of mid-term goals, to be achieved on a sustainable and permanent basis, adequately supported by micro reforms. In practice, the convergence to these benchmarks will be reached through paths that will be largely national, and therefore, specific to each of the candidate countries.[15]

The relationship of the set of monetary and fiscal targets in the criteria with the exchange rate regime is one of dependence and concordance with the macro setting of reforms. The exchange rate regime is not an independent aim by itself, and cannot be seen as such. This is not only the position of the

Commission, but of the national governments themselves (among others, see CEC 1998a; Nemenyi 1998; Polanski 1999). As such, the analysis of the subject separately from the wider macro framework is artificial.

As a general rule, most transition economies adopted, at some point early in their transition process, macroeconomic stabilization programmes[16] with some form of exchange rate anchor. Most of these initial peg strategies were later abandoned or softened, in the face of growing external imbalances, either relatively swiftly, as is the case in Poland, or spectacularly, in the midst of a speculative attack, as was the case in the Czech Republic.[17]

It must be noted that the learning curve of these countries (some of them newly independent – namely, Estonia, Latvia, Lithuania, Slovakia and Slovenia – which had to build national institutions virtually from scratch, including their monetary authorities) had to be very steep: barely ten years ago, the currently universal two-tier bank structure was not only absent, but irrelevant. The central bank, for all practical purposes, was a department of the ministry of finance, and its only real function was to produce the means of exchange to allow the trading of predetermined quantities among individual consumers.[18]

The development of the institutions able to carry out monetary policy actions, as well as the development of the necessary instruments to carry them through, took time. Initially, more blunt direct monetary control instruments were used (interest rate and credit caps, high reserve requirements, 'moral persuasion' and so on) since (i) the monetary authorities themselves had not learned how to use modern monetary policy tools,[19] (ii) the transmission channels for the proper use of those tools – namely, working financial markets – were absent in these economies (and still are today, but to a lesser degree) and (iii) there was a lack of stable relationships among the central bank's target variables and its instruments. Only more recently have market-based indirect monetary policy instruments – repos, Lombard facilities, government securities auctions – been introduced.[20]

The primary goal of a central bank is to maintain price stability. This can be accomplished through direct or indirect strategies. To try to meet an inflation target indirectly assumes some sort of stable link between the final target and an aggregate(s), which the central bank attempts to influence. These aggregates are the so-called intermediate targets, but inflation is the final target. There are two possible types of indirect strategies, one based on a stable rate of exchange between the domestic currency and the currency of a low-inflation country, and the other based on controlling the growth rate of a domestic money supply aggregate. The use of any type of pegging regime is, therefore, equivalent to the use of indirect inflation targeting. No single exchange rate regime is optimal for all nations at every time, but, nevertheless, it is usually considered that only a free float is sustainable in a long-term perspective, since other strategies are unstable to exogenous shocks and ultimately collapse.[21]

The extreme case of the peg strategy is the currency board arrangement (CBA), which requires the official foreign exchange reserves to be at least equal to the amount of domestic currency issued (at a given fixed exchange rate): under a strict CBA, there is no actual domestic monetary policy, since both the monetary base and the level of interest rates are endogenously determined. Modified CBAs, though, may perform limited monetary policy actions, through the use of some types of central bank instruments, such as lender-of-last-resort (LLR) facilities or limited open market operations.[22]

Usually, the choice of a CBA is linked to the need to give credibility to a stabilization policy, or, in the case of Eastern Europe, to sheer inexperience in terms of conduct of monetary policy by the monetary authorities of these countries. Among its stated advantages, a CBA entails automatic balance-of-payment adjustments (essentially in the same way that a gold standard exchange system would operate: in the case of a deficit in the capital and current accounts, money supply is reduced, causing, *ceteris paribus*, the interest rate to rise, which will lead to (i) reduced domestic activity and reduced imports, and (ii) an increase in foreign capital inflows). It should also result in reduced inflation expectations (depending on the anchor currency chosen). Finally, it should also, in principle, encourage sound fiscal policy, as the CBA does not automatically endogenize fiscal policy. For transition economics this does not necessarily mean a constant supply of the quantity of money, as money demand during transition can be assumed to be notoriously unstable.

Among its drawbacks, a CBA means not only the loss of monetary policy as a countercyclical tool, but it can actually be *procyclical* (reinforcing economic booms and troughs). In general the monetary authority's lack of LLR features such as foreign currency reserves could potentially increase both the short-run probability and the effects of financial sector crisis (regardless of the beneficial long-run effects caused by the reduction of moral hazard). The need to perform active policy actions is heightened in periods of market instability, as was clearly the case in Eastern Europe after the Russian crisis of 1998 and during the series of Baltic banking crises of 1993–95. A CBA also discourages the development of domestic money and capital markets.

Nevertheless, the most fundamental problem[23] of a CBA lies in its 'exit strategy'. There is no clear optimal staircase leading from the almost complete absence of monetary policy under a CBA regime to a fully-fledged and even independent central bank, but an interesting and useful example can be taken from Lithuania's exit strategy from its CBA arrangement (see Box 9.1).[24]

Since the application countries currently have several different ways of linking their national currencies to the eurozone, we shall make a condensed

BOX 9.1   LITHUANIA'S 'EXIT STRATEGY'

Lithuania uses a modified CBA, introduced in 1994, which pegs the Lithuanian litas to the US$. Its monetary authority, the BoLi (Lietuvos Bankas, Bank of Lithuania) has available to it certain types of market-based instruments, and it also has a clear strategy to evolve towards a fully-fledged central bank.

The rouble was initially replaced, as in Latvia, by an interim coupon currency issued by the newly created BoLi, from May to October 1992, and then by the talonas, which in its turn was replaced by the litas in June 1993. The talonas, initially in a floating regime, lost over 50 per cent of its value between its introduction and April 1993. Some exchange rate stability was regained with the introduction of the litas. Nevertheless, the government, with the support of the IMF, decided to press for the institution of an Estonian-type CBA in October 1993, against the will and the advice of the BoLi. The CBA was introduced in April 1994 – although the administrative structure of the BoLi was unchanged. Therefore, since the very beginning its CBA has been characterized as a modified CBA, since some central bank instruments were preserved (such as reserve requirements and short-term credit facilities, including for LLR operations: all those tools were necessary and duly used during the great 1995–96 banking crisis).

The Lithuanian strategy, presented at the 'Monetary Policy Programme for 1997–1999', is to move towards a fully-fledged central bank. It has three phases: during the first one (already completed), the aim is to introduce and develop open market operations and a Lombard facility with the currency board still in existence (1997–99); during the second phase (1999–2000), the 'Law on the Credibility of the Litas' is to be amended; the third and final phase (2000 onwards) would aim to link the litas to the euro or, temporarily, to a basket that would include it. By that time, the BoLi plans to be prepared to meet the requirements of ERM-II membership.

Recently, the BoLi has partially modified the timetable described above (see Bank of Lithuania, 1999). It has resolved:

a.   not to carry out the planned re-peg of the litas exchange rate to the euro in 2000;
b.   to re-peg the litas directly to the euro in the second half of

2001, skipping an intermediate peg to a US$/euro currency basket.

The pegging of the litas directly to the euro is defended on the basis that 'no principal decisions concerning the litas exchange rate will be taken in 1999–2000; therefore, in the future, this plan will have to be carried out faster' (Bank of Lithuania 1999, p. 40). In addition, such a peg would be more transparent and easily understood by the agents, and, at the same time, would send a clear signal to them to increase the use of the euro in their international trade settlements with the European Union.

presentation of those different linkage strategies. The current arrangements are itemized in Table 9.2.

The transitional linkage strategies and the degrees of preparation – and, indeed, the very perception of the need to start preparing immediately – for eventual integration into the eurozone vary widely from country to country.

This will necessarily change, as the need to prepare becomes apparent in the next few years. The European Commission, during the ongoing negotiation process, through the pre-accession treaties, with the advice and technical support from the European Central Bank, will have to define a clearer and more gradual monetary integration strategy for these countries. Until then, their disparate, even informal linkages with the eurozone – shadow and sliding pegs, free and dirty floating, currency boards – will remain.

The question is whether all the application countries will with time, converge to a common optimal strategy for their progressive integration in the common currency monetary framework or whether currency competition will continue until the very end. For the national economies the initial convergence rate to the euro is crucial for their competitiveness. Competition would then make sense, assuming that when these countries join EMU, market exchange rates will be the basis of the euro convergence rate. However, any joint convergence strategies for the applicant countries should be necessarily specific to the individual countries' national conditions.

The President of the ECB, Wim Duisenberg, in a speech on 26 September 1999 at the headquarters of the US Central Bank System, indicated that some flexibility can be expected in the use of the criteria for the application countries:

Against the background of different starting-points and degrees of economic transition, and the difficulty of ascertaining the lead time for further headway towards real and nominal convergence, a plurality of approaches should be feasi-

Table 9.2   Exchange rate linkages in the year 2000

Countries	Currency	Exchange rate regime	Date of introduction
Bulgaria	Lev	Currency board regime (anchor is the euro)	July 1997
Cyprus	Pound	Peg with intervention bands (+/– 2.25%) towards the euro	1992
Czech Republic	Koruna	Managed float, with informal shadowing of the euro	May 1997
Estonia	Kroon	Currency board regime (anchor on the euro)	June 1992
Hungary	Forint	Sliding peg –0.3% monthly – with intervention bands (+/– 2.25%) towards a basket made up of the euro and the US$ (70%, 30%)	March 1995
Latvia	Lats	Peg with the IMF's special drawing rights, with intervention bands (+/– 1%)	October 1993
Lithuania	Litas	Currency board regime (the anchor is the US$)	March 1994
Malta	Lira	Peg +/– 0.25 fluctuation bands, towards a basket of euros, GB stg and US$ (56.8%, 21.6% and 21.6%)	1971
Poland	Zloty	Free float	April 2000
Romania	Lei	Managed float with informal shadowing of the euro	August 1992
Slovakia	Koruna	Managed float with informal shadowing of the euro	October 1998
Slovenia	Tolar	Managed float with informal shadowing of the euro	October 1991

Sources: European Central Bank; European Union; International Monetary Fund.

ble without compromising equality of treatment. This may apply, in particular, to the timing of EU accession, ERM-II membership, monetary policies (including exchange rate strategies) before EU accession and the development of sound financial market infrastructures (see ECB 1999c).

The same use of flexibility was indicated, in less strong terms, in Duisenberg's first speech after the 13 October recommendations, delivered at the Bank of Greece, on 15 October 1999. He said that, 'against a background of different starting points and varying degrees of economic transition, a plurality of approaches should be feasible without compromising equality of treatment' (see ECB 1999b).

The first formal meeting between the ECB and the monetary authorities of the accession countries to discuss matters concerning their relations with the eurozone was held in Helsinki, from 10–12 of November 1999. The need for flexibility was also expressed in the final communiqué of that meeting, which stated:

> [B]y modifying their economic structures in line with those prevailing within the EU and by implementing appropriate structural reforms, accession countries will speed up the process of 'catching up,' whereby their living standards will progressively evolve towards levels closer to those of the EU member states. Historical experience shows that this process should go hand in hand with price stability and sound public finances (nominal convergence). The progress towards fulfilling the Maastricht criteria as a condition for the adoption of the euro is therefore fully compatible with structural reform. The accession countries need to continue to implement monetary policies that are geared to achieving and maintaining price stability, and to support this process with prudent fiscal policies and adequate structural reforms. No common path should be prescribed for all 12 accession countries with regard to the orientation of their exchange rate policies prior to accession, the inclusion of their currencies in ERM 11 or the later adoption of the euro. Against this background of different starting-points for the economic reform process and the difficulty of ascertaining the lead-time for further headway towards nominal and real convergence, a plurality of approaches should be feasible without compromising equality of treatment. The smooth functioning of banking and financial markets is of the utmost importance for the applicants to be integrated successfully into the Single Market and, at a later stage, into the euro area. The Helsinki Seminar followed a number of bilateral visits and contacts between the European Central Bank and the monetary authorities of the accession countries. National central banks that are part of the Eurosystem have long-standing relationships with accession countries and will develop them further in the Eurosystem. In particular, to enhance the mutually beneficial working relationship between the Eurosystem and the central banks of accession countries, the Eurosystem stands ready to provide technical assistance in its field of competence. (ECB 1999a p. 1.)

The views of the ECB on the accession process were exposed more extensively in an article published in the ECB's *Monthly Bulletin* of February 2000 (see ECB 2000).

5   STRATEGIC CHOICE AND BEST PRACTICE

In the context of economic development as a process of catching up to the more advanced Western industrialized countries, an optimal strategy could be based on a stability-orientated undervaluation strategy (see Hölscher 1997, Hölscher et al. 2000) of entry candidates. This would promote export-led growth within the transition countries and speed up convergence towards eurozone GDP levels due to domestic income creation. In addition, it could provide an insurance against the Balassa–Samuelson effect. This effect does not necessarily disappear with the institution of a common currency area; it is a real phenomenon with real and nominal effects and, if we deal with different currency areas, one additional nominal effect, namely, the exchange rate imbalances. The configuration of a common currency area eliminates this nominal effect but not the others (capital, wage and labour adjustments still have to be made). However, this might be too tough and even unrealistic for some of the transition countries, since exchange rate policy has to be defined *vis-à-vis* the euro. The implication of undervaluation is that even if the entry candidate succeeds in maintaining a stable peg with the euro, the inflation rate has to be below that of the eurozone in order to increase competitiveness. Given the current situation, this would mean near-zero inflation. Considering the specific structure of the transition economies, which still have to face large relative price movements, which in turn will lead to greater variability in inflation levels than is usual among advanced economies, such a strategy is unlikely to be feasible. Among the more advanced transition countries, even Poland has, so far, failed to implement such a sustainable undervaluation strategy.[25]

In general such a strategy would have to rely on considerable support both within and outside the country. Internal support is limited due to political constraints, which were indicated by resistance to IMF-type stabilization programmes[26] and social hardship incurred by such a strategy of tight money. Also it seems to conflict with the common intuition of policy makers that a development strategy requires export-led growth rather than capital imports. The bottom line of this train of thought is that these capital imports would threaten exchange rate stability through the introduction of devaluation expectations. External support would require some kind of international monetary regime in analogy of the Bretton Woods system, which provided exactly that environment for West Germany (Hölscher 1994) after the Second World War. The dollar regime gave the opportunity of competitive advantages through lower inflation rates within other national economies such as West Germany. At the moment there is no indication that euroland is willing to play a similar role for Eastern Europe to the United States for Western Europe in order to pave the way for economic recovery.

As this 'optimal strategy' may contain a little too much wishful thinking, we are proposing a second-best strategy, which takes the Polish experience into account. Broadly speaking, there are three strategic options for the entry countries: a currency board arrangement; a band around an adjustable central parity; or a more flexible exchange rate arrangement (a crawling band or a managed float), perhaps augmented by an additional nominal anchor for monetary policy. The complexity of economic transition means that whatever strategy will be chosen, it has to be transitional.

6 CONCLUSION

In practice, such a second-best strategy could be based on – and culminate in – an early voluntary entry into an ERM-II-like mechanism (see Box 9.2). Such entry, however, would be advisable only after the implementation of the necessary macro structural reforms, with adequate micro underpinnings, had been undertaken in a sustainable fashion. Among these reforms, are:

1. the complete constitution of an independent and operational central bank;
2. the stability and adequate supervision of a privatized and liberalized financial system; and
3. the final and progressive opening up of these countries external accounts.

The optimal path towards that stage could be similar to the Polish integration strategy, in which the currency linkage evolves towards increased flexibility, culminating in a temporary float regime before ERM-II entry. This may indicate that CBA-type strategies should be, in the medium run, replaced by the applicant countries that use them, and attempts to develop fully-fledged central banks should be undertaken, but without undermining the hard-won stabilization and credibility gains. One implication for central banks is that they will have to give up direct inflation targeting in order to maintain a peg to the euro (Orlowski 2000, p. 153). Vigilance will be required to check that such a 'return to peg strategy' will not lead to a return of overactivist discretionary monetary policy.

Our proposal for the EU entrants is a hybrid system of exchange rate strategy, which contains a monetary policy aimed at internal price-level stability as well (see also Masson 1999). This proposal is not optimal, but takes the real world into account. Since this world might change, another market constellation might become feasible, one which would include the acceptance of export surpluses from transition economies into the EU. Under such circumstances, a switch towards the optimal strategy of stability-orientated undervaluation would be possible.

BOX 9.2   THE ERM-II MECHANISM

According to the Resolution adopted by the European Council in Amsterdam in June 1997, the European Monetary System from 1 January 1999, will be replaced by a new exchange rate mechanism (ERM) that will link the currencies of non-eurozone area EU member states to the euro.

ERM-II aims to ensure that non-eurozone EU-member states participating in it orient their policies towards stability and convergence, and help them in their efforts to adopt the euro. Participation in it will be voluntary for all non-eurozone member states. An EU member state that does not participate in ERM-II from the beginning may join later. The operating procedures for the new ERM have been so defined by the ECB and the non-eurozone national central banks: the currency of each member state participating in ERM-II will have a central rate against the euro and bands of ± 15%, supported by automatic unlimited intervention at the margins. However, the ECB and the participating non-eurozone national central banks can suspend this in a situation of conflict with internal price stability. The exchange rate coordination in ERM-II can eventually be increased by tighter currency bands, if deemed necessary. Also, after a political decision process, the parities in the currency exchange rates grid can be adjusted to new levels.

Until March 2000, only the Kingdom of Denmark and the Greek Republic had joined this structure. Also, in March of 2000, the Greek Republic officially requested entry into the eurozone *proper*, which is expected to take place in early 2001. In preparation for that move, the Greek drachma had its central grid parity in the ERM revalued in January of the same year and the Bank of Greece reduced its reference rates.

NOTES

1. Malta was only added to this list in October of 1998, when the Council accepted Malta's request to reactivate its candidature, which had been presented in 1990 but withdrawn following the change in government in the island after the general elections of 1996. A new government, elected in September of 1998, reverted this position.
2. See CEC (1998a).
3. It must be noted that the specific political situation in Cyprus, namely, its division be-

tween a Greek Cypriot south and a Turkish-occupied north, casts doubts on the final outcome of the accession negotiations.

4. Some numerical benchmarks, aiming to guarantee the stability of the new single currency area, were defined in the framework of the Maastricht Treaty. They are the four so-called *EMU or convergence criteria*, which aim to ensure monetary and fiscal stability in the joint currency area: their assessment is not obligatory for application countries at this stage of the process. Two of them are monetary, one is linked to currency rate stability, and the final one is fiscal. They are: (i) *the inflation convergence criterion*, defined as an inflation rate which should not exceed by more than 1.5 per cent the average inflation rate of the three best-performing countries; (ii) *the interest rate convergence criterion*, meaning that the average long-term nominal interest rate should not be more than 2 per cent above the average interest rate of three countries with the lowest inflation rate; (iii) *the ERM criterion*, which postulates that the currencies of future EMU members should have been in the ERM (exchange rate mechanism) without devaluation or revaluation for at least two years; (iv) *the excessive debt criterion*, which is composed of a budget deficit component, which declares that a country's budget deficit should not exceed 3 per cent of its GDP, and of a stock of debt component, which states that the stock of outstanding government debt should not exceed 60 per cent of that country's GDP (or otherwise be in a descending sustainable trajectory towards these benchmarks).

   In addition, an 'operational' element was also set, concerning the legal and institutional features of the national central bank, namely, its independence from government interference, a mandate towards price stability, the prohibition of monetary financing of deficits, and the availability of a set of market-based instruments that enable the CB to conduct monetary policy actions.

5. Note that the eurozone benchmarks for long-term interest rate and inflation used in Table 9.1 do not conform to the strict Maastricht criteria definition, since they are ECB-produced GDP-weighted averages of the national figures. Strict Maastricht criteria benchmarks would be much more stringent. As an example, the non-weighted average HICP (Harmonized Index of Consumer Prices) for the three best-performing eurozone countries – Austria, France and Germany – for the same period is a mere 0.67 per cent, with the result that only Bulgaria and Lithuania would fall within the 2.2 per cent upper boundary for the 'inflation criterion'.

6. The literature on OCAs was initiated by Robert Mundell in his seminal 1961 paper, entitled 'A theory of optimum currency areas' (for which he was awarded the 1999 Nobel Prize in Economics). This work, of a clear Keynesian theoretical underpinning, can be truly called a classic in its field (see Mundell 1961). Nevertheless, its actual usefulness as a tool for assessing the outcomes of a currency union has been seriously doubted in several studies (see Ministério das Finanças 1998, and Bordo and Jonung, 2000), but it still remains one of the most used types of analysis. Mundell himself updated this concept somewhat in a 1997 work (see Mundell 1997).

7. *Conditional* in the sense that they assume the *adequate* use of the monetary/exchange rate instrument by the authorities to 'soften the blow' of adjustment, which is not necessarily confirmed by empirical studies (see Ministério das Finanças 1998). Also, even if this was the case, private capital markets, federal transfers or increased labour market flexibility (see Buiter 1995) could replace this instrument.

8. Other criteria are usually also added to the testing procedure, such as the degree of openness of an economy (measured by the ratio of trade to GDP), and the degree of geographical concentration of its trade flows. The rationale is that very open countries that trade a lot with specific countries/areas would have added incentives to participate in a common currency zone with these countries/areas.

9. His discussion is related to the question of the so-called OCA endogeneity: even areas that are not OCAs at the start could become so, as integration progresses. The United States itself actually only became a currency union about a generation after independence. This also underlies another serious limitation of the OCA theory: its *static* feature.

10. De Grauwe and Aksoy (1999) seem to have come to the conclusion that the Eastern European countries, as a group, might be an OCA with the EU. Nevertheless, their results

are preliminary and tentative, and, as they themselves indicate, should be treated with caution. Horvath and Jonas (1998), for the Czech Republic, in a country study, came to the conclusion that it is not, at this moment, an OCA with the EU.

11. Buch (see Buch and Döpke 1999), in a study on financial integration which also uses the Southern European states as a benchmark for the new entrants, concludes that the benefits derived from EU accession will be smaller for the latter, since their degree of integration is already greater than the former at a similar stage, and will increase before actual accession. This 'convergence from outside' is actually one of the standard features of the successive expansion waves of the EU (see Vinhas de Souza 1996).

12. These results are obtained from the updating of the endogenous growth model developed by Gaspar and Pereira in 1995 (see Gaspar and Pereira 1995).

13. Such conclusions seem to be supported by the recent results of a series of studies that try to estimate cost and benefits of EU accession for a specific set of Eastern European accession countries through CGE models, under the PHARE ACE Project no. P96-6033-R, 'Measurement of costs and benefits of accession to the European Union for selected CEECs': for general results, see Mortensen and Richter (2000). For the country-specific studies, see, for Hungary, Szemlér (1999), for Poland, Wyrzykowska (1999) and for Slovenia, Majcek (1999).

14. Some national modelizations (see Wdowinski and van Aarle 2001 for the case of Poland) would seem to agree with this conclusion. Of course, other – non-economic –considerations (political, strategic, security related) also underpin the new entrants' will to integrate themselves into the EU and to participate in EMU (see Bordo and Jonung 2000).

15. The time span required for the convergence process of Eastern European countries, according to an IMF study (see Fischer et al. 1998), using the average development level of the southern EU member countries (Greece, Portugal and Spain) as a benchmark would be: 28 to 29 years for Bulgaria, 11 to 15 years for the Czech Republic, 16 to 17 years for Estonia, 20 to 22 years for Hungary, 23 to 25 years for Latvia, 23 to 24 years for Lithuania, 18 to 23 years for Poland, 34 to 36 years for Romania, 15 to 19 years for Slovakia and 19 to 24 years for Slovenia. In other words, it will be a generation-long process, even with sustainable macro policies.

16. These macro programmes encompassed, of course, several different policy actions. On the monetary side, one of the main initial concerns was the elimination of the monetary overhang: centrally planned economies traditionally generated a surplus of legal tender, given the limited amount of goods and services available for consumption. A substantial part of this overhang was held by households outside of the former mono-bank financial system. The liberalization of prices and external trade, besides the macro balance and allocative micro-efficiency issues involved, aimed at eliminating part of this surplus.

17. For a stylized description of the general trajectory, see Halpern and Wyplosz (1997).

18. Among the state enterprises and government departments, not even this means of exchange function of money was necessary: barter – inter-unit transfers of goods and services for settlement – was used instead.

19. Which, even in Western Europe, were introduced only slowly and progressively between the 1950s and the 1990s.

20. It is estimated that, on average, only three years separated these two distinct phases: it was a much faster process than its counterpart in Western Europe (see Radzyner and Riesinger 1998).

21. The 'shock-isolation' capabilities of a float regime can be intuitively demonstrated in a simple IS–LM analytical framework (see Visser and Smits 1995). Both foreign demand and foreign price shocks are cushioned by a floating exchange rate. Nevertheless, a foreign interest rate shock is cushioned neither by a float nor by a peg, but the shock works in opposite directions (in a float, a fall in the 'world' interest rates results in a capital inflow and an appreciation of the exchange rate, causing the IS curve to shift to the left; conversely, in a peg regime), but, in the case of the float, an activist monetary policy can be used as an effective instrument by the domestic policy maker.

22. A comprehensive discussion of alternative exchange rate regimes, and of several other

subjects related to the integration of the accession countries into the eurozone, can be found in the Forum Report on Economic Policy Initiative (1999).

23. Other weaknesses of peg regimes are: it is very difficult to determine the equilibrium exchange rate of a national currency in a peg; the economy becomes vulnerable to shocks in the country to which the national currency is pegged and the actual shock correction arrangement has to be defined; and the destabilizing effects of capital inflows, when a misaligned fixed exchange rate violates the uncovered interest rate parity condition (by creating exploitable 'risk-free' interest rate differentials), forces the central bank to make costly and ultimately ineffective sterilization operations.

24. It must be noted that some authors (see Äimä 1998) have a much more negative interpretation of the monetary policy developments in Lithuania and the very institutional design of the Lithuanian monetary authority, linking them to, in essence, a power struggle within the Lithuanian government.

25. This is supported empirically by an initial estimation of the Balassa–Samuelson effect for the accession countries, in terms of sustainable inflation differentials, which indicates a difference of several percentage points compared with the eurozone (see CEPS 2000).

26. For an example of the political implications in the course of the implementation of an austerity package in Hungary, see Stephan (1999).

References

Agell, J., L. Calmfors and G. Jonsson (1996), 'Fiscal policy when monetary policy is tied to the mast', *European Economic Review*, **40**, 1413–40.

Äimä, K. (1998), 'Central Bank independence in the Baltic countries', *Review of Economies in Transition*, No. 3, Bank of Finland.

Akerlof, G.A., W. Dickens and G. Perry (1996), 'The macroeconomics of low inflation', *Brookings Papers on Economic Activity*, **1**, 1–76.

Alesina, A. and S. Ardagna (1998), 'Tales of fiscal adjustment', *Economic Policy*, **27**, 489–545.

Alesina, A. and R. Perotti (1995), 'Fiscal expansions and fiscal adjustments in OECD countries', *Economic Policy*, **21**, 205–48.

Alexander, V. (1994), 'Die deutsche Vereinigung: Public-Choice-Aspekte, langfristige Perspektiven und Konsequenzen für die europäische Integration' (German unification: public choice aspects, long-run perspectives and the consequences for European Integration), Dresdner Beiträge zur Volkswirtschaftslehre 1/94, Dresden.

Andersen, T. and J. Sørensen (1988), 'Exchange rate variability and wage formation in open economies', *Economics Letters*, **28**, 263–8.

Artis, M.J. (1994), 'Stage II: feasible transitions to EMU', in D. Cobham (ed.), *European Monetary Upheavals*, Manchester: Manchester University Press, pp. 188–225.

Artis, M. and Z. Kontolemis (1998), 'The European Central Bank and inflation targeting', *International Journal of Finance and Economics*, **3**, 27–38.

Artis, M.J. and M.P. Taylor (1988), 'Exchange rates, interest rates, capital controls and the European Monetary System: assessing the track record', in F. Giavazzi, S. Micossi and M. Miller (eds), *The European Monetary System*, Cambridge: Cambridge University Press, pp. 185–206.

Artis M.J. and M.P. Taylor (1994), 'The stabilising effect of the ERM on exchange rates and interest rates', *IMF Staff Papers*, **41**, 123-48.

Aschauer, D. (1989a), 'Is public expenditure productive?', *Journal of Monetary Economics*, **23** (2), 177–200.

Aschauer, D. (1989b), 'Does public capital crowd out private capital?', *Journal of Monetary Economics*, **24**, 171–88.

Asdrubali, P., B.E. Sorensen and O. Yosha (1996), 'Channels of interstate risk sharing: United States 1963–1990', *Quarterly Journal of Economics*, **111**, 1081–110.

Baffes, J. and A. Shah (1998), 'Productivity of public spending, sectoral allocation choices and economic growth', *Economic Development and Cultural Change*, **46**, 291–303.

Balassa, B. (1982), *Development Strategies in Semi-industrial Economies*, Oxford: Oxford University Press.

Baldwin, R., J. Francois and R. Portes (1997), 'The costs and benefits of Eastern enlargement: the impact on the EU and Central Europe', *Economic Policy*, **24**, 125–76.

Bank of Lithuania (1997), 'Monetary Policy Programme for 1997–1999', Vilnius.

Bank of Lithuania (1999), 'Statement of the Bank of Lithuania', Vilnius, 13 October.

Barro, R.J. (1991), 'Economic growth in a cross-section of countries', *Quarterly Journal of Economics*, **106**, 407–43.

Barro, R.J. and D. Gordon (1983), 'A positive theory of monetary policy in a natural rate model', *Journal of Political Economy*, **91** (4), 589–610.

Barry, F. and M.B. Devereux (1995), 'The expansionary fiscal contraction hypothesis: a Neo-Keynesian analysis', *Oxford Economic Papers*, **47**, 249–64.

Bayoumi, T. and B. Eichengreen (1993), 'Shocking aspects of European monetary integration', in F. Torres and F. Giavazzi (eds), *Adjustment and Growth in the European Monetary Union*, Cambridge: Cambridge University Press.

Bean, C. (1989), 'Comment on "Economic policy and adjustment in Denmark", by C. Vastrup', in M. Monti (ed.), *Fiscal Policy, Economic Adjustment and Financial Markets*, Washington: IMF.

Bean, C. (1994), 'European unemployment: a survey', *Journal of Economic Literature*, **32**, 573–619.

Begg, D., P. De Grauwe, F. Giavazzi, H. Uhlig and C. Wyplosz (1998), 'The ECB: unsafe at any speed? Monitoring the ECB', London: Centre for Economic Policy Research, October.

Bernanke, B.S., T. Laubach, F.S. Mishkin and A.S. Posen (1999), *Inflation Targeting: Lessons from the International Experience*, Princeton: Princeton University Press.

Blanchard, O.J. and P. Muet (1993), 'Competitiveness through disinflation: an assessment of the French macroeconomic strategy', *Economic Policy*, **16**, 11–56.

Blanchard, O.J. and J. Wolfers (2000), 'The role of shocks and institutions in the rise of European unemployment: the aggregate evidence', *Economic Journal*, **110**, C1–33.

Blinder, A.S. (1997), 'What central bankers can learn from academics – and vice versa', *Journal of Economic Perspectives*, **11**, 3–19.

Bordo, M. and L. Jonung (2000), 'Lessons for EMU from the history of monetary unions', Institute of Economic Affairs, London.

Bougheas, S. and P. Demetriades (1997), 'Infrastructure, specialisation and economic growth', unpublished MS, Keele University.

Brissimis, S.P. and H.D. Gibson (1997), 'Monetary policy, capital flows and disinflation in Greece', *Economic Bulletin*, Bank of Greece, **9**, 21–38.

Brissimis, S.P., H.D. Gibson and E. Tsakalotos (1998), 'A unifying framework for analysing offsetting capital flows and sterilisation: Germany and the ERM', mimeo, September.

Bröcker, J. and B. Raffelhüschen (1997), 'Fiscal aspects of German unification: who is stuck with the bill?', in B. Huber and F.L. Sell (eds), Transition in Eastern Europe: Current Issues and Perspectives, *Applied Economics Quarterly*, **45**, 139–62.

Buch, C. and J. Döpke (1999), 'Real and financial integration in Europe – evidence for the accession states and for the pre-ins', Kiel Working Papers, no. 917.

Buiter, W.H. (1995), 'Macroeconomic policy during a transition to monetary union', CEPR Discussion Paper, No. 1222, London: Centre for Economic Policy Research.

Buiter, W.H. and K. Kletzer (1991), 'Reflections on the fiscal implications of a common currency', in A. Giovanni and C. Mayer (eds), *European Financial Integration*, Cambridge: Cambridge University Press, pp. 221–44.

Buiter, W.H., G. Corsetti and P.A. Pesenti (1998), *Financial Markets and European Monetary Cooperation*, Cambridge: Cambridge University Press.

Buiter, W.H., G. Corsetti and N. Roubini (1993), 'Excessive deficits: sense and nonsense in the Treaty of Maastricht', *Economic Policy*, **16**, 58–100.

Burgess, S. and M. Knetter (1998), 'An international comparison of employment adjustment to exchange rate fluctuations', *Review of International Economics*, **6** (1), 151–63.

Buti, M., D. Franco and H. Ongena (1997), 'Budgetary policies during recessions: retrospective application of the stability and growth pact to the post-war period', European Commission Economic Papers, No. 121.

Buti, M. and A. Sapir (eds) (1998), *Economic Policy in EMU*, Oxford: Oxford University Press.

Button, K.J. and E.J. Pentecost (1999), *Regional Economic Performance within the European Union*, Cheltenham, UK and Northampton, MA: Edward Elgar.

Calmfors, L. (1998a), 'Macroeconomic policy, wage-setting and employment: what difference does the EMU make?', *Oxford Review of Economic Policy*, **14** (3), 125–51.

Calmfors, L. (1998b), 'Monetary Union and precautionary labour market reform', Stockholm University, Institute for International Economic Studies (IIES) Seminar Paper No. 659.

Calmfors, L. and J. Driffill (1988), 'Bargaining structure, corporatism and macroeconomic performance', *Economic Policy*, **6**, 14–61.

Calmfors, L. and A. Forslund (1990), 'Wage formation in Sweden', in L. Calmfors (ed.), *Wage Formation and Macroeconomic Policy in the Nordic Countries*, Oxford: Oxford University Press.

Calmfors, L. and H. Horn (1985), 'Classical unemployment, accommodation policies and the adjustment of real wages', *Scandinavian Journal of Economics*, **87** (2), 234–61.

Canova, F. and M.O. Ravn (1998), 'The macroeconomic effects of German unification: real adjustment and the welfare state', CEPR Discussion Paper No. 2038, London: Centre for Economic Policy Research.

CEPS (2000), 'Annex II: The Balassa-Samuelson effect', mimeo, Brussels.

Clarida, R., J. Gali and M. Gertler (1998), 'Monetary policy rules in practice: some international evidence', *European Economic Review*, **43**, 1033–67.

Clarida, R. and M. Gertler (1998), 'How the Bundesbank conducts monetary policy', in C. Romer and D. Romer (eds), *Reducing Inflation: Motivation and Strategy*, Chicago: Chicago University Press, chapter 10.

Clausen, V. and M. Willms (1994), 'Lessons from German monetary union for European monetary union', *Journal of International and Comparative Economics*, **3**, 195–228.

Coffey, P. and J.R. Presley (1971), *European Monetary Integration*, London: Macmillan.

Commission of the European Communities (CEC) (Werner Report) (1970), *Report to the Council and Commission on the Realisation by Stages of Economic and Monetary Union in the Community*, Luxembourg: Office for Official Publications of the European Community.

Commission of the European Communities (CEC) (1990), 'One market, one money: an evaluation of the potential benefits and costs of forming an economic and monetary union', *European Economy*, No. 44, October.

Commission of the European Communities (CEC) (1993), 'Growth, competitiveness and employment: challenges and ways forward into the 21st century', *Bulletin of the European Communities*, Supplement 6/93, Brussels.

Commission of the European Communities (CEC) (1995), 'Broad economic policy guidelines', *European Economy*, No. 60, Brussels.

Commission of the European Communities (CEC) (1997), 'Agenda 2000', Brussels: European Commission.

Commission of the European Communities (CEC) (1998a), 'Composite paper', Brussels: European Commission.

Commission of the European Communities (CEC) (1998b), *Euro 1999, deel 2 (Part 2) Verslag*, Luxembourg: Europese Gemeenschappen, May.

Commission of the European Communities (CEC) (1999a), 'Final Statement of the First Meeting between the ECB and the Monetary Authorities of the Accession Countries', Bank of Finland, Helsinki, 12 November.

Commission of the European Communities (CEC) (1999b), Speech by Mr Romano Prodi, President of the European Commission, 'Enlargement', Brussels: European Commission.

Committee on the Study of Economic and Monetary Union (Delors Committee) (1989), *Report on Economic and Monetary Union in the European Community (Delors Report)*, Luxembourg: Office for Official Publications of the European Communities.

Connolly, B. (1995), *The Rotten Heart of Europe: The Dirty War for Europe's Money*, London: Faber & Faber.

Costa, C. and P. De Grauwe (1999), 'EMU and the need for further economic integration', in W. Meeusen (ed.), *Economic Policy in the European Union*, Cheltenham, UK and Northampton, MA: Edward Elgar, pp. 27–48.

Crafts, N.F. and G. Toniolo (1996), 'Postwar growth: an overview', in N.F. Crafts and G. Toniolo (eds), *Economic Growth in Europe Since 1945*, Cambridge: Cambridge University Press, pp. 1–37.

Cukierman, A. (1992), *Central Bank Strategy, Credibility and Independence: Theory and Evidence*, Cambridge, MA: MIT Press.

Currie, D.A. (1992), 'European monetary union: institutional structure and economic performance', *Economic Journal*, **102** (1), 248–64.

Currie, D.A. and J. Whitley (1994), 'What route to European monetary integration?', in D. Cobham, (ed.), *European Monetary Upheavals*, Manchester: Manchester University Press, pp. 167–83.

Danthine, J.-P. and J. Hunt (1994), 'Wage bargaining structure, employment and economic integration', *Economic Journal*, **104**, 528–41.

De Grauwe, P. (1988), 'Is the EMS a DM-zone?', CEPR Discussion Paper, No. 297, London: Centre for Economic Policy Research.

De Grauwe, P. (1990), 'The cost of disinflation and the European Monetary System', *Open Economies Review*, **1** (2), 147–74.

De Grauwe, P. (1994), 'Toward European Monetary Union without the EMS', *Economic* Policy, **18**, 147–85.

De Grauwe, P. (1997a), *The Economics of Monetary Integration*, 3rd edn, Oxford: Oxford University Press.

De Grauwe, P. (1997b), 'Core–periphery relations in EMU', unpublished.

De Grauwe, P. (1997c), 'Exchange rate arrangements between the ins and the outs', CEPR Discussion Paper No. 1640, London: Centre for Economic Policy Research, May.

De Grauwe, P. and Y. Aksoy (1999), 'Are Central European countries part of the European optimum currency areas?', in P. De Grauwe and V. Lavrac (eds), *Inclusion of Central European Countries in the European Monetary Union*, Dordrecht: Kluwer Academic Publishers.

Diamond, D. and P. Dybvig (1983), 'Bank runs, deposit insurance and liquidity', *Journal of Political Economy*, **91** (3), 401–19.

Dornbusch, R. (1982), 'Stabilisation policies in Latin America: what have we learned?', *World Development*, **10**, 701–8.

Dornbusch, R. (1996), 'The effectiveness of exchange rate changes', *Oxford Review of Economic Policy*, **12** (3), 26–38.

Dornbusch, R., C. Favero and F. Giavazzi (1998), 'Immediate challenges for the European Central Bank', *Economic Policy*, **26**, 15–64.

Dowd, K. and D. Greenaway (1994), 'Currency competition, network externalities and switching costs: towards an alternative view of optimal currency areas', *Economic Journal*, **103**, 1180–89.

Easterly, W. and S. Rebelo (1993), 'Fiscal policy and economic growth: an empirical investigation', *Journal of Monetary Economics*, **32**, 417–58.

Edwards, S. (1984), *The Order of Liberalisation of the External Sector in Developing Countries*, Princeton, NJ: Princeton University Press.

Ehrenberg, R. (1994), 'Labour Markets and Integrating National Economies', Washington DC: Brookings Institution.

Eichengreen, B. (1990), 'One money for Europe? Lessons from the US currency union', *Economic Policy*, **10**, 118–87.

Eichengreen, B. (1991), 'Is Europe an optimal currency area?', National Bureau of Economic Research, Cambridge, Working Paper 3579.

Eichengreen, B. (1993), 'European monetary unification', *Journal of Economic Literature*, **31**, 1321–57.

Eichengreen, B. (1996), 'Institutions and economic growth: Europe after World War II', in N.F. Crafts, and G. Toniolo (eds), *Economic Growth in Europe Since 1945*, Cambridge: Cambridge University Press, pp. 38–72.

Eichengreen, B. and C. Wyplosz (1998), 'The stability pact: more than a minor nuisance?', *Economic Policy*, **26**, 67–113.

Elmeskov, J., J.P. Martin and S. Scarpetta (1998), 'Key lessons for labour market reforms: evidence from OECD countries' experience', *Swedish Economic Policy Review*, **5** (2), 205–58.

Erkel-Mousse, H. and J. Melitz (1995), 'New empirical evidence on the costs of European monetary union', CEPR Discussion Paper No. 1169, London: Centre for Economic Policy Research.

European Central Bank (ECB) (1998), 'A stability-oriented monetary policy strategy for the ECB', Press Release, 13 October.

European Central Bank (ECB) (1999a), *Monthly Bulletin*, October.

European Central Bank (ECB) (1999b), Speech by Dr Willem F. Duisenberg,

President of the European Central Bank, 'EU enlargement, some views from the ECB', Bank of Greece, Athens, 15 October.

European Central Bank (ECB) (1999c), Speech by Dr Willem F. Duisenberg, President of the European Central Bank, 'The past and future of European integration: a Central Banker's Perspective', Washington DC, 26 September.

European Central Bank (ECB) (2000), *Monthly Bulletin*, February.

European Monetary Institute (EMI) (1995, 1997), *Annual Report*, Frankfurt: EMI.

European Monetary Institute (EMI) (1997), *The Single Monetary Policy in Stage Three: Elements Of the Monetary Policy Strategy in the ECB*, Frankfurt: EMI.

European Monetary Institute (EMI) (1998), *Convergence Report*, Frankfurt: EMI.

Fischer, S. (1995), 'Central bank independence revisited', *American Economic Review, Papers and Proceedings*, **85**, 201–6.

Fischer, S., R. Sahay and C. Végh (1998), 'How far is Eastern Europe from Brussels?', IMF Working Paper, WP/98/53, Washington, DC: International Monetary Fund.

Flood, R.P. and P. Garber (1984), 'Collapsing exchange rate regimes: some linear examples', *Journal of International Economics*, **17**, 1–13.

Forum Report on Economic Policy Initiative (1999), 'Monetary and exchange rate policies, EMU and Central Eastern Europe', London: Centre for Economic Policy Research.

Franz, W. (1995), 'Die Lohnfindung in Deutschland in einer internationalen Perspektive: Ist das deutsche System ein Auslaufmodell?', (An international perspective of wage determination in Germany: is the model in decline?) *Konjunkturpolitik*, **43** (3), 31–57.

Fratianni, M. and J. von Hagen (1990a), 'Asymmetries and realignments in the EMS', in P. De Grauwe and L. Papademos (eds), *The European Monetary System in the 1990s*, London: Longman, pp. 86–113.

Fratianni, M. and J. von Hagen (1990b), 'German dominance in the EMS: the empirical evidence', *Open Economies Review*, **1** (1), 67–88.

Fuhrmann, W. (1994), 'Currency board system', Working Paper 9403, Universität-GH-Paderborn.

Gaspar, V. and A. Pereira (1995), 'The impact of financial integration and unilateral public transfers on investment and growth in EC capital-importing economies', *Journal of Development Economics*, **48**, 43–66.

Giavazzi, F. and A. Giovannini (1987), 'Models of the EMS: is Europe a greater DM area?', in R.C. Bryant and R. Portes (eds), *Global Macroeconomics*, New York: St Martin's Press, pp. 237–65.

Giavazzi, F. and A. Giovannini (1989), *Limiting Exchange Rate Flexibility: The European Monetary System*, Cambridge, MA: MIT Press.

Giavazzi, F. and M. Pagano (1988), 'The advantage of tying one's hands: EMS discipline and central bank credibility', *European Economic Review*, **32**, 1055–75.

Giavazzi, F. and M. Pagano (1990), 'Can severe fiscal contractions be expansionary? A tale of two small economies', in O.J. Blanchard and S. Fischer (eds), *National Bureau of Economic Research Macroeconomics Annual*, New York: NBER, pp. 75–110.

Giavazzi, F. and L. Spaventa (1990), 'The "new" EMS', in P. De Grauwe and L. Papademos (eds), *The European Monetary System in the 1990s*, London: Longman, pp. 65–84.

Gibson, H.D. (1996), *International Finance*, Harlow: Longmans.

Gibson, H.D. and E. Tsakalotos (1991), 'European monetary union and macroeconomic policy in southern Europe: the case for positive integration', *Journal of Public Policy*, **11** (3), 249–73.

Gibson, H.D. and E. Tsakalotos (1993), 'Testing a flow model of capital flight in five European countries', *Manchester School*, **61** (2), 144–66.

Gibson, H.D. and E. Tsakalotos (1994), 'The scope and limits of financial liberalisation in developing countries: a critical survey', *Journal of Development Studies*, **30** (3), 578–628.

Giovannini, A. (1990), 'European monetary reform: progress and prospects', *Brookings Papers on Economic Activity*, **6**, 218–91.

Giovannini, A. (1991), 'On gradual monetary reform', *European Economic Review*, **35**, 457–66.

Greiner, U., H. Maaß and F.L. Sell (1994), 'The East-German disease: Volkswirtschaftliche Anpassungsprozesse nach der Deutschen Einheit' (The East German disease: the adjustment process of East Germany's economy after unification), *Zeitschrift für Wirtschaftspolitik*, **43** (3), 271–99.

Gros, D. and N. Thygesen (1992, 1998), *European Monetary Integration: From the European Monetary System towards Monetary Union*, London: Macmillan.

Grubel, H. (1970), 'The theory of optimum currency areas', *Canadian Journal of Economics*, **3** (2), 318–24.

Haberler, G. (1971), 'Reflections on the economics of international monetary integration', in W. Bickel (ed.), *Verstehen und Gestalten der Wirtschaft*, Tübingen, pp. 269–78.

Halpern, L. and C. Wyplosz (1997), 'Equilibrium exchange rates in transition economies', *IMF Staff Papers*, **44** (4), 430–61.

Henrekson, M., L. Jonung and J. Stymne (1996), 'Economic growth and the Swedish model', in N.F. Crafts and G. Toniolo (eds) (1996), *Economic Growth in Europe Since 1945*, Cambridge: Cambridge University Press, pp. 240–89.

HM Treasury (1989), *An Evolutionary Approach to Economic and Monetary Union*, London: HMSO.

Hochreiter, E. and G. Winckler (1995), 'The advantages of tying Austria's hands: the success of the hard currency strategy', *European Journal of Political Economy*, **11** (1), 83–111.

Hoffmann, L. (1993), *Warten auf den Aufschwung* (Waiting for the recovery), Regensburg: Transfer-verlag.

Hofmann, V. and F.L. Sell (1993), 'Credibility, currency convertibility and the stabilisation of the rouble', *Intereconomics*, **28** (1), 11–21.

Holmes, M.J. and E.J. Pentecost (1995), 'Changes in the extent of financial integration within the European Community between the 1970s and the 1980s', *Applied Economics Letters*, **2**, 184–7.

Holmes, M.J. and E.J. Pentecost (1996), 'Some econometric tests of changes in the degree of financial integration in the European Community in the 1980s', *Journal of Economic Studies*, **23**, 4–17.

Hölscher, J. (1994), *Entwicklungsmodell Westdeutschland* (West Germany's economic development), Berlin: Duncker & Humblot.

Hölscher, J. (1997), 'Economic dynamism in Central–East Europe: lessons from Germany', *Communist Economies and Economic Transformation*, **9** (2).

Hölscher, J., E. Owen Smith and G. Pugh (2000), 'The DM-undervaluation and Germany's economic performance', in Hölscher, J. (ed.), *Fifty years of the German Mark*, Basingstoke: Pulgrave, pp. 125–53.

Horvath, J. and J. Jonas (1998), 'Exchange rates regimes in the transition economies: case study of the Czech Republic 1990–1997', ZEI Working Papers.

Hughes Hallett, A.J. and Y. Ma (1993), 'East Germany, West Germany, and their Mezzogiorno problem: a parable for European economic integration', *Economic Journal*, **103**, 416– 29.

Huizinga, H. (1993), 'International market integration and union wage bargaining', *Scandinavian Journal of Economics*, **95** (2), 249–55.

Institut für Weltwirtschaft (IfW) (1999), 'Macro and microeconomic progress in East Germany's economy', Kiel Discussion Papers, Nos 346/347.

Johnson, H.G. (1970), 'The case for flexible exchange rates', in G.N. Halm (ed.), *Approaches to Greater Flexibility of Exchange Rates*, The Bürgenstock Papers, Princeton, NJ, pp. 91–111.

Kenen, P.B. (1969), 'The theory of optimum currency areas: an eclectic view', in R.A. Mundell and A.K. Swoboda (eds), *Monetary Problems of the International Economy*, Chicago: University of Chicago Press, 41–61.

Kenen, P.B. (1995), *Economic and Monetary Union in Europe. Moving Beyond Maastricht*, Cambridge: Cambridge University Press.

Kenen, P.B. (1996), 'Sorting out some EMU issues', Princeton University, Reprints in International Finance.

Keynes, J.M. (1936), *The General Theory of Employment, Interest and Money*, London: Macmillan (1973 edition).

Khan, M. and M. Kumar (1997), 'Public and private investment and the growth process in developing countries', *Oxford Bulletin of Economics and Statistics*, **59** (1), 69–88.

Kindleberger, C.P. (1967), 'The pros and cons of an international capital market', *Journal of Institutional and Theoretical Economics*, **23**, 600–617.

Kormendi, R. and P. Meguire (1985), 'Macroeconomic determinants of growth', *Journal of Monetary Economics*, **16**, 141–63.

Krugman, P. (1989), 'Economic integration in Europe: some conceptual issues', in A. Jacquemin and A. Sapir (eds), *The European Internal Market: Trade and Competition*, Oxford: Oxford University Press, pp. 357–80.

Krugman, P. (1991), *Geography and Trade*, Cambridge, MA: MIT Press.

Krugman, P. (1993), 'Lessons of Massachusetts for EMU', in F. Torres and F. Giavazzi (eds), *Adjustment and Growth in the European Monetary Union*, Cambridge: Cambridge University Press.

Lamfalussy, A. (1996), 'The operation of exchange rate policy in Stage Three of EMU', *Economic and Financial Review*, Winter, 178–87.

Lane, P. (1998), 'Irish fiscal policy under EMU', *Irish Banking Review*, Winter, 2–9.

Layard, R., S. Nickell and R. Jackman (1991), *Unemployment: Macroeconomic Performance and the Labour Market*, Oxford: Oxford University Press.

Levine, R. and D. Renelt (1992), 'A sensitivity analysis of cross-country growth regressions', *American Economic Review*, **82**, 942–63.

Lucas, R.E. (1973), 'Some international evidence on output–inflation trade-offs', *American Economic Review*, **63**, 326–34.

Maastricht Treaty (Treaty of European Union) (1992), CONF-UP-UEM 2002/92, Brussels.

Magnifico, G. (1973), *European Monetary Unification*, New York: Wiley.

Majcek, B. (1999), 'Measurement of costs and benefits of accession to the EU for selected CEECs: country report Slovenia', WIIW (Vienna Institute for International Economic Studies) Research Reports, No. 256, Vienna.

Mankiw, G., D. Romer and D. Weil (1992), 'A contribution to the empirics of economic growth', *Quarterly Journal of Economics*, **107**, 407–37.

Masson, P. (1999), 'Monetary and exchange rate policy of transition economies of Central and Eastern Europe after the launch of EMU', IMF Policy Discussion Paper No. 99/5, Washington DC: International Monetary Fund.

McCauley, R.N. and W.R. White (1997), 'The euro and European financial market', in T. Krueger, P. Masson and B. Turtelboom (eds), *European*

Monetary Union and the International Monetary System, Washington DC: IMF.

McKinnon, R.I. (1963), 'Optimum Currency Areas', *American Economic Review*, **53**, 717–25.

Meyer, C. and D. Neven (1991), 'European financial integration: a framework for policy analysis', in A. Giovannini and C. Meyer (eds), *European Financial Integration*, Cambridge: Cambridge University Press, pp. 112–35.

Ministério das Finanças (1998), 'O Impacto do Euro na Economia Portuguesa' (The impact of the euro on the Portuguese economy), Lisbon.

Mishkin, F.S. and A.S. Posen (1997), 'Inflation targeting: lessons from four countries', *Federal Reserve Bank of New York's Economic Policy Review*, **3** (3), 9–11.

Morin, P. and F. Thibault (1998), 'Performances macro-économiques françaises et policy-mix: quelques interrogations sur les années quatre-vingt-dix' [French Macroeconomic performance and the policy mix: some questions on the years 1990–1995], *Revue d'économie financière*, **45**, 63–94.

Mortensen, J. and S. Richter (2000), 'Measurement of costs and benefits of accession to the European Union for selected countries in Central and Eastern Europe: Final Report', WIIW (Vienna Institute for International Economic Studies) Research Report, No. 263, Vienna.

Mundell, R.A. (1961), 'A theory of optimum currency areas', *American Economic Review*, **51**, 657–65.

Mundell, R.A. (1997), 'Updating the agenda for monetary union', in M. Bleijer, J.A. Frenkel, L. Leiderman and A. Razin (eds), *Optimum Currency Areas, New Analytical and Policy Developments*, Washington DC: IMF.

Naylor, R. (1998), 'International trade and economic integration when labour markets are generally unionised', *European Economic Review*, **42**, 1251–67.

Naylor, R. (1999), 'Union wage strategies and international trade', *Economic Journal*, **109**, 102–125.

Nemenyi, J. (1998), 'Challenges of monetary policy in the run-up to European Union accession', mimeo.

Nickell, S. (1997), 'Unemployment and labor market rigidities: Europe versus North America', *Journal of Economic Perspectives*, **11** (3), 55–74.

Niehans, J. (1984), *International Monetary Economics*, Deddington: Philip Allan.

Nordhaus, W.D. (1975), 'The political business cycle', *Review of Economic Studies*, **42** (2), 169–90.

Obstfeld, M. (1996), 'Models of currency crisis with self-fulfilling features', *European Economic Review*, **40**, 1037–47.

Organization for Economic Cooperation and Development (OECD) (various issues), *Economic Outlook*, Paris: OECD.

Ogrodnick, R.A. (1990), 'Optimum currency areas and the international monetary system', *Journal of International Affairs*, **44** (1), 241–61.

Orlowski, L. (2000), 'Direct inflation targeting in Central Europe', in *Post Soviet Geography and Economics*, **41** (2), 134–54.

Ozkan, F.G. and A. Sutherland (1995), 'Policy measures to avoid currency crisis', *Economic Journal*, **105**, 510–19.

Pentecost, E.J. (1997), 'Currency substitution and exchange rate policy within the European Union', in P. Karadeloglou (ed.), *Exchange Rate Policies for Europe*, Basingstoke: Macmillan, November, pp. 110–31.

Polanski, Z., (1999), 'Poland and international financial turbulence of the second half of the 1990s', in J. Hölscher (ed.), *Financial Turbulence and Capital Markets in Transition Countries*, London: Macmillan; New York: St. Martin's Press.

Pscharopoulos, G. (1994), 'Returns to investment in education: a global update', *World Development*, **22** (9), 1325–43.

Putnam, R.D. and N. Bayne (1987), *Hanging Together: Cooperation and Conflict in the Seven–Power Summits*, Cambridge.

Radzyner, O. and S. Reisinger (1998), 'Central bank independence in transition: legislation and reality in Central and Eastern Europe', Österreichische Nationalbank, Vienna.

Rudebusch, G. and L. Svensson (1999), 'Policy rules for inflation targeting', in J.B. Taylor (ed.), *Monetary Policy Rules*, Chicago: University of Chicago Press, chapter 5.

Sala-i–Martin, X. and J. Sachs (1992), 'Fiscal federalism and optimum currency areas: evidence for Europe from the United States', in M. Canzeroni, V. Grilli and P. Masson (eds), *Establishing a Central Bank: Issues in Europe and Lessons from the US*, Cambridge: Cambridge University Press, pp. 195–220.

Scarpetta, S. (1996), 'Assessing the role of labour market policies and institutional settings on unemployment: a cross-country study', *OECD Economic Studies*, **26**, 43–98.

Schmidt, K.-D (1994), 'Treuhandanstalt and investment acquisitions: how to ensure that contracts are kept?', Kieler Diskussionsbeitrag No. 632, Kiel.

Sell, F.L. (1993), 'Liberalisierung des Kapitalverkehrs und makroökonomische Stabilisierung' (Liberalization of the capital account and macroeconomic stabilization), in *List Forum für Wirtschafts-und Finanzpolitik*, **19** (1), 64–75.

Sell, F.L. (1994), 'Wettbewerb unter erschwerten Bedingungen: Ostdeutschlands außenwirtschaftliche Achillesferse' (Facing competition under unfavourable conditions: East Germany's foreign trade sector under pressure), in U. Blum, E. Greipl, H. Hereth and S. Müller (eds), *Wettbewerb und Unternehmensführung* (Competition and entrepreneurship), Stuttgart: Schaffer-Poeschel Verlag, pp. 64–75.

Siebert, H. (1990), 'The economic integration of Germany – an update', Kieler Diskussionsbeitrag No. 160a, Kiel.

Siebert, H. (1992), Five traps for German economic policy', Kieler Diskussionsbeitrag No. 185, Kiel.

Siebert, H. (1993), 'The Big Bang with the Big Brother', Kieler Diskussionsbeitrag No. 211, Kiel.

Siebert, H. (1994), 'Integrating the Eastern Länder: how long a transition?', Kieler Diskussionsbeitrag No. 229, Kiel.

Sinn, G. and H.-W. Sinn (1991), *Kalstart* (Jumpstart), Tübingen: J.C.B. Mohr Verlag (Paul Siebeck).

Sinn, H.-W. (1997), 'International implications of German unification', Centre for Economic Studies Working Paper No. 117, University of Munich.

Sinn, H.-W. (1999), 'EU enlargement, migration and lessons from German unification', Centre for Economic Studies and Institute for Economic Research Working Paper No. 182, University of Munich.

Sørensen, J.R. (1993), 'Integration of product markets when labour markets are unionised', *Recherches Economiques de Louvain*, **59** (4), 485–502.

Statisches Bundesamt, Fachserie 18, Reihe 1.3: Volkswirtschaftliche Gesamtrechnung, Hauptbericht 1997, Wiesbaden 1998.

Stephan, J. (1999), *Economic Transition in Hungary and East Germany – Gradualism and Shock Therapy in Catch-up Development*, Basingstoke: Macmillan.

Sutter, M. (1999), 'Voting and voting power in the stability pact', *Homo Oeconomicus*, **15** (4), 521–42.

Svensson, L. (1997), 'Inflation forecast targeting: implementing and monitoring inflation targets', *European Economic Review*, **41**, 1111–46.

Svensson, L. (1999), 'Monetary policy issues for the Eurosystem', CEPR Working Paper No. 2197, London: Centre for Economic Policy Research.

Szemlér, T. (1999), 'Measurement of costs and benefits of accession to the European Union for selected CEECs: country report for Hungary', Institute for World Economics of the Hungarian Academy of Sciences, Budapest.

Tavlas, G.S. (1993), 'The "new" theory of optimum currency areas', *The World Economy*, **16**, 663–85.

Taylor, J.B. (1993), 'Discretion versus policy rules in practice', *Carnegie-Rochester Conference Series on Public Policy*, **39**, 195–214.

Teltschik, H. (1993), *329 Tage-Innenansichten der Einigung* (329 days. Interior views on Germany's unification), Munich: Goldmann Verlag.

Todaro, M.P. (1977), *Economics for a Developing World. An Introduction to Principles, Problems and Policies*, London: Longman.

van Poeck, A. (1998), 'Leidt een vermindering van de bijdragen van Sociale Zekerheid tot meer werkgelegenheid in Belgie?' (Does lowering social security contributions lead to more employment in Belgium?), *Cahiers Economiques de Bruxelles*, **157**, 35–63.

van Poeck, A. et al. (1999), *Economishe politiek: principes en eruaringer*, Leuven: Garant.

Vaubel, R. (1976), 'Real exchange-rate changes in the European Community: the empirical evidence and its implications for European currency unification', *Weltwirtschaftliches Archiv*, **112**, 429–70.

Viñals, J. and J. Jimeno (1996), 'Monetary union and European unemployment', CEPR Discussion Paper No. 1485, London: Centre for Economic Policy Research.

Vinhas de Souza, L. (1996), 'The Portuguese legal framework for foreign direct investment', in D. Dimon, A. Tomlimson and S. Nichols (eds), *Competitiveness in International Business*, Vol. I, College Station, TX: A&M University Press.

Visser, H. and W. Smits (1995), *A Guide to International Monetary Economics: Exchange Rate Systems and Exchange Rate Theories*, Cheltenham: Edward Elgar.

Von Hagen, J. (1991), 'A note on the empirical effectiveness of formal fiscal restraints', *Journal of Public Economics*, **44**, 199–210.

Von Hagen, J. and M. Fratianni (1994), 'The transition to European Monetary Union and the European Monetary Institute', in B. Eichengreen and J. Frieden (eds), *The Political Economy of European Monetary Unification*, Boulder CO: Westview Press, pp. 129–48.

Von Hagen, J. and M.J.M. Neumann (1994), 'Real exchange rates within and between currency areas, how far away is EMU?', *Review of Economics and Statistics*, **76**, 236–44.

Wallerstein, M., M. Golden and P. Lange (1997), 'Unions, employer associations, and wage-setting institutions in Northern and Central Europe 1959–92', *Industrial and Labour Relations Review*, **50** (3), 379–401.

Wdowinski, P. and B. van Aarle (2001), 'Economic performance in Poland under fixed and flexible exchange rate regimes', in C. Papazoglou and E.J. Pentecost (eds), *Exchange Rate Policies, Prices and the Supply-side Response*, Basingstoke: Palgrave, pp. 140–56.

White, W. (1998), 'The coming transformation of continental European banking?', Bank for International Settlements Working Paper No. 58.

Wyplosz, C. (1986), 'Capital controls and balance of payments crises', *Journal of International Money and Finance*, **5**, 167–79.

Wyrzykowska, E. (1999), 'Measurement of costs and benefits of accession to the European Union for selected CEECs: country report for Poland', Warsaw School of Economics and Foreign Trade Research Institute, Warsaw, Poland.

Index